THE
COLOUR
OF HOME

THE COLOUR OF HOME

Growing up in 1970s Britain

SAJID JAVID

abacus
books

ABACUS

First published in Great Britain in 2026 by Abacus

1 3 5 7 9 10 8 6 4 2

Copyright © Sajid Javid, 2026

The moral right of the author has been asserted.

All rights reserved.
No part of this publication may be reproduced, stored in a retrieval system, or transmitted, in any form or by any means, without the prior permission in writing of the publisher, nor be otherwise circulated in any form of binding or cover other than that in which it is published and without a similar condition including this condition being imposed on the subsequent purchaser.

A CIP catalogue record for this book
is available from the British Library.

ISBN 978-0-349-14762-8

Typeset in Bembo by M Rules
Printed and bound in Great Britain by
Clays Ltd, Elcograf S.p.A.

Papers used by Abacus are from well-managed forests
and other responsible sources.

Abacus	The authorised representative
An imprint of	in the EEA is
Little, Brown Book Group	Hachette Ireland
Carmelite House	8 Castlecourt Centre
50 Victoria Embankment	Dublin 15, D15 XTP3, Ireland
London EC4Y 0DZ	(email: info@hbgi.ie)

An Hachette UK Company
www.hachette.co.uk

www.littlebrown.co.uk

*For Sophia, Suleiman,
Rania and Maya*

Contents

1. Run, Paki, run — 1
2. Partition — 9
3. Hiya, Rochdale — 19
4. Dettol and determination — 31
5. Crammed in — 45
6. Bristol beginnings — 55
7. Flat out — 69
8. Britain's most dangerous street — 81
9. Punches and canes — 107
10. This is our house, you need to leave! — 121
11. Strimming by the sea — 133
12. Back to Bedminster — 147
13. Reading my way out — 157
14. The big one — 161
15. TV repairman — 175

16.	Trading games	189
17.	Laura	195
18.	Exeter initiations	205
19.	Son, you're already engaged	213
20.	Savage Javage	233
21.	Boys, go and get your hockey sticks!	241
22.	Who are you and what do you want?	255
23.	Goodbye Dad and Tariq	269
	Epilogue	285
	Acknowledgements	289

1

Run, Paki, run

1975: Rochdale

The rumour was that you could tell the kind of skinhead a person was by the colour of their laces. As young as five years old, I knew to check their Dr Martens. Then I would know if I had to run. We were told that black laces were safe. Red laces indicated that someone was a supporter of the National Front and was probably racist. Yellow laces were the worst. They meant that someone particularly hated Pakistanis.

My nine-year-old brother Tariq was theoretically in charge of the walk to school. But he and my second-oldest brother Khalid would often race ahead, leaving my cousin Rozina and me, both five at the time, to meander behind and make our way to school. It was just the two of us, creating games and ducking in and out of the path. We weren't scared of ogres under bridges or stray dogs. We were only scared of the skinheads who gathered in the subway under the dual carriageway.

The tunnel was dimly lit and the often-blinking strip lighting added to the sense of menace. The walls were graffitied with various racial slurs and pledges of allegiance to the NF. Even without a loitering gang, it was an intimidating part of the journey. They weren't often gathered early enough in the morning to cross paths with us on the way to school but it did happen from time to time. And on this day, we turned the corner into the walkway, to see them gathered. We were too far away to see the colour of their laces but we didn't need help working out what kind of skinheads they were.

'Oh, when the lights go flashing, we go Paki bashing . . . !'

The words reverberated down the underpass, enhanced by the echo. The members of the group would have been fifteen or sixteen years old. Children by many standards, but to me they were adults. We steadily approached, maintaining our pace, but keeping as far to the other side of the walkway as possible. I made sure Rozina was between me and the wall, acting as a small barrier between her and the gang. If she was hurt, I knew my dad would ask why I hadn't kept my cousin safe.

We kept walking forward, eyes directed into the distance past them. Maybe that was the stubbornness or foolishness of youth. Maybe that was the strength of character and fearlessness that we would need in life as a part of a minority in an area that didn't want us.

There was a crack on the floor, again with its partnering echo. I looked around to see that one of the teens had smacked a heavy stick on the ground. They had stones and rocks in their hands. As we got level with them, the stick-wielding skinhead crouched down to our eyeline and said, 'Run, Paki, run.'

I put my hand on Rozina's arm and pushed it forwards and shouted 'Puj-yeh!' (Punjabi for 'Leg it!'), while breaking into a run myself. The rocks chased us down the passage, clattering as they ricocheted off the walls. None made contact. We got to the end, swung around the corner and kept running until we were on a busy street with other parents and children walking to school.

Over the years, I wondered if Tariq and Khalid had seen them. If they had been subjected to the same treatment. If they had considered hanging back to warn us. Or just saw it as a gauntlet we would all have to get used to.

We were scared but Rozina was defiant. Growing up with one brother and five male cousins just a few doors down meant she had been forced to play the boys' games. She was feisty.

The next day, we took the same route. The alternative was crossing a busy motorway, and the skinheads were only sporadically waiting for us, so the underpass felt like the safer of the two options. As we rounded the corner, we saw that the tunnel was empty. I took a long, deep breath. I felt lighter. Rozina smiled and stopped. With a big grin she plunged her hand into her pocket.

'Look what I brought,' she said, pulling out a chunky stub of chalk that was usually in the wooden frame of her play chalkboard at home.

'What are you going to do with that?' I asked, keen to get through the tunnel and out the other side as quickly as possible.

'We're going to write. Look!' She walked up to the wall where someone had written 'NF' in big letters using a similar chalk. She drew in shaky, child's handwriting a big capital 'A' before it.

'What's that for?' I asked, starting to worry that someone would come along and see us.

'It's an "A", it stands for "Anti". It means the "Anti-National Front".'

'What is Anti-National Front?'

'I don't know, but I've seen other people do it, and we will do it too. It means we're against them and they will see that we don't like them when they see the "A". We won't be scared of them any more.'

She walked down the passage, adding her big 'A' to any 'NF' graffiti she could reach.

We both started to carry chalk from that point and, if any new graffiti popped up, we made it our mission to adapt it. We could take action too. In time we started putting an 'A' before 'NL' signs as well, indicating our 'anti' position to the Nazi League.

Of course, we didn't understand the manifestos of the National Front or the Nazi League. But we knew they were bad. We knew they hated us and our families. We knew that if you came across them, you ran.

Britain offered financial security to my parents when they moved over from Pakistan but, in those early years, that was the only type of security. The 'othering' of racial minorities was extreme. It's worlds apart from the modern London in which I raised my children. For my parents to integrate, if that was even possible, would have been for them to accept prejudice and a 'second-class citizen' status in the social hierarchy. They were used to being called Pakis or people joking that they smelled like curry. My mum's poor English meant that she was protected from some of the depths of the insults. But she got the gist. On the whole, my parents believed the more they mixed with white folk, the more they would be exposed to racism. And in seventies Britain, that proved to be correct more often than not.

Even as a boy I remember the rage and sense of injustice I felt when my brothers and I left for school only to see the windows of my dad's ladies' fashion shop smeared with the words 'Paki go home'. The sense of dread as we played rock, paper, scissors to decide who would go back up to the flat to tell my parents this time. The pit-of-my-stomach feeling as I walked into the kitchen, and told Mum, 'It's happened again.'

She never swore. She didn't even look angry. She just hung her head and closed her eyes for a moment before slowly moving away from the sink to get the bucket and sponge. I would help her carry the sloshing soapy water down the stairs and then leave for school as she knelt, trying to clear the graffiti away before the start of business. I felt hot with embarrassment but there was no one to take my anger out on. The drunken racists from the night before were long gone. Although, years later, my mum told me that sometimes a group of skinheads would make a point of walking by in the morning jeering at her as she scrubbed. She felt sure it was them. She was probably right.

It wasn't just us. The same hateful artwork was found on other Pakistani-run businesses in the area. And the Sikhs who ran the corner shop by my mosque got similar treatment. At least we didn't live in a high rise. Poor Mrs Ul-Haq had to run the gauntlet of terrifying German shepherd dogs that had been trained to snarl and bark at her as she got to her door. Even when she was inside, she often had to step over a puddle of urine; a little gift from any of the young male neighbours who had come home late from the pub the night before. Integration wasn't welcomed by either side, for some because of hatred, but for all because of fear.

This perspective isn't one many fellow Conservative MPs shared. I'm not the only Tory from a Pakistani background but, on the whole, my party is a homogenous collection of people from some of the finest educational institutions money can buy. Not me. My ending up as Chancellor of the Exchequer and Home Secretary, among other roles, was unlikely, to say the least. It hinged on the stranger who left a copy of an intriguing pink newspaper on the bus every day, the bike I finally persuaded my dad to buy me, the bank loan meeting I set up in my dad's name, the tutor who carried on teaching me well after my money ran out and people like the college teacher who told me I had a gift. There were no easy wins for me. No inheritance or trust funds. Just days of attempting to dodge scammers, including those in our extended family, and stopping the bailiffs clearing out Dad's shop.

In our family, my dad held the purse strings. His women's fashion business started from a market stall, but over the years he built it up. At its height, he owned two shops and a warehouse in the roughest parts of Bristol. He sold a range of low-cost skirts, dresses and tops but takings were variable. Everything rested on 'the total' for the day, or 'toe-taal' as my dad pronounced it with his Punjabi accent. On a good Saturday, the shop till receipt would be long and would report more than £400 of sales. This would put him in an excellent mood. He would sit at the dinner table joking with Mum and asking each of his sons about their day. It was at these times that my mother would take the opportunity to ask him for money for new trainers for one of us, or replacement towels, or whatever else was on her long shopping list. On a bad day, when the sales were closer to £150, there were no jokes. Sometimes Mum would come upstairs early to warn us that 'the total' had been bad, so we needed to be on our best behaviour. He would sit at the table in silence and, on those days, his temper was short.

We didn't get pocket money. So, if we wanted something, we had to persuade Mum it was necessary so she would add it to her list and try and get the cash from Dad. There were other occasional opportunities to get money. At Eid, a twice-annual Muslim celebration, our friends and family would give cash gifts to all the children. It would just be a couple of quid, or a fiver from the most generous, and our favourite, relatives. When she could, Mum would slip us some coins but, otherwise, we were on our own.

My life is so different now that I reflect on my childhood with a sense of nostalgia, but also disbelief. Speeches and articles have hinted at the trials I experienced in childhood, but I've never shared my story in its entirety. As I step away from politics, I want to share our story as a Pakistani immigrant family in seventies, eighties and nineties Britain.

I'm proud to have overcome the exclusion, racism and poverty that marked my formative years. To be surrounded by poverty and hatred is no life, but there is hope to be found in such hardship. I believe that difficulties didn't preclude me from success and I believe that's the same for everyone. That success may not look like mine; it may be success as a teacher, or working for the council, it may be dutifully raising your family or pounding the corridors of a high-flying firm in the City. It doesn't matter what your race, religion, socio-economic background or political leaning, I wrote this book in the hope that it would inspire you.

2

Partition

1947: India and Pakistan

When partition came, there was confusion about where the line fell. Everyone knew that Punjab had been split down the middle. Jalandhar stayed part of India and Lahore was in the new state of Pakistan. The stretch of seventy miles between them was anyone's guess.

My mother's family had always lived in the predominantly Muslim area that was now a part of Pakistan. My father's was closer to Jalandhar, caught up in the turmoil. They weren't wealthy compared to their British occupiers, but over hundreds of years, they had built up one of the biggest farms in their town. Aside from acreage, the affluence of a farm was measured by the number of wells housed on the land. Water was critical and easy access to it was a luxury. Their farm had eight. It was considered particularly large at the time. In the fertile lands of Punjab, known as 'the breadbasket of India', they successfully grew spinach, corn, sugar cane and cotton. My grandad was well respected in the neighbourhood as a landowner, and the family was well known. His father, my great-grandfather, had been affectionately called Baba Koolo, meaning 'wise old man'.

The family owned a reasonably sized home, with a central courtyard for the goats and chickens to roam and where the women would cook outside on cauldrons suspended over a fire. The rooms were sparse, as most of the real living was done in the shade outside. Each bedroom had a *manja*, a simple wicker bed on four legs, and that was all. When it was too hot in the night they would pull their *manja* outside and sleep in the open air to benefit from the breeze. The women managed the home and the children would be running around the courtyard amusing themselves, or when they got older out playing cricket on the street. The men would all be working the farm during the day.

By the time my dad was born in British India in 1941, the country was in a time of change. The occupation was on the way out and people were starting to wonder what life would be like when the British left.

In previous years, Muslims, Sikhs and Hindus had largely lived alongside each other as neighbours. But as the political unease mounted and prominent politicians began to incite division, people began to experience a looming feeling that those who were different to them couldn't be trusted. Gradually members of each religion closed ranks, relying only on those who shared their beliefs.

When partition was announced in 1947, as Muslims living in Punjab, my father's family found themselves on the wrong side of a poorly defined line. Overnight they became refugees. They hadn't moved, but their country had. The resulting migration was overwhelming. There was one train line connecting Amritsar, the nearest major city to Jalandhar, and Lahore. It was a lucky few who crammed themselves onto the train. Others had to walk for days on end in search of safety, carrying what was left of their lives on their backs. The caravan of hundreds of thousands of people was matched by another running parallel walking in the opposite direction: the hordes of Hindus and Sikhs who also found themselves on the wrong side of the line in Pakistan and faced similar persecution.

For a few months my dad's family stayed where they were, confident that those they'd lived alongside for generations wouldn't turn on them because of their religion. They had lived in peace and prosperity alongside their friends, neighbours and business associates for years, and they couldn't see that changing. But their confidence waned with every day.

They weren't welcome in the new India. The government never told Muslims they had to leave, but the rising tensions made it impossible for them to stay. So close to the divide, my father's family were living in a pressure cooker. They started looking over their shoulders at people they'd known their whole lives wondering who would be the first to turn on them. Reports came through of Muslims having their homes torched in the night. Mobs started patrolling the country in search of clusters of Muslims. People were slaughtered in their thousands. As the violence escalated, my grandfather knew it was time to leave.

They made a plan to head to a small village called Lasuri, a hundred or so miles west of Lahore, where they already had family and were confident of a warm reception. But they needed to get there by dirt road and rail without being killed. My grandfather and grandmother had four children, and she was seven months' pregnant with their fifth. My father, Abdul-Ghani, was five years old, his older brother Munir was eight, his only sister Salima was three and the youngster was Majeed, who was just a year and a half.

They knew the journey to get the entire family over the border and to the township would be treacherous. Travelling down dirt roads, in the blistering heat, only moving as fast as a heavily laden bull cart could take them would make them conspicuous and easy targets for rape, robbery or worse. My grandfather was a big, imposing man. He was tall and respected, but he knew he alone wouldn't be able to protect them against any baying mobs.

He decided they would leave everything behind. All the possessions they loved and cherished. Packing would raise suspicion. He asked my grandmother to make up some food. She made dense balls of a Punjabi snack called *panjiri* from wheat flour, nuts, spices, ghee and lots of sugar. They were tasty, wouldn't go off in the heat and were easy to hide in the bull cart, away from people driven crazy by the famine.

The supplies, children and women sat in the bull cart. My grandfather rode on his beloved horse Savan, named after the fifth month in the Punjabi lunar calendar, and packed only his prized sword strapped to his belt for the journey. The train station was fifty miles from their home and they only travelled at night, seeking shelter where possible in the daytime.

Days of uncomfortable, slow progress saw them finally reach the station. The scene was one of frantic chaos. Not only were there terrified throngs of Muslims, caught on the wrong side of the divide, trying to make their way to safety, but the incoming trains were releasing mobs of Hindu and Sikh refugees in a similar frenzy, desperate to reach India. It was a dangerous meeting point with tensions running high.

Trains were packed to the point of suffocation with people hanging out the windows, on the outsides and sitting on the roofs. People were jumping on the tracks in a bid to mount moving trains, some losing their lives in the process. The searing heat only amplified the distress. People were starving and terrified. And it showed.

My grandfather gathered his family, abandoned his bull and cart and tied his treasured horse up to a railing. It pained him to walk away, never knowing what would happen to her. By some miracle, he managed to get the whole family on to one of the packed trains. The carriages were arranged so that women and children sat on one side and men were crammed into the other. The family were divided but he stayed as close as he could in the same overflowing carriage.

Getting on the train wasn't an automatic ticket to safety. It was commonplace for vigilantes and terrorists to put rocks on the tracks, causing a train to come to a stop. They would then board the train and walk through the carriages, forcing men at knifepoint to strip from the waist down to establish who was circumcised, and therefore Muslim, at best slicing off their penis, at worst slitting their throat.

The train moved slowly. Even if you did avoid a makeshift blockade, the atmosphere was toxic, with everyone stuffed together in the sweaty compartment, and many of the passengers vomiting where they stood. My five-year-old dad was also unwell on the journey. As a child he had contracted polio. It left him weak. Between the journey and the lack of good food and rest, he was very frail. His skin was grey, and he became increasingly unresponsive as the train lumbered on.

There was no space for any additional cargo, so there was a rule that passengers could not bring their dead with them. Bodies had to be left in Amritsar before boarding the train, no matter how painful it was to leave a loved one without a proper burial.

In order to ensure this was being adhered to, the guards that patrolled the carriages would look out for dead people. If they saw one, they threw the body out of the door of the moving train.

Towards the end of a horrific journey, just when there was a feeling of having made it, the patrolling guards locked eyes with my grandmother. She was heavily pregnant, cradling my dad, a small, barely conscious boy. They moved over to inspect him more closely. After poking him and satisfying themselves that he hadn't reacted, one guard said: 'He's dead, he can't stay on the train.'

She could feel the faint pulse in his neck and his shallow breaths, she knew he was alive. 'He's not dead,' she pleaded. 'Please, touch his pulse, you will feel it.'

They refused to indulge her. 'No, this boy is dead. You have to throw him from the train. No dead bodies.'

She screamed as they tried to pull him from her arms, her muscles tensing with a strength that surprised even herself. As the scuffle continued, my grandad, having caught wind of the commotion, pushed his way down the carriage. He prised himself through the crowd to get to his wife and children. As he made it, he drew his sword. The guards and my grandmother stopped and stared at him.

'Touch my child again, and I swear by Allah I will slice your heads off,' he said, brandishing the impressive weaponry. His stature was imposing and he towered over the guards. They released their grip on my father and stepped back, hands raised in a sign of submission. As they left, my grandad installed himself in front of his family for the rest of the journey, refusing to leave the women and children's area, standing guard over them. If he had not prevailed, you wouldn't be reading this book.

The family made it to Lahore. They were the lucky ones. They knew where they were headed and who would be there to greet them. Hundreds of thousands of others got off the train in those months with no idea where to go, how to work or eat.

Their relatives in Lasuri had their own farm. It was smaller than the one that they had left behind in India, but it gave my grandad work and he started to build up his own farmland alongside theirs. My dad's health slowly returned. The transition wasn't easy, but they considered themselves some of the most fortunate, compared to the horror stories produced by the conflict on both sides.

Two months after they arrived in Pakistan, my grandmother went into labour and gave birth to another son, their fifth child. He was named Hamid. This would have been the source of great joy and celebration, had she not suffered complications in childbirth and died a few days later. My father's lasting, faint memories of his mum were from that dreadful passage to safety and he had none of the everyday life they were robbed of afterwards.

Death in childbirth wasn't uncommon. My grandfather was left with five children to raise and feed, while working on the farmland seven days a week. Without remarrying, he and his children would be in dire straits. He arranged a second marriage with the family of a young local woman and it was settled within months. He replaced a loving relationship with one that was transactional. My dad's stepmother was a seventeen-year-old girl, informed of the match by her parents and handed a household and five unknown children to raise with virtually no money to do so.

Over the next seven years, my father's stepmother had five daughters of her own, each given a name starting with the letter 'N'. She was devoted to them, and as a mother of young children, much of her energy and affection centred on their needs. Adjusting to the role of stepmother to an existing brood was likely not easy. Over time, my father and his siblings sometimes felt as though they were in the background, asked to take on more and more household chores. The boys, especially, seemed to attract criticism, and discipline in the household could be stern – perhaps shaped as much by the era and its expectations as by personal temperament.

As the boys grew older, they were given more freedom to spend time outside the home, which offered them a degree of escape from the daily routines. For my father's younger sister, Salima, life was more confined. As the only girl among the older siblings, she found herself shouldering much of the domestic workload. Household expectations often fell heavily on her, and she had little choice but to meet them. Life at home was strict, and discipline was not uncommon. I've often wondered if Phopo (Punjabi for auntie) Salima's slight frame and quiet presence today hint at the difficult experiences she endured during those formative years.

However, while Phopo Salima endured a tough home life, she did enjoy some privileges. Her village was the only one for miles around to have a school for girls. It was basic when compared to the boys' school but she was taught reading and writing at a time when most girls, my mother included, were not offered an education. When her brothers graduated from their own schooling, two of them became teachers. My dad taught English and their eldest brother Munir was a science teacher. He would take Salima into the lab so that she could look through the microscopes and see the test tubes and Bunsen burners. He also taught her English at home and when he was convinced that she was as good as any of the boys at the school, he booked her in to sit the high-school exam so she could get the formal qualification.

My father Abdul-Ghani resolved to get out of the house as soon as possible. By this time, he was nineteen years old. It was the early sixties, and Brits were constantly coming to Pakistan to recruit manual labourers. There were rumours of good jobs in mills, farms and factories in the UK. Some people even heard reports from those who were already over in England, claiming they were making good money. He decided he wanted to go.

My father's English was known to be excellent. He'd been attentive in school and, knowing that he may want to move to the UK in the future, had paid particular attention to his language studies. If anyone needed to complete a form or write a letter in English, he was summoned to their village to assist. He was as prepared as he would ever be for England. The only problem was that he had no money for the journey. With very few options for raising the funds, Abdul-Ghani went to see his great-uncle, who lived in the same township. He persuaded him to mortgage the little farmland he had and lend him the money for the journey. He bought the cheapest ticket he could find, an Egyptair flight with a one-night stopover in Cairo. After buying the ticket, he had one British pound note left.

In the summer of 1961, his flight landed at Heathrow. To this day, this area of west London has a huge Indian and Pakistani population. Many people who flew over didn't have the money to travel any further so just settled where they were, plus the airport provided plenty of jobs for baggage handlers and the like. But my father had a family friend who lived in Birmingham, so set his sights on the Midlands. He bought the cheapest possible overnight coach ticket and, the following day, was sitting on a tatty sofa in his friend's flat in Rubery, near Birmingham, outlining his plans. Fifty years later, that flat would be in my parliamentary constituency.

After much discussion, his friend convinced my father to travel further north, where he assured him there were more jobs, especially in the cotton mills. He told him that he'd heard of a place where they were desperate for workers, and it was cheap to rent a room. A place called Rochdale.

3

Hiya, Rochdale

1962: Pakistan to Rochdale

My mother Zubaida, or Beydi for short, was striking. The deep brown of her saucer-like eyes caught the attention of many admirers. I know because my dad was one of them. Distantly related, when they were young teenagers they found themselves at some of the same events. At the family wedding when they first met, she caught his attention immediately. He was passing by where she and her friends were standing and caught a whiff of her face cream. Mum kept a small tub of Oil of Ulay that, as it was expensive, she used only on special occasions. The rose perfume drew him in, or at least he pretended it did in order to have an excuse to interact with her.

He sent over one of his friends to tell the girls that he liked the way she smelled and to cheekily request that he could use some of the same cream. Coy, but amused by the request, she obliged and handed his friend the pot. Abdul-Ghani sparingly applied the cream as part of his flirtation and the two of them continued the party with an identical floral smell.

The culture dictated that girls didn't have conversations with boys. When she was old enough, her dad would choose a man for her to marry. He would make all the arrangements with the groom's family and she would be told when it was settled. That's how it was for her and every woman she knew who had come before her. She had never grown up expecting anything different. There was no notion of falling in love. You met your husband and then worked to build love in your relationship.

Despite this, my mum had also spotted my dad. In his day, before the hair loss that, I'm sorry to say, is a feature of our family, he was what my aunties would describe as 'dashing'. He was well presented and handsome. When she subtly asked around with her younger sister and friends, the women she spoke to said they had only heard good things of his character. While she wasn't able to choose her husband, she did give hints to her sisters that she would be interested in this man Abdul-Ghani. And, if they followed the proper, unspoken procedure for such circumstances, they would have gently made sure their mum was aware of the attraction. As such, Zubaida held out hope that, when her father decided on her husband, it would be him.

My mother grew up in an affluent household. Again, not affluent like their British occupiers, but wealthy when compared to their neighbours. Her dad grew cotton and was the owner of the largest farm in the area. He was a village chief, a *lambardar*, a position he inherited from his own father. A wise man, he mediated disputes in the community. There was no mechanism of enforcement for the decisions he made other than the respect the locals had for him, and it was all he needed. He worked hard to support his family, gave money to charity and attended the local mosque.

As with most girls, my mum didn't go to school and instead performed chores around the house. She spent most of her time making clothes; she could knit, crochet and sew like a professional, and was so fast that she could turn out a cardigan in a day. Her handiwork provided clothes for the whole household. As her family had help with the animals and the cleaning, her responsibilities were limited. With no obligation to stay out in the sun for hours on end, her skin was soft and her hands youthful.

Zubaida was the fourth child of six, with four brothers and one sister. In Pakistani culture, having a boy was worthy of great celebration. Families would hand out delicious sweets to their neighbours to celebrate the blessing, while no such treats were distributed for the birth of girls. With their dowries and inability to enter into gainful employment, girls were expensive. My grandfather did not buy into this tradition. He flung the sweets around with the same enthusiasm at the birth of his first daughter Zubaida, as with the three sons who came before her. To treasure a daughter was not as common as it should have been in forties Pakistan. This was an extraordinary gesture. He started as he meant to go on and delighted in his eldest daughter every day. My mother was adored by both of her parents. It's that nurturing that I believe shines out of a person. She held her head high, took care of her appearance, her skin and her clothes. She was content and cared for.

My mother's family didn't experience the same traumatic forced relocation during partition. When the news hit, they found themselves on the 'right side of the line' already in Chichawatni, an area of Punjab assigned to the new state of Pakistan. The women and children were kept completely protected from news of the devastation that had hit the outside world. When asked of her memories of partition, my mum simply says that she has none. She was only a four-year-old girl and, even as she grew up, the men of the family never discussed the war with her.

Unbeknown to my mum, life in Pakistan was in turmoil. Any non-Muslim friends or neighbours they had previously spent time with had left, often in the dead of night, leaving lifeless, abandoned houses in their wake. They were quickly inhabited by some of the eight million displaced Muslims seeking safety from India. But these desolate homes weren't enough to meet the housing demand and large buildings like colleges and offices were shut down and turned into refugee camps.

All of Pakistan was in crisis. Food was scarce and people were desperate. There were riots in all the major cities. Just as Muslims were being slain in India, mobs were marching around Pakistan in search of Hindus and Sikhs to do the same. The Indian government sent convoys of army trucks to evacuate the families that survived before the culling. No one knows how many people died in those years, but it's estimated at around a million. There were no winners, just pain, destruction and death on both sides of the line.

Zubaida got to see Abdul-Ghani again when he graduated from high school. His English had become so good that he was a respected advisor in the local area. If someone needed a form filled out or a formal letter written in English, they solicited his help. That included her father. From time to time she would see Abdul-Ghani arrive at the house. Unable to have a conversation, they were confined to eye contact when she brought in the tea. As frustrating as this was, she had no other option. To approach him would have been shameful and meant that her father would never consider him as her match.

Nine days before Abdul-Ghani was due to fly to the UK, Zubaida's father died. The whole village and many people beyond showed up to pay their respects to the man who had enjoyed such a high profile in the area. Abdul-Ghani was among the mourners. But once again they were in a situation where it would have been inappropriate for him and Zubaida to speak. Once again, they politely passed by each other.

When my dad arrived in Rochdale in Lancashire, he thought he would only be there temporarily. The whole UK adventure had been a short-term solution for him to get away from home, make some money and then return to Pakistan to start a business. He was proud of Pakistan. He'd lived through the growing pains of partition and war. He was patriotic.

He found himself a space in a boarding house with a group of other Pakistani men, each with their own, albeit similar, aspirations. The house was owned by one of the earliest immigrants from Pakistan to settle in Rochdale, Cha Cha (meaning uncle) Sardar. Among the eight men who slept in sleeping bags on the floor was Anwar, one of Zubaida's older brothers. They cooked together on a burner stove, making curries and other dishes that reminded them of home. Abdul-Ghani never cooked in Pakistan, as that was considered women's work. But he picked up the recipes the others had cobbled together and started to enjoy the days when it was his turn to be chef.

They were all looking for work and were in competition with each other for the few labourers' jobs that were available each day. Full-time employment with a salary and benefits wasn't available to the Pakistani immigrants – or any immigrants for that matter. They would stand outside the gates of a cotton mill first thing in the morning, hoping that the foreman would be short staffed that day. The foreman would stride out to the gate ten minutes or so after the regular, white workers had traipsed in and announce the number of people he needed. He would then point into the crowd to select his temporary staff from the hopefuls. Everyone else was sent home. Sometimes my dad would be picked, sometimes he wouldn't. Just because he managed to get work on one day didn't mean there would be a place for him the next.

My dad was competitive. He didn't want to miss out on work. He didn't want to stand around for two hours only to be sent home for the day. He wanted to make his money so he could move on and start his own business. He started turning up at the factory gates before sunlight. He was always first there, aiming to arrive an hour before even the foreman showed up. The foreman would have to walk past Abdul-Ghani every morning on his way into the factory. He would stand there on his own, at the crack of dawn, keen to work. As the foreman made his way in, my dad would politely greet him. 'Good morning, Mr Foreman,' he would say.

The enthusiasm paid off and he became the go-to temporary employee at the Courtaulds cotton mill. Slowly they increased the duration of his employment, initially offering a week here and there, then two and finally a six-month contract. His work was mundane and boring: he would clean, mount the cotton on wheels, pack boxes into lorries and any other jobs that were required.

Abdul-Ghani's drive and ambitions didn't end there. When he arrived in Rochdale there was no mosque in the area where he and his fellow Muslims could worship. People would just pray in their living rooms or, more likely given the demographic of young men away from home for the first time, allow their religious practices to lapse. Along with a group of other Pakistani men, they petitioned and fundraised to be able to rent a space to use as a mosque.

After a year working in the UK, my father's savings grew. He kept only a fraction of them for himself. On arriving, his first objective was to send back enough money for his great-uncle to release the mortgage. It would have been financially crippling for his great-uncle to keep up the repayments on his own. Once he had done that, he wanted to contribute towards the cost of schooling for his younger brothers. Each week he joined the long queue of immigrants outside Western Union, all sending a proportion of their meagre earnings to their families back home.

Dad may have been struggling, but he knew it was nothing compared to the need that his family experienced in Pakistan. This is a familiar story for any immigrant family. These remittances play an important part in Pakistan's economy. They put food on the table, provide healthcare for the unwell, fund schooling and secure houses. Being able to help elevate your family from the poverty you left them in is a motivator for so many who leave their home country, my dad included.

After paying off the debt to his great-uncle and putting aside a little extra money, Dad started to think about returning to Pakistan. But the few pieces of news he got from home painted a bleak picture. He heard from his family through airmail letters. They would take three or four weeks to arrive and were never long enough to satisfy his longing for home. The country had entered into its second war with India over the disputed state of Jammu and Kashmir, soon followed by civil war. There wasn't conscription in Pakistan so he wouldn't have been forced to fight, but the country was in a state of unrest and good jobs were few and far between.

Abdul-Ghani was, however, ready to marry and he wanted to marry Zubaida. With her father now dead, he asked Anwar for his sister's hand in marriage. Together with her other two older brothers, Anwar had been tasked with finding matches for his sisters in his father's absence. They discussed the potential match and agreed, by committee, that it should go ahead. Zubaida's family were pleased with the engagement and were happy that Beydi would be going to experience new adventures in a wealthy country like the UK. Things were starting to come together.

Abdul-Ghani's younger sister Salima was the person he was most worried about. Her letters didn't mention the country's troubles or the state of the village. Instead, they spoke of wanting to leave. Life at home seemed heavy for her. The expectations were constant, and she often felt alone. Abdul-Ghani found it hard to think of her still caught in that world. While he wasn't living in luxury, Abdul-Ghani was safe, had work and friends, and was away from the neglect of their stepmother. Salima had none of those things. But there was comfort in knowing the situation would end.

Since birth, Salima had been intended for a second cousin, Mohammad Ali, known as Chaudary to all. Their parents planned the union and a marriage ceremony was performed to solidify the match when they were both children. As she got older, the time for her to leave home to move in with him and start their life together fast approached. Much like Abdul-Ghani, Chaudary had been attracted to the promises of more jobs and better pay in the UK. He too had moved to Rochdale, just a few months after Abdul-Ghani. He was tall and imposing, but with a gentleness that endeared him to everyone. Abdul-Ghani hadn't known him well before he had arrived in Rochdale, but in this strange, lonely country they had formed a tight bond. Chaudary started coming with Abdul-Ghani to the cotton mill in the mornings and was slowly ingratiating himself with the foreman too. Soon, once they had gathered enough money, Salima would join them in the UK and it was that knowledge that kept my dad going.

I will take a pause here to acknowledge that to modern, Western ears, the notion of matching children and performing a ceremony when they are still young sounds utterly ridiculous. Marriage was a tool used to strengthen familial bonds and consolidate wealth. People outside of your own family couldn't be trusted. You and your family had to work their fingers to the bone, day in and day out, in order to secure an income and build your standing in the community. To marry outside of your own family was to risk losing that income. It was to invite in an outsider. It was a risk too many had taken and too many had lived to regret. It doesn't sound romantic but it was seen as a necessary mechanism for protecting the family for thousands of years. In the Pakistan of my parents' and aunts and uncles' day, you didn't fall in love, you were obedient. They would accept the match, and out of duty and consistency, love would follow. That was how it worked. It was a custom my parents tried to carry forward with their own children in England many decades later.

It took my dad a few more months to save up the money for a flight back to Pakistan. Now twenty-two years old, he finally returned home. Zubaida's family greeted him like a new son. They had a large ceremony that lasted for days in her home village. He flew back to the UK and awaited Zubaida, who flew out six months later after arranging her visa and passport.

The process of applying for a passport was relatively straightforward; the authorities didn't demand much paperwork because very few citizens had any. If you ask any Pakistani person of my mum's generation their birthday, most will only be able to give you a rough date, like summer of 1942. They didn't register births like they do these days. Most mark their birthday on a nominal date around that time – my mother and father included.

Abdul-Ghani, Anwar and Chaudary bought a small house at 6 Freehold Street in Rochdale for £400 for themselves and their wives. Salima was happy in the UK, finally free from the torment she had endured in Pakistan. In contrast to Chaudary's height, Salima was slight and unimposing. They visually appeared a mismatched pair, but the reality was very different. Chaudary continued in the cotton mill for the rest of his working life, accumulating promotions over the years until he was finally named foreman. He retired against his wishes, aged sixty-five. He was one of the last employees standing when the mill's doors were finally closed for good in the 1990s.

When Salima first arrived, concerned about her low weight and ill health, Abdul-Ghani set about helping her build her strength. He took her to a local chemist where he proudly marched her over to a display of large bottles of Lucozade. In the sixties, the luminous drink was only stocked in pharmacies as it was considered to have medicinal qualities. He insisted she should drink it every day to help her build her strength. Salima has long come to the realisation that the energy drink won't solve her ailments but, even so, she still stocks it in her fridge to this day, sneaking it out to her grandchildren as a treat.

Initially, there was nothing about the UK my mother liked. The unending shades of grey took their toll. Phopo Salima and my mum became best friends, they needed each other in order to keep going in the foreign country. My mum didn't speak English, and when together they spoke in Punjabi. Phopo Salima continued learning English, teaching herself from books, but my mum never had enough time. Being unable to communicate was an isolating experience. Perhaps it was the difference in their education that meant they approached communication differently. Phopo Salima was shy and considered; she didn't want to say something unless she could be sure she was saying it correctly, while Zubaida just threw herself in, doing whatever she could to be understood. In shops she would use hand gestures and pointing to try and get her wishes across. In the days when food and supplies were bought over the counter, rather than from a shelf, even the simplest transactions posed problems. If she needed sugar or flour, she would take a pinch from the supplies in her own kitchen, put it on the palm of her left hand and point at it to communicate what she needed.

In those early days, everything felt foreign, but it was also made clear to them that *they* were foreign. While they never experienced physical violence, or even the threat of it, they endured comments and unkindnesses that only added to their sense of disconnection from their new home country. People made a show of avoiding the seats next to them on the bus, turning their nose up as they walked past. From time to time they would get shouted at in the street 'go home' or 'go back to where you came from'. Sadly I think my parents' generation tolerated incidents such as these as a necessary part of settling in a new country. They didn't complain or try to retaliate, they just kept walking.

A few years after they moved in, the council decided to build on Freehold Street so bought the house back from them for £1,100. Delighted with their profit, Abdul-Ghani and Chaudary bought a new house to share. Anwar and his wife moved into a house of their own closer to Manchester. The two couples now lived on Dunster Avenue. Zubaida and Salima looked after the house and kept each other company.

A year or so later, in 1965, they decided they would both start a family. With much excitement, the women became pregnant and, within weeks of each other, gave birth. My mum gave birth to my eldest brother Tariq in 1966, but devastation struck when Phopo Salima's baby boy was stillborn. She was inconsolable. Just as her life was picking up, she was hit with tragedy. The juxtaposition of the sorrow of loss and the joy of new life was difficult for the two families to bear. At the centre of it all was Tariq. A gurgling and giggling newborn.

The devastation took Phopo Salima years to overcome, and all the while she watched Tariq grow up as her son should have. Far from allowing this to come between them, she became strongly attached to the baby, helping Zubaida to care for him. On one occasion she was out walking Tariq in the pram in Broadfield Park when a woman came over with a camera and asked to take her picture. She agreed and the following week the same woman came back to show her the first real photo of herself, wrapped up in a warm coat, with one hand on the pram pushing Tariq in a padded romper suit and woolly hat.

My mum had her second child, Khalid, in 1968, but Salima wasn't ready to try for another. As time went on and the families built up some modest savings, Chaudary and Salima moved out to a house of their own. They relocated to 35 Merefield Street, no more than a sixty-second walk door-to-door from Abdul-Ghani and Zubaida. The houses were almost identical two-up-two-downs, with a cellar for coal and a small box yard at the back.

It was in early 1969 that each of the women once again decided they would have another child. And once again both women found out they were pregnant within a month of each other. Phopo Salima gave birth to a beautiful baby girl, Rozina, in November, and four weeks later, on 5 December, I was born. While my parents were grateful for a healthy third baby, by then they were desperate for a girl. They were even prepared with a girl's name for me: Sophia, which means wisdom. On realising that the name Sophia was out, they named me Sajid, which has the less catchy meaning: one who is devoted to God.

My mum had her fourth son, Basit, in 1971 and three years after that she gave birth to my youngest brother Atif, just five months after Salima had her third child, a boy she called Tehseen. Their families were complete.

4

Dettol and determination

1970: Rochdale

The network of roads that we lived on in Rochdale housed an array of immigrant families from different parts of the world. Some were Pakistani like us, but there were plenty of Ukrainian and Polish families on the street too. We mainly stuck with the other Pakistani families. There were two white children who would come out to play cricket with us in the street from time to time. But we always knew them as 'the white kids', and we were never invited into their homes, just as we didn't invite them into ours.

Our little corner of the neighbourhood was 17 Dunster Avenue. It was a compact terraced house with no frills. There was a coal chute to the basement that was in regular use. The coalman came every Wednesday and used the chute to restock our cellar. The living room's fireplace served as the source of heat for the whole ground floor. When it needed feeding, my mum or dad would go down into the basement and emerge with sooty hands and just enough coal to revive the embers.

Walking in through the front door took you straight into the living room; with space at a premium, there was no room for corridors or entrance halls. One room opened up to another by way of a door – or just a gap in the wall where a door could feasibly have been installed. The walls were covered in the thick textured wallpaper that was to become a feature of my childhood. I would run my hands along it as I went up the stairs.

Our privacy was maintained by a netting with a lace trim covering the downstairs window. With the living room abutting the street, Mum was always worried passersby would stop to peer in. At the back of the house was a box room that functioned as a dining room, with just enough space for a table of four when it was pushed up against the wall. My mum cooked in the adjoining cupboard kitchen.

Upstairs were two bedrooms and a bathroom with an indoor toilet – a relatively recent luxury. Without a fireplace of their own, the bedrooms would get unbearably cold in winter, so we used plug-in electric heaters for as long as our dad would allow before he marched in and turned them off, demanding that we cover ourselves with another blanket instead. My parents and baby Atif slept in one of the double bedrooms, and the other room was for me and my three brothers. There was a commode in a closet in the back garden, but by the time we moved in, this was defunct, and served solely as an additional spot for our games of hide and seek.

We didn't have a shower, but it wouldn't have mattered if we had. My mum washed all five of her boys, exactly as she would have done in Pakistan. Every evening, we would sit in the empty bathtub while Mum used the taps to fill a bucket with warm water. She would then scoop it out with a plastic cup to wet us all over and apply lathered Imperial Leather soap with her hands. When she was satisfied that we were sufficiently clean, she scooped more water to wash away the soap. Finally, she would take a bottle of Dettol liquid antiseptic. She poured a small amount into the cap of the bottle and tipped it into the remaining water in the bucket. She swirled her hand around in the bucket to make sure it was properly mixed in. Then she tipped the entire contents of the bucket over our heads, in a final flurry that brought great delight to us as young boys. We used to call it the 'best bit' and ask for it again and again. On the days when we bathed with one of our brothers, we would fight over who got the 'best bit', keeping track of who had the delightful torrent last time.

The Dettol had a distinctive smell; one that I always associated with cleanliness. For the entirety of my childhood, I believed that you hadn't really washed if you didn't smell of Dettol. I continued with this routine well into my teens. It took time for me to realise the Dettol and bucket were not standard practice among my peers and slowly I, and all my brothers, stopped. It wasn't until I was eighteen and in the safety of my long-term relationship that I described the routine to my girlfriend and future wife, asking if she had done the same. I was greeted with a kindly and sympathetic laughter as she explained that she had not, in fact, used buckets and Dettol in her ablutions.

When I was growing up my parents still used natural bark or *miswak* to clean their teeth. They bought toothbrushes and toothpaste for us boys but continued with the traditional Pakistani practice of chewing the fibrous bark at the end of each day for their own oral hygiene.

Our home may have been small, but my mum took pride in keeping it, and us, clean. We got fresh sheets weekly, and we put on clean pyjama bottoms, Pakistani shalwar – baggy cotton trousers with a drawstring – after our Dettol bath every night. On special occasions she would want her boys to look extra smart. We would fight her as she wet our hair to run the comb through it and apply Brylcreem. She would dress us in our best clothes, and for me that was trousers and a shirt with a collar that started life as Tariq's, then belonged to Khalid and were making a brief stop off with me before being handed down to Basit. To finish our ensemble, she would apply a lead liner to the waterline of our eyes. This was a popular Pakistani practice. She kept the powder, or *surma* in Punjabi, in a small clay container. She would use an applicator to pick up a little of the powder and apply it to our inner eyelids. We all felt that we looked girlie but Mum reassured us that it was for boys too.

In the seventies, the UK government had warned against this practice as it could result in lead poisoning. Rumours circulated in the Pakistani community that the government thought it was bad for your eyes. These were largely ignored. The feeling was that the UK officials didn't understand and didn't like our traditions. It wasn't until a Pakistani GP, who spoke Punjabi, told my mum that it could be very harmful that she finally stopped and told her friends to do the same.

As Dad worked long hours, I looked forward to the times when I would see him. Two years after I was born, he left the cotton mill and started working on the buses, where conductors were offered permanent contracts and the pay was better than at the mills. Initially he trained up as a bus conductor for what became Greater Manchester Transport. He would leave before sunlight to start his bus route. Sometimes I would hear him running water in the bathroom so I would go and sit at the top of the stairs, in the hope of snatching a few minutes with him before work. His conductor's hat and tie were a novelty, but I was most fascinated by the ticket machine.

He took an old Setright Speed with him every morning. It was fitted with a weighty brown leather strap that bore the wear and tear of many previous conductors. There were two slots at the front for money, one for shillings and the other for halfpennies. By the time my dad was on the buses the UK had moved over to the decimal system, so while the markings were still intact, it had now been adapted to accept pounds and pence. Dad printed the tickets by rotating a side lever, an action I was desperate to perform. On a couple of occasions he generated a ticket so I could see it emerge from the slot on the top of the machine. I would watch in amazement as the thin card curled round, mimicking the roll it had recently been released from. But he would never let me pull the ticket over the serrated edge to remove it. Instead, he'd roll it back in so it could be reprinted and issued officially to a passenger, and therefore not create a discrepancy in the takings.

From time to time, Mum would gather all of the boys together and hurry us down to the bus stop so we could ride on Dad's bus. This often meant a wait of half an hour or more, and sometimes waving buses on when we realised it wasn't Dad's. But when we mounted the back of the 454 and saw Dad in his uniform in charge of the bus, it felt like that little corner of Rochdale was ours and the other passengers were just invited for the ride. Children didn't pay for the bus but Dad always charged Mum for her ticket. He didn't bend the rules or give out freebies. He insisted that he would do every job with honour and respect for his employers.

Each conductor was paired with a driver and my dad's was called Mr Pudelski. A Polish immigrant, he was universally liked. Everyone called him 'mate'. So much so that the Pakistani community adopted it as his name. My mother only found out a few years ago that Mate was not his given name. Mate was fat and jovial and also lived on Dunster Avenue, and it was he who recommended it to Dad as a good area for families and children. He also told him that Marland Hill Primary School was the best in the area. After that, Dad insisted that each of us go there, rejecting any of the three schools that were closer by.

While Mate was an immigrant, he was made more welcome on the buses because he was white. In time, Dad decided he wanted to work as a driver. Greater Manchester Transport was crying out for drivers and the hourly pay was better than that of conductors. The problem was that while the law and theoretically the bus company supported non-white drivers, the local branch of the Transport and General Workers' Union was opposed to them. Bus driving was a higher paid and more highly skilled job and therefore should be protected and kept only for the white folk. It was one of the jobs some people were terrified the immigrants would steal from under their noses. Nevertheless, my dad was insistent. He had worked hard for the company as a conductor and had read up on his legal rights. He had heard about the Bristol Bus Boycott in the mid-sixties and drew a lesson.

Armed with these encouragements, he went to the recruitment office in Manchester. When faced with two queues – one for bus conductors and one for drivers – he joined the latter. He was the only non-white person in the line. When he got to the front, he asked for an application form to become a bus driver. The burly thirty-something-year-old woman behind the counter stared at him. From the way he told it, the sides of her face were hidden by a dramatic shock of blonde permed hair. What was visible of her face was tucked behind wide glasses that would only be worn by Deidre Barlow fans, but through the lenses her eyes looked large and pronounced. She cut them as she turned behind her and reached for a piece of paper. She pinned it to the counter with two fingers and slid it over without making eye contact. He looked down and saw 'Bus Conductor Application Form' in block capitals at the top of the page.

'Sorry, madam, no. This is for the bus conductors. I am already a bus conductor, you see.' He pointed to the name badge that was still attached to his lapel following his earlier shift. 'I want to train to be a driver.'

Her eyes widened in indignation. 'Well, you can't!' she said, raising her voice above the polite office murmur around them. 'It's whites-only for drivers.'

'That is not the law. I know the law and I am allowed to do this job. You must give me an application form.'

'No, I must not do anything. We don't want coloured drivers. You're a conductor and that's the job you're allowed.'

'I am allowed any job, madam. It is my right to apply. All I need from you is the application form.'

'You need to leave!' Her voice became so high pitched that there wasn't a person in the room who hadn't tuned into the ruckus. It had also caught the attention of a suited man behind the desk who my father assumed was a manager.

The man shuffled over, having kept his distance in the hope that the awkward incident would go away without his intervention. He asked the mega-permed receptionist what the matter was.

After ascertaining the situation and hearing my dad, for a third time, explaining that he knew himself to be lawfully entitled to apply for the job, the man let out a deep sigh and instructed the Deidre-style fan to hand over the form. She reached behind her, picked it up and then slid it across the counter and onto the floor. 'Oops,' she said with a flat, bitter tone.

Despite the local union's protestations, my father and a few other non-white applicants were accepted on to the training programme and, just three months later, my dad was a bus driver. Pressure had been mounting for the company to go against the union and start accepting all applicants. My dad wasn't the first to make a stand, and the impact of lots of men insisting on their rights meant that the policy was changed.

He took shifts as both a driver and a conductor. He took as much work as the hours of the day would allow him, often sleeping just four hours between shifts. Sometimes he would jump off the back of one bus as close to Dunster Avenue as possible, run back to the house, burst through the door and shout for a cup of tea. Mum would hand him a mug, he would tip out the top fifth, replace it with cold water, drink the entire mug in one and go straight back out to catch the next bus for work. His colleagues nicknamed him 'Mr Night and Day' as there was no time when he wasn't working. On the weekends, he would go to local markets and sell women's clothes. Initially he bought these from Pakistani-owned warehouses, but it quickly became apparent that it would be cheaper to buy the material and make them himself. So, Dad asked Mum if she would make the clothes. The pitiful dining table was replaced with a Brother standalone table sewing machine with space either side of the machine, one for cut fabric and another for fabric that was already sewn. While we were out at school, she would cut the fabric according to the pattern. By the time we came home, there would be piles of cut material dotted around the kitchen and living room. Once we were in bed, I would hear the hum of the chunky Brother sewing machine as she fired it up ready for four or five hours of garment assembling before bed. The whirring sound became a comforting white noise to accompany my sleep. In the morning there would be a folded pile of tank tops, flared trousers or blouses on the side ready for Dad to take to the market.

With both our parents constantly busy, my brothers and I were able to play on the street in front of the house from a young age. We would venture a little further out of sight every day until eventually we had free run of the neighbourhood. We played cricket and ball games on the road, while a network of garages provided settings for our other games. We would go in and out of any that were left unlocked, exploring the contents and using them as hiding places. There was an abandoned house just around the corner with broken windows and the door hanging off its hinges. Sometimes we would dare each other to go in and then run away squealing as soon as someone put a foot over the threshold. Our mum put a stop to that game by telling us the house was haunted.

When we were at home, we always wanted to put on the telly. It was a cumbersome appliance with a huge, deep back and an aerial that needed to be repositioned every time the channel was changed. Mercifully, with only three channels, that wasn't often. Everything we watched was in black and white. As a boy, I always hoped for *The Magic Roundabout* or Bill and Ben the Flowerpot Men and I would try to replicate their unintelligible noises. Sometimes the BBC would air a cartoon like Mickey Mouse or Bugs Bunny, and on those occasions I would run around trying to gather up my brothers to watch it together. We all knew to go and get Mum when Laurel and Hardy films were on. She loved them and would come out of the kitchen, wiping her hands on her apron, and sit for fifteen minutes or so to laugh along. Many of their films were silent, which removed the language barrier that prevented her enjoying much of the TV shows we watched.

I was four years old when I first started attending primary school in Rochdale. Aside from my two brothers, my cousin Rozina and me, almost everyone was white, from the pupils to the teachers. When I first started, I didn't speak English, having always spoken Punjabi with my parents at home. I liked Punjabi. It's a guttural language that sounds harsh to the untrained ear. Just as romance sounds better when spoken in French, jokes sound funnier when they're relayed in Punjabi. The same joke told in English sounds twice as funny in Punjabi. Each year group had two classes and the teachers deliberately separated Rozina and me, for fear that we would only speak in Punjabi to each other if we were kept together. We both adapted quickly to the new language. I had picked up words of English here and there from playing with the other kids in the street, from watching TV and from my older brothers when they came back from school. It didn't take me long to get used to and by the time I was six, I was speaking to my brothers and cousins in English and even dreaming and thinking in English too.

Language wasn't the only barrier I faced. Everything about my new classmates was alien to me. They had different food, different customs, a different religion and a different home environment. We ate with our hands at home, but in school we quickly had to learn to use a knife and fork. My parents were trying their best to adapt to the new culture, but heavily relied on the Pakistani customs that were most familiar to them. Despite being born and raised in Rochdale, I was a foreigner to the children at that school, and to their families.

Some new practices I welcomed with open arms. For example, my brothers and I embraced the concept of Christmas, enjoying the festivities rather than its Christian origins. The fact that we were Muslim didn't stop us from insisting on benefiting from the occasion in the same way as our white-British counterparts. As such, we would hassle our mum to take us to the Pioneer House department store in Rochdale to visit Santa. Every year the town centre's staple shop would house a modestly arranged grotto with an elderly Santa sporting an acrylic beard and brandy-induced rosy cheeks. We would pose for a photo with him, all dressed in our best clothes, with *surma* lining our eyes and cooking oil brushed into our hair to give it a shine.

Another British novelty that became a highlight of my day was being presented with an apple and a carton of milk during the school morning break. Lunches were batch-cooked English food and, compared to the flavourful curries and homemade chapatis we were given at home, it tasted bland. The dinner ladies would stand behind a row of tables dishing out scoops of ambiguous slop and insisting it was all finished before we were allowed to play. To add insult to injury, my mum told the school that we were vegetarian. We were Muslim and didn't eat pork. Other meat was fine, provided it was halal, but as that would never be available, they played it safe and opted us all in for the meat-free choice. This meant that we were only ever served the least appetising elements of the meal: the overcooked vegetables and sloppy mashed potato. The only days I looked forward to were Fridays, when the dinner ladies served fish fingers and chips. As for desserts, it was always a square of sponge cake swimming in lumpy custard, or occasionally jelly, but we weren't to touch that either as Mum had heard a rumour they had snuck some pork into it.

When it comes to people who weren't formally educated, I've found they often fall into one of two camps. The first is the 'I didn't learn to do that and it did me no harm' school of thought. They turned out fine, so they think we get too caught up in classrooms and should be more focused on the lessons life has to teach us. The second group are the people who are desperate for others to access what they couldn't. They wonder what would have been if they'd had a formal education; if they would have enjoyed history or found they had a surprising aptitude for maths.

My mum sat in the second camp. She was firmly convinced by the importance of education.

Far from being content with us replicating the lives and career choices of our parents, she wanted better things for her boys. The little she had, she took pride in. Even if we didn't have the newest or best fitting uniforms, they were perfectly clean and pressed for us in the mornings. Our satchels sat packed and ready by the door. Days off for sickness were distributed sparingly and only after in-depth questioning.

At the end of each day, when we got home, she would ask

each of her boys what they had learned in school. We would recite back the key topics, elaborating on request. Over the years the subjects we reported became increasingly complex but her poker face never faltered. She didn't know about iambic pentameter or trigonometry, but she didn't let on. Instead, she smiled and nodded.

Our after-school snack of pakora or samosa was only a brief break from the work as we were instructed to go straight to our room to complete our homework before dinner. Even if we hadn't been set any, we busied ourselves rather than telling Mum, otherwise she would threaten to send Dad into school to demand they handed out more exercises.

On a Saturday, Mum would take us all to Rochdale Library, one of the few services that didn't cost a penny and where children were welcomed with open arms. She would let us loose in the children's section and tell us all to pick a book and read it there and then. I immersed myself in classics like *Meg and Mog* and *The Cat in the Hat*. As we got older, and the books gradually changed from pictures to chapters, we would check out longer tales to finish at home like *The Wind in the Willows* and *Watership Down*. When I was old enough to venture out of the children's section, I immediately switched to non-fiction, focusing on history books to get my stories and sense of the past. As we read, Mum sat in a chair in the corner and knitted, occasionally looking up to offer us a satisfied smile.

Mum may not have been able to read books, but my mother could read people. She was shrewd, and savvy to the point of cynical. I've never known her not to be following, tracking, listening and remembering. In our world of reminders, notifications and even primitive prompts like the Post-it note, we can't imagine functioning without writing anything down. But that's what my mum did. She managed a household, husband and five sons with no means of recording anything. Recipes, appointments, phone numbers, dates, times, instructions, facts, jokes, information: she stored it all in her head. And she didn't miss a thing. Even so, she didn't want us to end up in her position. She wanted us to have careers that required serious qualifications.

I often wonder about the insistence of immigrant parents that their children become extremely well qualified. There's a stereotype that Asian parents all want their children to be doctors, lawyers, accountants . . . but mostly doctors. Lots of people from minority groups work towards these professions. In my musings, I wonder if it's because it's much harder to exercise racism in the face of valid certification. No one can consciously, or subconsciously, assume that a person won't be as good as their white counterparts when they have the same – extremely difficult to obtain – qualification. The paperwork reduces the risk of prejudice. I think my parents thought that education would become my protection as racist people could question my character and personality, but never my grades.

5

Crammed in

1974: Rochdale

The time came for Abdul-Ghani to leave the buses and realise his dream of becoming a full-time businessman. The clothes on the market stall were selling steadily and he saw an opportunity to expand. It was Dad's dream to be an entrepreneur. Mum's brother Anwar was now settled with his wife on the outskirts of Manchester and had been angling to work with Dad. He proposed that the two of them should be business partners.

My mum was adamant that it was a bad idea. She loved her brother, but she insisted that he had never been trustworthy, and he wouldn't start now. They argued about it a lot, before Dad finally overrode her instincts and decided to accept the offer, choosing to believe that he would use his cunning and smarts for the benefit of them both and the business. My dad took people at their word. My mum was sharper and more suspicious. She waited for people to prove themselves rather than allowing them to prove her wrong. Like most Pakistani families, my parents adhered to the patriarchal family structure that dictated my father was the head of the household. But regardless of the set-up, my mum made herself heard. While Dad may have had the final decision, he rarely got the final word. She was never disrespectful. She never highlighted a poor decision in public, but when they got behind closed doors, she would make her feelings known.

This would often be around financial choices. Dad was too trusting. He stocked his businesses from big Pakistani-owned warehouses, but he became known as gullible. Wholesalers would see him coming and take it as an opportunity to shift dead stock. They would launch into a patter about some brand-new skirts that were all the rage. 'They're selling like hot cakes!' they would announce before saying that — because they liked him — he could take a hundred units away with him, even though they were only planning on letting him have fifty. Most people are immune to these wheeler-dealer tactics, but not my dad. In a foreign country, where nothing had come easy, he wanted to trust fellow Pakistanis. I think it was more important to him to believe that he had the support of his brothers in business than to make money on some out-of-season skirts. He refused to believe they were looking after anything but his best interests. Having handed over a post-dated cheque, he would load the unsellable stock into his van and face the wrath of Mum when he got home.

When the skirts — or whatever that week's item was — didn't sell, he would get upset with himself. He would know that, once again, he'd made a mistake and they would be choosing between paying the electricity bill and buying groceries. Exasperated by the seemingly never-ending pattern, Mum didn't hold back in her criticism. Over his forty years as a businessman, every single enterprise he established would go bust. He was constantly in a state of losing money. And, with the benefit of hindsight, I wonder if 90 per cent of the failings came from his relying on the wrong people. The other 10 per cent was the Peacocks that eventually opened directly opposite his clothes shop in Bristol, spelling the end.

In fairness to my dad, my mum's distrust was not unanimously vindicated. There were times when his generosity would prove to be well placed. But when my dad's judgement served him poorly, the consequences were far more severe than when my mum was wrong.

The clothes manufacturing business started with Mum at her sewing machine and grew to a small factory space my dad and Uncle Anwar rented on Back Turner Street in Manchester. They also leased a shop in the original Manchester Arndale Centre, the same shopping centre that would go on to be destroyed in an IRA bombing in 1996. At its peak, they had twenty Pakistani women all making ladies' clothes at the rows of machines.

Anwar was convinced that the next step was to expand into another part of the country. He wanted them to establish a second shop in a new area and stock it with the clothes they had made themselves. Dad thought Bristol was the best area, simply because there were some Pakistani shop owners in the city, but not many. To his mind, Pakistanis were the only real competition. This move would take them away from market stalls and be the first step in establishing their empire. They hoped to grow into the next Chelsea Girl or C&A.

After settling on the location, Dad agreed that he would move to Bristol to continue their expansion. Mum was unimpressed. She had friends and family nearby in Rochdale. In Bristol, there would be fewer Punjabi speakers. But once Dad had made his mind up, it was set. She complied with his decision on the condition that they could still live in a house with space for her and the boys, and didn't end up in a flat above a shop.

Dad sold our house in Rochdale and, in order to save money to buy a new Bristol home, take out a lease on a shop and relocate his family, he packed us all up and moved us into Phopo Salima's house for six months. To this day I couldn't tell you how all eleven of us fitted in that compact terraced house.

Phopo Salima's home was welcoming. Yes, we were crammed in, but we were happy. She kept a Crawford's Rover biscuit tin full of treats on a high shelf. When we were good, she would allow us to pick between the KitKats, Penguins and the occasional Tunnock's Caramel Wafer – my fave – that she harboured inside.

Opportunities to get our hands on sweets didn't come often but when they did, we jumped on them. My mum's uncle, known to all as Cha Cha, had moved to the same area and regularly came round for a cup of tea. He planted himself on an armchair in the corner of the living room and stayed put, telling elaborate stories and chain-smoking Dunhill cigarettes. When his packet ran out, which happened frequently, he would jingle the weight of coins he carried in his right-side jacket pocket and say, 'What's all that? It's really weighing me down all this money . . . what shall I do with it?' We'd watch on, eyes wide, hoping to be the lucky child who got to help him lighten his load. He would pick one of us and tell us to go to the Beer Shop to get a packet of cigarettes for him and some sweets for ourselves with the change. If we were chosen, off we would run, five-year-old children going to buy a pack of Dunhill's and some Mojo sweets. Incidentally, it wasn't called the Beer Shop, but as a family that didn't drink, any shop that sold alcohol had a black mark against it. Our local newsagent and off-licence fell into that category. As soon as Cha Cha left, Phopo Salima would open the windows and waft around a damp tea towel to try and bring the air pollution levels in the front room back down to normal.

At night, Phopo Salima would slot a block of wood into the letterbox from the inside and loosely secure it with a nail. It was a practice she maintained for a number of years when we were young. The wooden block was given to her by John, a man who lived a few doors down who owned a hardware shop on Merefield Street. He came to the door one day and told her he was worried that some of the local kids might put fireworks through the letterbox while she and her family slept. He had fashioned the primitive device to block those attempts and showed her how to install it. He didn't say if he had overheard a direct threat or if he was just being cautious. They never had fireworks through their letterbox, whether that was because of the sturdy wooden blockade or because no one tried, we don't know.

We all secretly hoped Phopo Salima would be the one to put us to bed as she told elaborate stories. Often, they would be Pakistani folktales and fables, but if she'd been teaching herself to read English using an old fairytale book, she would tell us those too. I remember her retelling of Aladdin and the sense of tender familiarity with which she told the story of Cinderella. But our favourite was when she made the stories up herself. She would look around at the tiny, hopeful faces and pick the child who would feature in the tale. We all got our turn to be the pirate or the farmer or the superhero, and there was nothing more exciting than when yours came around.

One morning when I was five years old and we were all packed into the house, I woke up with a short, dull, stabbing pain in my stomach. Throughout the day at school, it got progressively worse and by the time I made it home, I was bent double. I couldn't eat or find any position that brought comfort. I was inconsolable and wailing constantly. No one knew what was wrong. Phopo Salima called for the doctor while both Mum and Dad tried to offer me some relief. Mum was convinced that I had gone into the scary abandoned house around the corner and was suffering the consequences of a curse.

My father cradled me in his arms and pulled me tight into his chest while I sobbed without restraint. He kept reassuring me that the doctor was on the way, and he would know how to help. To distract me while we waited, he took his gold-coloured Timex watch off his wrist and handed it to me. My little fingers clasped tight around the face. I loved his watch. I was fascinated by it.

'You can keep my watch,' he said. 'But you must stop crying.' I tried with all my might to suppress the screams. I clung on to the watch, desperate not to let the opportunity to keep it pass me by. But I couldn't contain myself, I burst into tears again. He went to fulfil the threat to take it back from me, but Mum stopped him.

'Leave him with the watch! If you think he's crying now, imagine him if you take it away!'

When the doctor arrived, he was ushered in by Phopo Salima. He spent all of three minutes examining me before telling my parents to call for an ambulance. I needed my appendix removed immediately.

My mum came with me in the ambulance, holding my free hand, while the other clung on to my dad's watch. I remember waking up in the hospital. By the time I came round, I wasn't feeling pain. My midriff was wrapped in bandages. 'Where is Dad's watch?' I asked Mum, on realising my hand was empty. She reassured me that Dad had it, but he would be coming in to see me later and he would bring it with him.

The following day I was allowed home. Tariq and Khalid had done drawings to welcome me back. I was off school for the following week, spending the days lying in bed and having warm, saltwater baths to help with the wounds. As the week was coming to an end and I was preparing to go back to school, I started to get another, sharper pain in my abdomen. It struck in the same place. Once again, the pain grew in intensity, until the following day when I couldn't walk and was in tears. The doctor was stumped. You can't remove someone's appendix twice. My mum once again convinced herself that the haunted, abandoned house was to blame. Unable to identify the cause of the pain, he told us to call an ambulance again.

An equally confused hospital team decided to do a scan to see if they could identify any irregularities. The scan showed that I had been sewn up with a surgical sponge still inside me. The shocked and apologetic surgical team rushed me straight into theatre, removed the sponge and patched me back up again.

In many families, this would have been a source of outrage, but my parents were just grateful. They had come from a country where a burst appendix would almost certainly result in death. In Pakistan they had no access to medical care. They couldn't afford it. It was a luxury enjoyed by the rich. Of course, they would have preferred that I didn't need the second surgery but, to them, the treatment I had received, however imperfect, was better than the alternative.

Fifty years later, when I was the Secretary of State for Health, a journalist asked if I had ever stayed in a hospital. I briefly relayed the tale, pausing for laughter as I finished only to see aghast faces. The story had become a funny family anecdote over the years, and with each retelling the gravity of it had chipped away. It was only when I brought it up in a new setting that I realised again quite how dramatic the experience was. The journalist did oblige me with a chuckle when he realised I had expected one. But I think his lasting impression was one of shock.

The six months with Phopo Salima continued with school on the weekdays followed by playing elaborate and imaginative games with my brothers and cousin Rozina on the evenings and weekends. One of our favourites was hide and seek. As one of the youngest, I could manoeuvre myself into small spaces, which gave me an all-important edge. On one Saturday afternoon, we hurtled around the house trying to find nooks to hide in while Khalid counted. Tariq and Rozina went into the back garden and squeezed into the defunct commode. It was an obvious choice and they were found almost immediately. I, rather unimaginatively, was behind the sofa. I had to push it away from the wall to squeeze behind it, so was less discrete than I had hoped. Bas tucked himself behind a curtain in the bigger of the three upstairs bedrooms. The babies Tes (Tehseen) and Atif were sleeping in the other double room so we all agreed it was off limits. His hiding spot was good. He got cold as he waited so switched on the electric heater to warm his feet. It took Khalid a few minutes to find him but when he did, he pounced, delighted at making the final catch of the game.

We all headed outside to the back alley to continue playing. We were halfway through a game of tag when we heard screaming coming from inside the house. Smoke billowed out of the back bedroom window in thick plumes. It was Phopo Salima screaming. The house was on fire. She ran upstairs to rescue Tes and Atif before the fire spilled out into the landing and second bedroom. My mum burst outside to check all the other children were on the street and hurriedly counted before turning back into the house. As Salima descended the stairs, she reached out and took Atif from her arms before they both flung themselves out of the back door.

We all stood in the alley looking up at the bedroom window helplessly, while a neighbour ran to call the fire brigade. Before they arrived, the glass panes in the window smashed under the high temperatures and we could see the flames spilling out and licking the brickwork either side. The smell was distinctive. A mix of burning plastic, wood and fabrics. Not the pleasant scent of a bonfire but a sickly, cloying smell of chemicals that were never meant to be burned, all up in flames.

No one was hurt, but it didn't stop my parents running through every possible, horrific scenario in their heads. When Bas left the bedroom, he had left the electric heater on. The scorching hot element touched the curtain that had previously been his hiding place and it went up in flames; a pile of laundry was next and soon nothing in the room was left unscorched. My mum was just relieved that all the children were safe and escaped unscathed. My dad was naturally relieved too, but also furious that one of his boys had been the cause of the damage. It took months to repair the decimated bedroom of the little house. Dad felt he should shoulder the cost of the repairs and the temporary house in which we all had to live in the meantime. It cost him dearly and meant we had to make compromises when we eventually moved to Bristol.

6

Bristol beginnings

1974: Bristol

Despite the setbacks, Dad was true to his word and bought a house for us in Bristol. He visited the city a couple of times while we were still living in Rochdale, but the day we arrived was the first time Mum and us boys had been to the area. When the moving day came, we packed up the grey Volkswagen Transporter van that Dad used to take clothes to market. Nestled between the driver's seat and the two passenger seats was a covered oil engine. This metallic engine cover was often used as the third passenger seat for the children. After about thirty minutes of driving, it used to become very hot, leaving the passenger with an uncomfortably warm bottom.

Dad drove, Mum was in the passenger seat with Atif in her lap, and Tariq was sitting on the engine cover. Khalid, Bas and I piled in the back once all the suitcases of clothes and boxes of kitchenware had been stacked in. Mum put a few poufs on the van floor and we were thrown about in the back for half a day while we slowly meandered down to the West Country.

We arrived in Downend, to the northeast of Bristol, in the late afternoon. The area felt less deprived compared to the Rochdale streets we'd lived on. We were in a suburb now. An area where the illumination of the lampposts signalled that it was time for the children to stop playing out. Where mums cooked meals from scratch while dads went out for work. Where, if they were well behaved, kids were given a few pennies on a Friday to spend at the sweet shop. It wasn't elaborate or wealthy, but simple and homey. It was completely white. We were surrounded by white working-class neighbours on all sides. Most difficult for my mum, there would be no one who spoke Punjabi.

Looking at the new house from the outside was exciting. To my untrained, five-year-old eye, it looked huge. Unlike our narrow Rochdale house, standing shoulder to shoulder with the other equally crammed homes next to it, this one was semi-detached. If I had been drawing a picture of it, I would have started with a square rather than a lean rectangle. It had a driveway and a front garden boxed in by a two-foot wall that I would climb and walk around every day on my way home from school. The house was set back from the pavement and there was even a garage at the end of the drive. It was adorned with a mushroom-coloured pebbledash that was a staple for well-groomed family homes up and down the country. As the exterior implied, the rooms were far bigger in every dimension.

The large rooms were made to feel even larger as they were totally empty. After Dad bought the house, the previous owners stripped it of everything. It was barren. There was no furniture, and even the stove had been ripped from the wall. My mum was furious. She had left an area she loved for a vast, empty house with no furniture and no money to buy any. My dad tried to make the best of things, setting up a camp stove as a temporary fix so Mum could cook while he saved up enough to furnish the house.

We brothers made a game out of sleeping on the floor, wrapped up in duvets and sleeping bags. We made a den out of the blankets and pillows and didn't mind that there were no sofas to sit on or tables to eat at. To us it was all one big game. In time, Dad gathered the furniture we needed for the house, but it was never what Mum wanted. He would always seek out the best deals and the lowest prices, insisting on shopping in Pakistani-owned warehouses rather than the catalogues and high-street shops that our neighbours used.

For Mum, it was too much to cope with. She felt completely alone. She cried almost every day. In those days, no one used language like 'depression'. There was no awareness of poor mental health or how to treat it. All my dad knew was that my mum wasn't OK. She stopped talking and didn't eat properly. Her previously plump cheeks became concave with the weight loss; her eyes looked heavy, propped up by the bags that emerged beneath them. The radiance she had exuded when they met in Pakistan had left only its shadow on her sunken, sullen face. Sometimes she just stayed in bed. She continued to care for her children but, on some days, she would do the minimum possible before going to lie down again.

Unsure how to help her, eventually my dad found a doctor in the area who spoke Punjabi and my mum met with him for what we would now describe as talking therapy. After establishing that she was suffering from some kind of melancholy, my mum later told me that the doctor didn't offer her any solutions or medical treatment. He just told her to get her act together. He said that her children and husband were relying on her and she had to sort herself out. The next day she woke up and thought: *I just have to keep going.* And that's what she did.

That kind of tough love wouldn't work for everyone. In fact, modern thought would say it wouldn't help many people at all. But exploring deep emotions was as foreign to my mum at the time as the shepherd's pie the next-door neighbour dropped around – which regrettably went straight in the bin as it wasn't halal. What she found inspiring and motivational was to be able to be dutiful. To provide for her children and her husband. Her biggest fear was that we would not be cared for. That we wouldn't have our Dettol bath and clean clothes for school. It was that job that gave her purpose. The job of giving us the best possible start.

All of us boys, with the exception of Atif who was only a few months old, attended Blackhorse Primary School. We joined as soon as we moved, in the middle of the year. I went straight into year one. I was too young to be thrown off by the uprooting. At that age, I was still at the stage where my parents could put any child between the ages of three and seven in front of me and I would have happily played with them like we were old friends. I hadn't formed great attachments and took each day as it came.

Bas was in the same year as me as they put two age groups together in one. We would walk to school together, trailing behind Tariq and Khalid who had characteristically run ahead. The whiteness of the area made it feel frosty, but not dangerous like in Rochdale. We were safe enough to make our own way home, as did many children of that age.

There was a local playground that we would frequent as often as we could get away with on our way to and from school. That playground was the setting for my earliest memories of trying to look cool in front of my friends. Bas was fearless on the seesaw, roundabout and any other piece of equipment that would no longer pass health-and-safety checks for children. I did my best to replicate his boldness. Respect was earned by staying on the monkey bars for extended periods and enduring the stomach-churning spin of the roundabout for as long as possible.

On one of my exhibitions of bravery, I had just descended

down the slide when a dog came pelting up to me. It was off the lead and bounding around the children's park untamed and untethered. Terrified, I was convinced it was going to bite me. We had been raised to fear dogs. In Pakistan, they weren't house animals. Dogs were considered dirty. You may have owned one for your farm or to guard your house, but they were undomesticated. They certainly didn't venture inside or cuddle up to you. When a dog was approaching us on the pavement, Mum would direct us to cross the road to avoid it. She insisted that they were wild and they would bite. We did all we could to stay away from them.

Armed with this knowledge, I did the only sensible thing on seeing an energetic, slabbering dog bounding towards me: I ran. Of course, far from taking this as an indication of a clear physical boundary, the dog saw it as all part of a game and did what dogs do best: took chase. It followed me all around the playground and then the grass beyond it before finally catching up to me, launching itself on to me and knocking me to the floor. The dog continued to pounce and play, taking nips out of my arms and locking its jaw on the sleeve of my coat. I rolled around trying to drag myself away from the rabid beast. After what felt like a torturous amount of time, the dog's owner came and pulled it off me.

I continued shouting that it had bitten me and stayed where I was on the floor crying until Bas came over to get me. He put his hand out to pull me up to my feet while loudly telling me I was fine and that I shouldn't be scared of dogs, they should be scared of me. No amount of roundabout endurance would be able to bring my credibility back after that display.

It was the last day of school before Christmas, just after my sixth birthday, and I had a festive project to finish. I had spent the night before working on a portrait of Santa Claus. The rest of my class had been set the same task, and just before the winter break, we would display our creations for everyone to enjoy. I'd opted for the traditional aesthetic. No big surprises. His hat and jacket were a signature red, created with my chunky felt-tip pens. The key features of his face – the eyes, nose, mouth etc. – were all represented in black felt-tip pen. But his beard was the most exciting flourish as it was fashioned from cotton wool balls that I'd pulled apart and stuck to the page with Pritt Stick. On running out of glue the night before, Mum said I could go to the VG shop across the road after breakfast to buy another and quickly finish it off.

Bas came with me and we ventured across the road to buy the glue stick. Snow had fallen overnight and there was a powdery layer over the driveway. We were the first out so we got to leave our footprints in the fresh snow. We bought the glue, plus a few penny sweets with the change. Bas rushed out of the shop and straight across the road. A few seconds behind him, I stepped out, unaware of my surroundings. A car slammed on its brakes but skidded on the ice and hit me square on. By the time it made contact it couldn't have been going more than ten miles per hour but it was enough to throw me a few metres down the road. I don't remember feeling any pain, just shock.

As I lay on the ground Bas ran into the house to get Mum. She rushed out, shouting at me. Was I breathing? Could I move? Could I talk? The answer to all three was yes but the shepherd's pie-eating neighbour, Ruma, who we started to call Auntie Ruma, called an ambulance and sat with Atif while Mum went with me to the hospital.

On getting into school Bas was so high on adrenaline that he announced the story to his whole class and, by first playtime, tales of my injuries had been exaggerated to the whole school. The other children were re-enacting me being thrown five metres into the air and slamming on to the road, leaving a dent in the tarmac. It was assumed they wouldn't see me for months and Bas had described the various broken bones that would need casts and the extensive treatment I would require to be able to walk again.

In the hospital, they were happy to sign me off with a warning to be more careful when crossing roads. Mum brought me home, where I insisted that I wanted to go into school. It was the last day, not a proper work day. The last day was always fun as the teachers had already mentally clocked off and the pupils were left to play games. Plus, I had a Santa portrait to showcase.

Mum assured me that I was better staying home, but I was adamant that I wanted to go in. She relented, so at lunchtime I sauntered into the playground to aghast faces. My classmates gaped at me like they were seeing a ghost. When they asked how I could move and where my multiple casts were, it became apparent that Basit's sense of showmanship had got the better of him. He responded to any questioning that day with a theatrical shrug, before doing what all four-year-olds do when they're in a bind. He ran away.

The following Easter, I hit a milestone that meant the world to me. I got my first bike. After a combined effort between the four older boys, as Atif was still a baby, Dad finally brought home bikes for us. He pulled up one evening after work in his VW van and wheeled three bikes into the garage. The first was the biggest and Dad announced that it was for Tariq and Khalid to share. The second was a mid-sized children's bike in red with a lightning bolt painted on the side and a bell that let out a shrill ding. Dad said that was for me. The third was smaller and had stabilisers fitted. That was for Bas.

They were all second-hand and showed some signs of wear and tear. It wasn't all we had dreamed of but it was all Dad could afford. As the only one of the four of us with a proper-sized kids' bike that I didn't have to share, I was delighted with the turn of events. The invitation for Tariq, who was nine at the time, to share with his seven-year-old brother Khalid was one that he didn't relish. Perhaps inevitably, Khalid got pushed out of the arrangement. The seat and handlebars were set too high for Khalid to ride the bike and he got a punch in the arm from Tariq if he tried to adjust them. Tariq was also extra cautious as we all knew Khalid couldn't ride a bike. He could in the sense that he was able to put his feet on the pedals and start the thing moving, but he was wobbly and unbalanced. He would often come off or roll into something without using the brakes. None of this was my problem though. I had my bike and, in a house where very few things were yours and yours alone, I was possessive of it.

I took my bike out for a ride every day after school and first thing on weekends. There were no cycling proficiency tests, there weren't even helmets. Just me, my five-year-old intuition and the open road. Realising that he was losing his grip on the bike that had been assigned to him, Khalid decided to turn his attention to my bike. He would announce he was taking it, which would always result in a wrestling match between the two of us. I would kick up a fuss at any suggestion of someone else using the bike and would run to Mum explaining that Khalid had a bike but he wanted mine.

One day I came home from school after a brief stint in the playground. Khalid had gone ahead and wasn't home when I got back, and neither was my bike. I went straight to Mum to say that Khalid had nicked my bike. Unfazed by my fury, she said to just wait as he would bring it back and then she could speak to him. I waited. I sat in the front garden. I walked up and down the street and a few of the neighbouring roads. A full two hours later there was a loud shout from the garden. A neighbour was carrying Khalid in his arms, and presented him to my mum over the garden fence.

My mum was desperately concerned. She took Khalid and laid him on the sofa in the living room. He didn't look too bad but was in shock. He had scratches on his knees and elbows and a bump was forming on his forehead. The neighbour had explained that Khalid had lost control of the bike going down a parallel road that had a steep hill. He'd gone careering into a parked car, came off the bike and knocked his head on the bonnet.

I was frantic. Not about Khalid. But about my bike. As the neighbour calmly and sympathetically relayed the events, I interjected like a hovering fly. 'Is the bike OK?' 'Did you leave the bike in the street?' 'What road was it?' 'Did the bike break?' The man ignored me and continued speaking to my mum until she snapped, 'What's the matter with you? It's not about your bike! Your brother is hurt!'

I skulked away. He seemed fine to me. I grabbed Bas and the two of us went in search of the bike. I knew which road the neighbour lived on and I knew it had a steep hill. That seemed like the sensible place to start. And there it was, my bike crumpled into a heap on the road next to a scratched Ford Cortina. I cursed Khalid as I picked it up and wheeled it home to survey the damage.

The handlebars were bent, the spokes had come off the front wheel and the chain had snapped. It wasn't fixable. I was gutted. I showed Dad when he got home and defiantly demanded a new bike to replace it. But there was no money for another. Dad told me to share Bas's stabiliser bike and told Khalid to stick to the one he shared with Tariq. At the time, it felt like a disappointment I would never recover from. I held on to it for a while.

Later that summer, Khalid and I were in the VG store. I had a few pence for Fruit Salad chews in my pocket. As we walked down one of the aisles, Khalid picked up a roll of Sellotape and put it into his pocket. My eyes widened as I saw the stationery disappear into his trousers. 'What are you doing?' I asked.

'Shut up!' he said. He walked out of the shop, leaving me alone to pay for my sweets.

I went to the counter and put my favourite chews on the counter. 'All right, Saj?' said the friendly shopkeeper. Unable to bear the weight of the crime, I didn't even respond to his greeting before saying, 'You know my brother Kal? He just stole some Sellotape.'

The man smiled and raised an eyebrow, 'Did he?'

'He just picked it up and put it in his pocket and then walked out.'

'Who did that? Your brother Khalid?'

'Yeah!'

'Just a moment ago?'

'Yeah!'

'That's not right is it?' he shook his head as he asked the question.

'No,' I replied, mimicking his gesture with an equally pious headshake.

'I tell you what,' said the shopkeeper. 'Why don't you go home and tell your mum what's happened and ask her to send him back with the Sellotape?'

I nodded in agreement, pocketed my sweets and headed back across the road to complete my mission. I walked straight into Mum in the kitchen and announced: 'Khalid stole something from the VG shop.'

He came running in behind me. 'No I didn't!' he protested. Mum shot him a stern look, 'Did you steal something, Khalid?'

'No!'

'Why does Sajid say you did then?'

'I don't know!' Tears of frustration started to well up in his eyes. 'But he's lying!'

'Khalid, tell me one more time, did you steal?'

The tears overwhelmed him and on the third time of asking, he confessed to his crime. Mum made him bring the Sellotape to her, which was mercifully still in its plastic packaging. 'Go and take this across the road and give it back to him now. You must say sorry, too.'

She turned to me, 'Sajid, go with him and support him.'

I puffed my chest out a bit as I walked behind him to oversee the confession. He walked into the shop, head hanging low, and shuffled over to the cash register. He pulled the Sellotape out from his pocket and put it back on the counter with a muffled 'I'm sorry.'

The shopkeeper picked it up and offered him a patient smile. 'It's OK, Khalid,' he said. 'But this is really serious what you did. I know you and your family and your parents, so I'm not going to get you into trouble but someone else might have called the police. You really mustn't do this again. Do you understand?'

Khalid nodded without breaking eye contact with his shoelaces.

'You see, my wife and I have paid money for this, and we only make money to buy food and clothes and things when people buy them from us. So we really need people to pay. Just like your dad in his shop.'

Khalid nodded once again.

'All right, boys, off you go.' He gestured us away to indicate that we were dismissed. As we turned away, he said, 'Hang on,' and handed us each a couple of Mojo sweets. 'Well done for telling me, Saj, and well done for coming back and saying sorry, Khalid.'

That was the last time I remember Khalid doing anything wrong. When the rest of us would continue to get into many scrapes ranging from cheeky to illegal, Khalid remained on the straight and narrow, helping Mum in the house and dedicating himself to Islam in a way none of the rest of us did. We branded him a Goody Two Shoes and a snitch on occasions when he told on us like I just had on him. But he could always be relied upon to do the right thing.

While we were settling into family life in the UK, other members of Dad's family were making the same move. His youngest brother Hamid, who was born just after that treacherous trip during partition, came to England while we were in Downend. He was living in Dad's village Lasuri when he met a British woman called Lucy. She had joined a humanitarian charity and was in Pakistan doing development work. Despite being in her mid-twenties, Lucy had already been married and divorced. She had a daughter called Katharine, who was about Tariq's age, from her first marriage. The pair met and started a relationship, eventually they married and Hamid moved to Bristol to live with Lucy and his new stepdaughter.

Lucy was from a middle-class white family and had been at Putney High School for girls. She faced challenges from some family members for her choice in partner. Interracial marriages were incredibly rare and it was the first mixed marriage I was aware of. But Lucy was strong minded and completely unfazed. For Lucy's family, she added insult to injury by taking Hamid's Pakistani last name.

The couple lived in what I would now describe as a modest four-bedroom semi-detached house, though at the time it looked palatial to me. I remember as a young boy living in Downend, we were invited to their house for tea. To my mum, tea was chai and it was very different to the pot of Earl Grey that Lucy brought out of the kitchen. Lucy's tea was served with crisps in a bowl and strawberry jam sandwiches. My mum couldn't get her head around the practice of inviting people to your home and not serving steaming hot pakoras. Driving back from their house on one of these occasions, she once again expressed this opinion, and I remember my dad saying, 'Stop it, Zubaida, this is just what English people do!'

7

Flat out

After just a year in Downend, my father's businesses were losing too much money for us to stay in the house. He decided to sell it and move the family to the two-bedroom flat above the shop on 109 East Street, Bedminster. I wasn't there when Dad broke the news to Mum, but I remember the months of anger in the fallout. Her one condition for moving to Bristol was that they would have a real family home for her and the boys. Now, just as they had finally managed to furnish the house and settle in, she had been told she would have to give it up.

Mum made her anger felt, but she didn't go on about it. There was no point. The decision had been made and we had to move. To argue about it daily would only make an undesirable situation intolerable.

The flat above the shop was small. It was a return to the close quarters of Rochdale but this time on a busy main road. Access was through the shop and up a dingy staircase to the front door. The whole of the first floor was taken up with the lounge and kitchen, the carpet curling at the edges and a breeze of unidentifiable origins coming from the windows. No amount of newspaper and T-shirt stuffing could plug the hidden valve that seemingly only allowed air in during the winter. We had a TV in the lounge, along with one small faux-leather sofa that we brought with us from Downend. There was no dining table. The family dining was done around the coffee table and those too slow to squeeze on to the sofa sat on the floor, or later, on one of the poufs that Mum piled in the corner. Mum was back to cooking in a cupboard kitchen and no longer had her drive or garage. We kept the van in a small car park around the back of the main road.

The flat was directly across the road from a rowdy pub, the Nelson. As neither of my parents drank, to them every pub was a den of iniquity. All they saw were the punters rolling out after a long session propping up the bar. There were often people shouting or singing or vomiting in the street into the early hours. Sometimes people would kiss up against the wall or, worse, a fight would break out. With our bedroom facing out on to the street, us kids would often be woken up by the noise and would then creep over to watch the commotion.

Mum was strict with us, saying that we shouldn't try and watch. Partly because she didn't know what we'd see and partly because she didn't want us to be seen staring at the drunk patrons who could then make a target of the shop below. She was worried that they would be offended by our curtain twitching and we would wake up to a brick through the window.

However, one perk of the move was that Dad no longer had to commute. We could see him whenever we wanted by just walking downstairs. Mum helped in the shop so wasn't up at the flat much during the day but, for the first time, they were both within reach. They didn't spend 'quality time' together in the way we think of now. They certainly didn't have date nights and only ever got dressed up for family events and weddings. But they paid each other compliments regularly. They were loving and made small physical gestures of affection when they thought we weren't looking, like a touch of a hand or the graze of an arm. They didn't kiss in front of us or hold hands. But they loved each other and showed each other little kindnesses.

To the right of our shop was a café, George's. The eponymous patron was a jovial Greek Cypriot who became friendly with my parents. Despite his nationality, the café's Mediterranean offering was limited, and instead George opted for the crowd-pleasing dishes of a greasy spoon. Mum and Dad never ate there. Eating out wasn't a good way to spend their money, especially when Mum would prefer to cook Pakistani food at home. Nevertheless, as neighbouring business owners, they got on well.

One day George asked Dad if he wanted a coffee. Until then, Dad had only ever had granulated instant coffee, like Nescafé. He didn't dislike coffee, he had it most mornings, but it wasn't a treat for him. George had a coffee espresso machine in the café. It had real ground coffee and steamed milk. My dad accepted the offer and, on taking his first sip of a frothy cappuccino, realised just how luxurious a coffee could be. He asked if he could take the mug with him into his shop next door. He took it through to my mum so she could taste this new indulgent coffee. From then on, every now and again, my dad would go to George's and bring Mum a cappuccino while she was in the shop. That was how they showed each other love.

We got to know all of the other local businesses and people who worked on the street, with the exception of the pubs and the butcher's, which we didn't go into at all. On the other side of George's was Regal Arcade, run by the larger-than-life Babs who smoked almost as much as she swore. We all got our hair cut at the Italian barbers, Napoli's on the corner – the barber being a man who we always called Napoli, on account of the fact that we had little idea of where Italy was, let alone Naples.

The shop is still in business now at number 163, although it's unlikely he still charges £1 for a trim.

Our favourite, however, was the sweet shop. Melville Confectionery was set back from the main road with a little side door. The tiny store of wonders was famous for its rosebuds – oval boiled sweets with stripes of yellow and red. They were stocked by a small sweet factory across the road. The smell on that corner was heavenly, particularly if you positioned yourself by one of the air vents – which we made a point of doing every time we were on the way home. As children of five and seven, Bas and I were almost exclusively motivated by sweets. My favourite was pineapple rock, while Bas was always excited by the idea of half a penny's worth of cola cubes. The short, elderly woman behind the counter had flushed cheeks and an aesthetic that would have been described as matronly if she didn't have such a warm smile.

Bas and I were desperate to get our hands on a few pennies here and there to buy sweets on the way home. For a month or so, there was a five-pence piece stuck in the grille of the vacuum cleaner. In order to get it out, Mum would have needed to remove the cover with a screwdriver. Something she hadn't yet done. One day after school I was so set on getting some sweets that I took the handle of a spoon and used it to lever the plastic on the grate. I snapped off two bars and was able to free the coin. It was Khalid who told Mum on me, although she just used her usual nickname for the snitch, 'a little birdie'. I had to apologise and Sellotape the grille back together as best I could, but it was worth it for the bag of Mojos Bas and I shared that day.

On one occasion, Bas and I had managed to get our hands on some coppers. They were enough for a small bag of one type of sweet, but not enough to pick multiple. We stood gazing up at the wall of jars on shelves above the counter. Our deliberations were precise and lengthy. With so little money, and everything charged by weight, any high-density sweets were out of the question. This was no time to buy vanilla fudge. Even Bas's preferred cola cubes could have been considered too dense for the occasion. As we weighed up our options, with the patient shopkeeper listening on with amusement, a man in his fifties walked in and stood behind us, forming a queue. He wore a suit and tie, and therefore stood out against the backdrop of windbreakers and tracksuits that usually clothed those who lived in the area. He stood in line, his smile slowly growing as our deliberations intensified. Eventually, I won the debate – I was the older of us, after all – and we ordered a quarter of pineapple rock. After she'd weighed them up, popped them into a paper bag and flipped it round by the corners to seal it, the woman asked: 'Anything else, boys?'

'No,' we chorused, reaching up to hand over the coins in payment.

The man behind leant forward towards us and said, 'Are you sure you don't want anything else?'

Slightly taken aback by the unexpected question, we quietly reassured him that was all. 'Oh, go on, get some more, boys,' he said. 'I'll pay.'

Bas and I looked at each other, 'What does he want?' Bas said to me in Punjabi.

I craned my head up to look at the man, who was still smiling down at us. 'I don't know,' I said. 'He looks fine, doesn't he?'

'I don't know,' Bas said. 'I think we should get the sweets though.'

I agreed and we said thank you to the man, before ordering a quarter each of cola cubes, fruit salads and lemon sherberts. After further encouragement from him that he didn't mind, we ordered another seven sweets while he watched on in amusement.

When the bags were lined up on the counter and he had confirmed one final time that we were definitely done, he ordered a bag of fizzy cola bottles for himself and paid for the lot. We took up the bags, repeating our thank-yous as we left the shop. We never saw that man again. He didn't want anything at all. But I remember the overwhelming feeling of excitement having all of those sweets. Days of plenty were rare for us, and that feeling never left me.

Every man in my family lost his hair at around the age of thirty. In our most honest moments, we would say that the event was foreshadowed long before. Unlike my brothers, it took my dad until well into his fifties before he finally succumbed to his retreating hairline and shaved his head. In his thirties, he tackled the problem in a different way: with a toupee.

We all knew Dad wore a wig, but as children, we didn't think anything of it. Dad had his regular toupee that he wore every day, and a backup. This was usually his previous full-time toupee that had become worn down and been replaced, only to be relegated to the role of substitute.

There were all sorts of specialist glues and tapes designed to discreetly attach the hairpiece to his head. He opted out of all of them in favour of the cheaper and less specialist alternative of double-sided sticky tape. He kept his tape, a pair of nail scissors and a comb with more than a couple of missing teeth in the mirrored cabinet above the bathroom sink.

The problem for my dad was that we all knew where the tape was kept. Often we would have an idea, an invention or a piece of homework that we couldn't possibly pull off without tape. Unable to locate any anywhere else, or having not bothered to try, we would go for Dad's tape in the bathroom and inevitably not return it. About once a month, Dad would stomp down the stairs and into the living room, one fist clenched on his mop of faux hair and the other just clenched and demand that we return his sticky tape.

'Where's my sticky tape? Who's taken it?' When this was greeted with no response, he would launch into the second part of the familiar speech. 'I'm late! I have to open the shop and here I am with no hair. I can't believe it! I have so much to do. I need to put my hair on!' When his shouts still elicited no response, he demanded my mum track down the thief and the stolen goods. 'Zubaida, how many times have I told you not to let the kids take my sticky tape?'

Mum's reaction went one of two ways. On her less patient days she would retort that if we had a bigger house, with two bathrooms, he could keep the tape away from the kids and always know where it is.

More often, though, she set to work trying to find the tape. Nothing was truly lost until my mum couldn't track it down. Her usual plan of action was to attempt to revive yesterday's toupee sticky tape as a temporary measure so that he could open up the shop with his head covered and she could come down later with some new tape to swap it over. This would always be met with the same protests: 'It's not strong any more. My hair's going to blow off at the first sign of wind. This is your fault!'

We would watch this all play out and make no attempt to stifle our giggles. It was only when Mum turned to us and told us to stop that we stopped. 'This is not a joke, boys, this is serious. Your dad needs to go to work with his hair on.' Whether she found it funny or not, she would not allow us to laugh at our dad. She would look each of us in the eye and ask where the tape was. When no one owned up, we would have to leave our breakfast at the table and go to find it. Meanwhile, she would try and rush him downstairs with her short-term solution. She knew how quickly the situation could turn from farce to fierce, and she didn't want him taking out his frustration on us boys.

*

Bas and I walked to the local primary school together every day. South Street Primary was ten minutes down East Street and up British Road, past a park which promised no more than a poorly kept patch of grass and a few trees. Our main source of amusement on the walk was playing knock-down ginger: the adrenaline-inducing practice of knocking on people's doors and running away before they could catch you. It was outrageously annoying for the residents and completely pointless ... but utterly thrilling. We would usually save the game for the walk home, when the first half of the journey was down a residential street with rows and rows of modest terraced houses. There were four of five of us who participated and we focused our energies on the houses that had shown themselves to be most annoyed by the game in the past. The approach to the door had to be silent and steady but once the knock was complete, you had to get out of there as quickly as possible. Whether you hid somewhere close to watch the reaction, dashed across the road to duck behind a hedge or just hit the pavement and kept running, was the knocker's choice. We toyed with every option at one time or another. I preferred the adrenaline of continuous running, imagining yourself being chased by hordes of angry residents. In reality I never was.

The school was, once again, with the exception of a Chinese boy called Wing Wang Chang, all white. Milk and an apple were also available at South Street school, only this time our parents had to cover the cost. Most of the children got the breaktime treat but there was one family whose children never did. They were the really poor kids. Their clothes were always tatty and they were rarely clean. The other kids used to joke that they smelled. When we first joined the school we got the milk and apples like anyone else, but after the first term, my parents decided they couldn't justify the expense so we stopped. I was ashamed to be in the same category as the neglected and deprived family everyone ridiculed. I was desperate to make sure people didn't think we were like them.

As it was a Christian school, the day started with prayers and hymns. I remember asking my dad if it was OK for us to participate in the Christian practices but my dad reassured me that I didn't need to kick up a fuss. He said that, as Muslims, we believed that Jesus was a prophet and that he is in the Qur'an.

At lunchtime everyone sat together, including the teachers. There were no food options and packed lunch wasn't allowed, you were just given what you were given. With halal meat out of the question and the risk of being served pork, we once again opted for a vegetarian approach. The dinner hall, a room that felt like a vast, expansive space at the time, had rows of tables and each was hosted by a different teacher who ate with us and generally made sure the pupils kept in line. One such lunch, Basit and I sat together when the deputy principal, Mr Edwards, took his place at the head of the table. The dinner ladies handed bowls of food to the teacher on each table who doled out a plate for each child. It was sausage and mash day so we each asked for a plate with mashed potato and peas but nothing else. We never risked the gravy.

Mr Edwards, a wiry old man who wore a trademark V-neck knitted tank top over his shirt, served the plates and then handed them to the pupils. When it came to me, he surveyed me before saying, 'And you're sure you won't have a sausage, Sajid?'

'No, sir,' I said. 'We don't eat sausages.'

'Nonsense, you can have one sausage.'

'No thank you, sir, I'm not allowed sausages.'

The idea that a boy at a Christian school would shun the food he was offered was offensive in Mr Edwards's eyes. Understanding of other cultures and belief systems was low. Even I, as a young boy, didn't understand the Islamic theology behind the decision to abstain from pork. All I knew was that

Mum said we didn't eat it. Clearly unimpressed, he decided to take matters into his own hands and, while I was distracted, snuck a piece of sausage into the middle of my potato and then disguised it with more mash. I was oblivious to the non-halal stowaway but Bas had clocked it. He kicked me under the table and said in Punjabi, 'Don't eat it, he's put pig in your potato.'

'What?' I replied. 'What are you talking about?'

But Mr Edwards intercepted the conversation, 'What are you doing? What are you saying? I don't want to hear that gibberish. How many times have I told you not to speak that gibberish in school?'

We apologised but Bas continued to throw meaningful looks directly into my eyes and then into my mashed potato. I dug through my plate and found the offending article, discreetly removed it, tucked it into a tissue and pocketed it without saying anything to Mr Edwards. I ate the rest of my food and then showed the teacher my empty plate – a prerequisite for being dismissed to go and play in the playground. He took the plate off me with a self-satisfied grin and told me I was free to go.

Once we were outside Bas and I couldn't contain our indignation. 'That bastard!' Bas said.

'Yeah, wait till I tell Mum!'

'What did you do with it?' he asked.

'I put it in tissue, it's in my pocket.'

'Let's feed it to the school cat!' he exclaimed with childish glee.

I was delighted with the plan and we went in search of the cat who we found licking her fur on a big planter by the main entrance. We fed her the sausage, broken up into smaller chunks and then went straight to rinse our hands in the water fountain. Mum had a sixth sense for when we were unclean and she would be furious if she knew we'd been feeding a cat.

I told my friends in school but none of them understood the

significance of what Mr Edwards had tried to do. They joined the bandwagon of fury, because everyone enjoys a new reason to hate a teacher, but they weren't really outraged at all.

When I got home and told my mum, that's when I saw someone truly rage at the situation. She marched downstairs to the shop before dinner to vent to my dad. Dad was also upset but tentative. He didn't want to be the brown family that rocked the boat. Dad felt grateful that we had places at the school and he didn't want to complain. He decided not to say anything: he felt lucky his boys were there and he didn't want to risk us being told to pack our bags and go elsewhere.

As I moved up into the junior school the focus of most of the young boys shifted from superheroes and pirates to sport. At the start of every break, a gaggle of young boys would steam across the road to the field where we could play football or cricket. I was not good at competitive sports. In the chicken-and-egg scenario of my believing myself to be bad at sports and me being bad at sports, I can't tell you which came first. But to know wouldn't have affected my performance. I was terrible. After a few attempts to be one of the lads and join a game, I gave up, opting to spend my breaks playing other games like marbles or tag.

It will come as no surprise, then, that I didn't look forward to physical education classes. They were just another opportunity for me to be highlighted as one of the weakest members of the team. My dislike for PE peaked in year four when we all, once again, marched across the road to play football on the grass field. The teacher split the class in two and assigned the teams. I was glad we didn't have to line up for captains to choose, as that never ended well for me. The whistle blew and the game started. I stood directly next to the opponents' goal. I didn't know much about tactics but I was sure that if I could get hold of the ball from that position, a goal would soon follow.

Sure enough, one of the other players kicked the ball in my direction. I stopped it with my right foot and before allowing the time for myself to overthink it, kicked it right into the back of the goal. I couldn't believe it. I had actually scored! I started running and whooping with delight, only to slow my celebration down when I realised none of my team were cheering. If anything, they looked angry.

'What the fuck, Saj?' one of the children shouted over to me. I had scored in the wrong goal. The others were furious and I got barged and ignored by my own team for the rest of the game. My team lost that match 1–0. My own goal was the only score of the game.

Feeling equal parts annoyed and embarrassed, I got dressed in the changing room, packed my school bag and left with the intention of skipping knock-down ginger and heading straight home. I left the school grounds down a small stairwell at the side of the building only to be greeted with three boys from my class, Kev, Martin and James. Kev grabbed me and pinned me up against a wall while Martin punched me in the stomach. 'Don't ever do that again,' he spat while landing a second punch. I took another couple of hits before they released me from their grip and sent me on my way.

If I didn't like football before, I now did all I could to avoid playing. I never wanted to make another mistake on the field.

8

Britain's most dangerous street

The premises that Dad and Anwar owned in Manchester struggled to show any return. With takings low up north, but potential for a decent set-up in Bristol, Anwar packed up his family of four and moved them to 309 Stapleton Road in Eastville, just south of Bristol city centre, so that they could focus their efforts on the one area.

My mum was still suspicious of her brother and his handling of the business's finances. Not least because, when they were up north, his family lived in one of the new-build Barratt Homes that were constantly advertised on TV by the man in the helicopter, while we were crammed into the tiny flat above the shop.

When he arrived, he took charge of the new site on Stapleton Road, a warehouse space they called Kaiza Fashions where they would sell directly to trade. The 'K' in 'Kaiza' was the first letter of Anwar's wife's name, Khalila, one 'A' was from his name, and the 'Z' and the other 'A' were from those of my parents.

Dad continued to run the shop on East Street in Bedminster. The split remained like this for a couple of years before Anwar decided he wanted a change. He told my dad he was sick of England and wanted to move, with his family, back to Pakistan for good. They wouldn't be coming back and it was Abdul-Ghani's lucky day, as he would be handing the whole business over to him to run as he pleased. I don't know if my dad did feel lucky when he heard this news. To run a multi-site business when he was low on funds to employ people would be hard work but then, his empire was growing. He had always dreamed of being a successful entrepreneur and now he would indeed be stepping into the role as sole owner of a fashion business.

My dad decided that we would move across Bristol again to the flat that Anwar and his family would be vacating above the warehouse, as that was his primary source of income. That way, he could be on hand for the wholesale customers. We rented out the Bedminster flat and Dad drove Mum there every morning to look after the shop. There she sat, day in and day out, sometimes with help and sometimes on her own, only coming home in time to arrange our food and make sure we got to bed.

Anwar's big move included a five-month road trip where he and his family would drive to Pakistan, taking various stops along the way. We all came over to Stapleton Road to wave them off as they started their trip. The boot of the brown Audi hatchback car was crammed so tight that the rear-view mirror was rendered redundant. They had stacked a mountain of cases on the roof, strapped together and covered with a bedsheet in an attempt to keep them in place. Anwar and Khalila sat in the front of the car while their four children were in the back seats. There was excitement as the laden vehicle took off down Stapleton Road and we all continued waving until it turned a corner and was out of sight.

Just three weeks later, my dad's business cheques started to bounce. At first, it was a supplier with a large cheque. Dad reasoned that if there was a delay in an incoming payment clearing into the account, then perhaps the cheque could have bounced. But then he got calls about other, far smaller amounts that he was certain the company could cover. Unsure of what was going on, he requested a meeting with his bank manager and went up to Barclays on Stapleton Road to meet with him.

'Thanks for coming in so quickly, Mr Javid, and I'm sorry that there's been so much confusion,' the man said as they settled into uncomfortable office chairs on either side of his desk. 'I think this can all be cleared up if you speak to your partner, Anwar.'

My dad furrowed his brow. 'Thank you, sir. I am not able to speak with Anwar though. He is travelling and decided not to come back to the business. He's moving back to Pakistan.'

The bank manager pushed his head back into his neck, creating chin rolls that his weight wouldn't have otherwise allowed. 'But he's told us he's *expanding* the business, not leaving it.'

'I don't understand, he came in and met with you about growing the business?'

'Yes, that's right. About a month ago, he came in and said he needed to remove all the money from your account as he would be using it to invest in new equipment and new premises. He had a plan to show us as he wanted a loan as well.'

'A loan? He borrowed money from you?' my dad asked.

'Yes, he said the company wanted to borrow twenty-five thousand pounds, but surely you knew.'

'I did not know. I knew nothing about this. Don't you need us both to approve a loan on the business?'

'Well, no. One account holder is usually sufficient.'

'So, he took all the money from our account and a twenty-five-thousand-pound loan?'

'Yes, that's right. He withdrew it all. Once we'd given him

the twenty-five thousand and then another fifteen thousand from your accounts, he walked out with forty thousand pounds.'

'Forty thousand pounds?!' My dad started hyperventilating. 'In cash?'

The account was barren. Anwar had barely left a few pounds for Dad to cover bills and wages that month. Not only would Dad have to find the money to keep the business afloat, he was now liable for a £25,000 business loan and the associated interest. He was furious with himself, he was furious with my mum for her warnings (even though she was right) and he was furious with Anwar, whom he had trusted to behave honourably.

I remember the despair that filled our house in the days after. Dad paced, unable to rest or sit down, drumming his fingers on the counter, repeating the same question to Mum, over and over again: 'What will we do?'

Mum struggled to hide her annoyance and lack of sympathy. She had warned him and she didn't mind reminding him. There was no way to contact Anwar while he was on the road. It would be months before he reached Pakistan and longer still before they would be able to get an address for him and reprimand him by airmail. There was no hope of recovering the money and no hope of making Anwar answer for his fraud.

Everything got tighter. We swapped to cheaper cuts of meat, or no meat at all for dinner. There were no treats and no new clothes. Anything we did buy had to be an absolute necessity. Dad worked longer hours, pushed for more deals and negotiated the prices of his incoming stock down as far as he possibly could. They scoured the house for anything of value to sell and after months of stress and frugality, we managed to get back on to an even keel.

In the meantime, however, Anwar and his family had reached Turkey. Conscious that they were carrying a suitcase packed full of cash, they made sure to find a hiding place for it in each place they stopped. In their overnight hotel in Ankara, they had opted to put it right at the back of the cupboard, tucked behind the extra blankets and towels. Then, as they left the next morning, they promptly forgot to take it with them. Each assuming the other had possession of the cash, they carried on their journey for an additional two days before realising their mistake and rushing back.

In the meantime, the story goes that the cleaning staff found the bag and did the honourable thing, handing it in to the management. The management, also displaying great moral fortitude, handed it to the Turkish police. The bag contained some paperwork, including the bank details for an account and loan at a Barclays Bank in England. The police made contact with the branch manager, who was delighted to hear that such a large sum had been discovered. He arranged for it to be collected, and he restored it to my father's business account.

The improbability of these events was so astounding that we could barely believe what had happened. My dad was able to breathe again for the first time in months. It felt like divine retribution. A higher power had stepped in to right a colossal injustice.

When Anwar got back to the hotel and was informed of what had become of the cash, he was frantic. He phoned my dad and, in a long conversation, he admitted that he had taken the money but maintained that, as Dad would have the premises and stock, he was entitled to it as his share of the business. He implored my father to show him kindness as he was now stranded with his wife and children in Turkey with no money for the onward journey and nothing to get them started in Pakistan. He begged my dad to send him back some of the money. He said that the lives of his children depended on it.

To the disgust and outrage of my mother, my dad wired £20,000 back to him the following day. My dad could not bear the idea that his nieces and nephews could be in trouble. To him, they were innocent and shouldn't be punished with their father. His only stipulation was that he never wanted Anwar, or his family, to contact us again.

The week that Anwar embarked on his road trip, our family moved into the flat above the Kaiza warehouse on Stapleton Road. The street was dubbed 'Britain's Most Dangerous Street' in the 1990s. In 1979, when we moved in, it wasn't safer, the press just weren't writing about it yet. Running from Eastville in the north all the way down to the centre of town, it was a hotbed for crime. In the winter months, I would walk down the dreary street in the dark, my face illuminated by the neon signs in the shops and the red glow from the windows above. At nine years old, I didn't know why women stood out in their doorways in miniskirts and thigh-high boots, faces weighed down by excessive make-up and heavy smoking. One woman, Jackie, would always shout over, 'Afternoon, boys,' as we walked past. We'd smile and wave and politely shout back, 'Hi, Jackie!' as we continued on our way home.

The streets were dirty. Rubbish piled up and we would run the gauntlet of old mattresses and shopping trollies spilling out from unkempt front gardens and on to the pavement. Needles were commonplace but mainly collected under the railway arches. There was a corner of the street, right by the KFC, that was surrounded by a pungent earthy smell. I wouldn't be able to identify it as cannabis until I was older. This was also the area most heavily affected by graffiti. These days those railway arches are still covered in graffiti but brightly coloured and well designed, bearing messages like 'Welcome to Easton' and 'Good vibes'. Back then it was a series of unartistic tags with the occasional 'fuck off' scattered between them.

The shops on the street appealed exclusively to ethnic groups that were a minority anywhere else in Bristol. There were many halal butchers, fabric shops for saris and takeaways from the four corners of Asia and most of the Caribbean. Despite the diversity, we still experienced racism on Stapleton Road. Some of the most vicious prejudice can come from one minority to another, and relations between different groups weren't always amicable.

Just six months after we moved in, we were warned by our parents not to stray into the neighbouring area of St Pauls. It was a fifteen-minute walk down the road from where we lived, and was a part of Bristol almost exclusively inhabited by Afro-Caribbean residents. One Asian family we knew well lived in the area but otherwise it was only Black friends, including Joe and Moses, the Barbadian handymen that Dad hired to help in the shops.

Previously we had been free to roam into any area and we hadn't felt any threat wandering around St Pauls. It housed a grandly named cinema, Metropole de Luxe, that showed Bollywood films. Occasionally we would get to go. But now my parents were serious that it was off limits. Race relations between the Black residents and police had been strained for a while. But in that year, 1980, a clash between police and residents at the local Black and White Café on Grosvenor Road resulted in a hundred and thirty arrests and twenty-five people being taken to hospital. Our friends in the area stayed at home for days. Cars were burned out and windows were smashed while the situation was still volatile. Smaller riots broke out in surrounding areas. It was a precursor to the Brixton riot that would happen in London the following year. While the unrest didn't spill out to Easton, there was sympathy for those involved. The Asian community knew discrimination and what it was to be patronised. People in our community did have problems from the police and experienced profiling, but nowhere near to the same extent as our Black neighbours.

Kaiza Fashions' small warehouse sat in the middle of the long street. The building was dilapidated to say the least. It had the standard-issue square ceiling tiles and strip lighting of any industrial building in the seventies and eighties. The front had a long series of windows where Dad would line up the latest fashions on mannequins. He also leased the shop next door. It was an extension of the warehouse, with more haphazard piles of clothes lining the walls. We lived above the smaller, second premises. The one-bedroom flat wasn't big enough for the seven of us, so Dad cut in half the office space between the shop and the flat. He used one side to store his paperwork and on the other he laid a double mattress and a single mattress. This would become the boys' room where Tariq, Khalid and Bas slept.

It was separate from the main flat, in that they would have to come up a small flight of stairs and in through the front door in order to speak to Mum and Dad when they were in. They had access to their own toilet near that bedroom, but only if they were willing to walk through the warehouse's storeroom to get there. In the night, this was a terrifying nightscape of shop equipment and shadowy mannequins. Under these circumstances they often preferred to hold it in till the morning, but Tariq came up with his own solution. He kept an empty milk bottle in a cabinet and, if nature called in the night, he would fill it and empty it again in the morning. Only, some mornings, he wouldn't bother. This practice was detested by Khalid and Bas, who insisted they could constantly smell it and would occasionally have to empty it the next day when Tariq forgot.

In the main flat, there was one bedroom, a living room, kitchen and bathroom. Having packed only what they could strap on the top of a hatchback, Anwar and his family left most of their furniture in the pokey flat. This comprised two small sofas in the living room and, just like in our previous flat above the shop, we would eat all our meals at a coffee table, although it wasn't big enough for everyone, so two of us had to eat off plastic trays on our laps. In the hallway they left a small mahogany cabinet on thin legs, and inside it were two speakers and a radio. We called it the gramophone, even though it had no record-playing function.

The bedroom had two double beds, divided by a chest of drawers. Mum and Dad slept in one bed and me and Atif were in the other. I didn't tell my friends that I stayed in the same bedroom as my parents and I avoided telling them anything about my home life. Having visited the houses of other children I went to school with, I knew that our living conditions weren't normal. Other people had space, they had gardens, bedrooms to themselves or shared with one sibling. They had furniture that matched and a proper dining table. A lot of the kids I went to school with would invite people over all the time, while I was desperate to hide my home at all costs.

Once again, Dad worked all hours. The warehouse, unlike the shops, stayed open till 9 p.m. every night. This allowed shop owners to come and stock up after closing their own stores. Often, the only time us brothers would get to spend with Dad was when we woke early in the morning and the others would come bursting into the room and get into my parents' bed with him. Mum, desperate for more sleep, would tell him to go with the boys into their room. I would follow on behind and we would jump on him. We would test out his feet to see how ticklish they were and climb all over him. He slept in a vest and lungi, a cotton sheet wrapped around the waist and extending to the ankles. We would nuzzle into his rotund stomach, pulling up his top to bounce on his belly and then flopping down and falling asleep on top of him.

Another new home meant another school and this time we went to Glenfrome Primary. I was used to being shuffled about by now. This school didn't have a huge amount of diversity, but there were a handful of non-white children that I befriended quickly.

Halfway through the first year a new girl joined our class. Mrs Walker finished taking the register and then invited the girl to stand up so she could introduce her. Her name was Monique. Her family had just moved to the UK from Mauritius. She was mesmerising. She had wide doe eyes and hair in plaits that reached to her waist. When she smiled she revealed two dimples. I couldn't take my eyes off her.

At break time I gathered with some of the other boys and one of them, John, said, 'What did you think of that new girl? She's pretty, right?' He'd spotted it too. I had competition.

'What?' Another replied. 'You can't fancy a Black girl!'

'Yeah,' agreed a third. 'She's not pretty. She's Black.'

John made a hasty retreat, raising his hands in submission. 'No, no. I mean she's pretty *for* a Black girl! I don't fancy her. I don't! I don't fancy her!'

Teasing John lasted for the rest of the day, but by the next we had found something else to wind each other up about. I'm ashamed to say I participated. I was grateful that he had said it before me so I wasn't the one being ridiculed. I didn't know the rule about not fancying Black girls but I wouldn't forget it after the response John was given.

Monique, the only Black girl in our class and one of just five or so across the whole school, found her friends and settled in over the coming weeks. In time, the girls' gossip mill started churning and rumour had it that Monique fancied Saj. I didn't have much interest in girls at this point but I knew she was beautiful. I would have been delighted if my friends hadn't made it abundantly clear that you couldn't fancy Black girls. The merciless teasing I endured when this news reached my friends only confirmed this. I was worried that people would think we had to date because we were both brown. In reality, having Monique as a girlfriend would have been a major catch for me. But I knew I couldn't entertain the idea.

I told my friends in the harshest terms I could muster that I was not interested in her. Thankfully, she hadn't approached me so I didn't need to renew my rejection to her face.

In our English classes, every now and again, Mrs Walker would take us to the school library. We would read for the session and two lucky pupils, always one boy and one girl, could sit up at the cassette player and use headphones to listen to a book on tape. On this occasion the teacher picked me and then scanned the room for a female companion. A number of hands shot up but Monique was particularly enthusiastic so she was also chosen. I could see my friends nudging each other and laughing as we sat down side by side.

We each put on the headphones and started listening to Kipling's 'How the Camel Got His Hump'. Every now and then she would nudge me and make a comment about the story. I remained stoney faced, committed to not encouraging her. After she let out a particularly loud laugh and put her hand on my arm, I knew I had to take action.

'Can you stop talking to me, please?' I said. 'I don't want to talk to you.'

I made sure I said it loud enough that my compatriots could hear the rebuff. She froze in horror. Buoyed by the reaction of my friends, who were now laughing, I added, 'I don't want to be your friend.'

Monique's eyes welled up. Tears rolled over her cheeks and dripped off her chin. I got up and walked back to my friends and she was joined by a posse of her own, who shot disapproving glances over to our group as they asked her what had happened. I never stopped regretting that interaction. Even recently, I relayed the story to my adult children, who insisted I track her down and make amends. I wouldn't know where to start but I did feel sorry, instantly, and I still do now.

Monique wasn't the only Black kid to experience racism at the school. There was a boy in my year called Trevor who got picked on regularly. I only had one class with him, so we didn't hang out often, but I was aware that he didn't have many friends. During one of these classes, I left the room to go to the toilet and came across Trevor. He was standing in a small nook in the corridor, not far from the toilets. With class still in session, no one else was around. He was huddled in on himself. I couldn't work out why he was there.

'Trevor,' I said. 'What are you doing?'

He swung round, tucking one hand behind his back. His other arm visibly hung free and it was grazed like he had fallen and scraped his skin.

'What happened to your arm?' I asked more out of curiosity than concern.

'Nothing, it's nothing,' he said, shuffling to tuck his arm away and out of sight.

'What is it? What are you doing?'

'Seriously, Saj, it's nothing.'

'It's not nothing, show me.'

He reluctantly pulled both hands forwards and showed me what he'd been concealing: a piece of glass paper.

'What's that for?'

'I'm rubbing the black off. I want the colour off my skin.'

'Why?' I asked, completely aghast and cringing at the sudden realisation that he inflicted the scrape on his arm on himself. 'Why would you do that?'

'I don't want to be black any more. They keep calling me nig-nog. I don't want this any more.'

'But that's not going to make any difference. You're just hurting yourself, it won't stop you being black.'

'I can try though. Don't tell anyone, Saj. You can't tell anyone.' He reached into his pocket and brought out a second piece of glass paper. 'Here, you can try too.'

I politely declined his invitation but I did keep the incident to myself. I thought that if I told people, it would only make the bullying worse for him. The children would have identified a weakness and they would have latched on to it.

I had experienced racism but none of it had made me truly hate myself. There was an element of feeling displaced and unsure where I fitted in best, but that made me want to find the right environment rather than adapt myself to fit the one I was in. I knew Trevor must have felt desperately unhappy with himself and the way he was being treated to take such painful action. Before, I had acknowledged racism and knew it was there, but this was the first time I really started to think about its impact.

Much like any school, Glenfrome Primary encouraged its pupils to do good and give back to those in need. In the term that I joined, the school decided the best way to do this was through a sponsored walk in aid of Help the Aged. We would all spend two weeks asking our families and neighbours to donate money and then we would complete a three-kilometre walk around Eastville Park for the charity. I collected a stack of sponsorship forms, optimistic that I would be able to get a fair few backers. The initiative was for the whole school, so Bas had the same assignment. The two of us started with family, gathering pledges of 50p here and £1 there. Then we moved on to the surrounding shops and their staff. We were surprised by how easily we could collect this money. We handed our earnings in to the school, successfully completed the walk and learned a good lesson about giving to charity.

That summer holiday, with both our parents constantly

manning the shops, we were free to roam as we pleased. With six weeks ahead of us, we plotted things we could do to keep busy over the summer. We remembered how easy it was to convince people to give us sponsorship money, so dug out the remaining unused forms. Fortunately for us, they still had the school's logo and the details of the activity, but no date. We picked a new stretch of shops and canvased people for their support for Help the Aged. Once again, we found generous donors willing to chip in small amounts here and there that soon added up. We continued this the next day and the day after, each time visiting a different street with a different set of shops.

On the fourth day, we were told by Mum that we had to look after Atif, who was five at the time. Undeterred by our younger charge, we pressed on. Taking it in turns to go into different shops asking for people to donate money in exchange for our physical activity. By the end of the summer, we'd done this routine frequently enough to have made more than a hundred pounds. We were never caught and when the holidays were over so was our latest money-making scam.

I never forgot that we had kept the money that was intended for the charity. When I saw an advert on TV for Help the Aged or heard the name, I would cringe. When I got my first bonus in banking, I made a hefty personal donation to the charity, now called Age UK, making sure I more than made up for what I did.

When November that year, 1980, came around, Bas and I saw another opportunity to collect some extra pocket money. Plenty of people in the area made a 'Guy' for Guy Fawkes Night, parading him around the streets asking, 'Penny for the Guy?' from passersby in exchange for the spectacle. We never missed the opportunity to ask for money, so we always made our own Guy.

Due to my dad's fashion business, we were never short of clothes. We started by stuffing a jumper and jeans with bits of old fabric to pad them out. We would ball up material into a pillowcase for the head, and use a felt-tip pen to draw eyes, a nose and a mouth on to him. Then we would top him off with one of Dad's jackets. One year we stole his spare toupee to give the Guy a more sophisticated air. We would march him out on to the street and position him in a nearby arcade, collecting the money.

After being caught one year pilfering bits and pieces of our dad's clothes from the flat, he got fed up and demanded them back. This meant that we had to disassemble our Guy. But rather than start from scratch, we elicited the help of Atif. We dressed him up in scruffy, oversized clothes, ruffled his hair and plonked him, as lifeless as he could maintain, in St Catherine's Place, a rundown shopping arcade in Bedminster. We got some quizzical looks, but overall people seemed impressed by the ingenuity and we gathered more with our fake Guy than the one we had built ourselves. People particularly enjoyed it when Atif moved or gave them a smile after they had given their donation.

It was at that school, Glenfrome, that I had my first crush. I'd noticed girls before, including Monique. I knew that they were different; there were some that I even thought were pretty. But none had made me feel nervous or self-conscious like Emma did. She was white, blue-eyed with blonde hair that was slowly transitioning to brown. She was sweet and a little quieter than the others in her class.

Having never had a crush before, and unsure of the procedure, I confided in a friend, a boy who was also in our class called Rob. He was delighted to hear the news as he, himself, also had a crush on her. Far from launching us into a masculine rivalry, we bonded over our mutual interest. She became something we had in common.

One Friday Rob came into school having hatched a plan. 'Saj,' he said, 'I know where Emma lives.'

'Oh yeah, where?'

'She's on the other side of Easton, on Beaumont Street. It's a bit of a walk for me, but it's only ten minutes from your house. I think we should go!'

'Go to her house? Why? We haven't been invited.'

'No, I think we should go tomorrow and surprise her. We should serenade her!'

It was the first time I'd heard the word serenade. I had no idea what he was proposing we should do.

'What's serenade?' I asked.

'Saj, we'll sing to her! Like they do in the films. Then that way, she'll know we love her!'

I was sold. What better way to catch the eye of the girl you fancy than with a romantic song? It was genius. Rob walked up to my house after lunch the following day, having nicked his older brother's guitar. Then we marched down Stapleton Road, instrument in hand, ready to romance the girl we loved.

When we got to the house we didn't knock on the door. Instead we stood on the small patch of lawn in her front garden. As we geared up to start the song, I realised we hadn't agreed which song to sing. Rob seemed unfazed by the idea of formally written music or even pre-established song lyrics, and instead sung straight from the heart.

'Emma,' he wailed to no discernible tune, 'You are our friend and we love you! Yes, we loooove you.' As he projected this, he earnestly strummed on the guitar. It was at this moment that I realised he didn't actually know how to play it.

Still, not to be outdone by my friend, I stepped up to take on the second verse of the ballad. 'Emma, we play with you in the playground. And we loooove you.' It was both factually accurate and steeped in romance. By this point Emma had been alerted by the noise and was standing watching us at the upstairs window. Buoyed by her presence and the faintest of smiles she was sending us, we continued to add lyrics to the song accompanied by whichever string made contact with Rob's fumbling fingers first.

We stopped abruptly when her dad came to the door. He made a soft approach, with a smile usually used by nurses to tell people in A & E that their abdominal pain is just trapped wind.

'Hello, boys,' he said. 'Can I just ask what you are doing?' He furrowed his brow in mock confusion and awaited our response.

Rob piped up, 'We wanted to see Emma so we made her a song.'

'Oh, so you know Emma do you? Are you in her class?'

'Yes,' we agreed. 'We go to school with her.'

'Emma,' he turned backwards and shouted towards the door.

She appeared behind it wearing a flannel dress and a playful grin.

'Do you go to school with these boys?' he asked, verifying the facts.

'Yes,' she replied. 'That's Rob and that's Saj.' She pointed at us in turn and when her finger directed towards me, I took it as my queue to greet her with an exaggerated wave.

Her dad retook control of the situation. 'Listen, boys,' he said, bending slightly to meet our eyeline. 'This is a very nice thought. But I think you should head home now. It won't be long before it's dark.'

'We got Emma some Mojos!' I said, finally feeling empowered to contribute.

'Well, that's kind,' he said, holding out a hand to take custody of the sweets. 'I'll see that she gets them.'

As we started to walk away he called to us again, 'And boys, probably better not to come back again.'

Emma, Rob and I never spoke of the incident when back at school. But it didn't matter that we'd hardly seen Emma or that we'd been sent packing. We were Casanovas who wrote love songs for women and took gifts to their house. We were men who knew how to woo a woman. We were romancers.

I was obsessed with electronics. Much to the annoyance of my parents, I would sometimes pop the TV's back cover off just to look at how it all worked. On weekends I would walk into town and hang about in Tandy and Comet. I would look at all the new products coming in and try to understand how they worked. I committed the specs to memory and even helped browsing shoppers with their purchases. I never bought anything, I couldn't afford to, but the shop assistants didn't seem to mind. When they were busy, I often served as an extra pair of hands on the shopfloor. I think they found my enthusiasm both bizarre and amusing. I also hung around the electronics market stalls and the non-branded odds-and-ends electronics stores near me. There, I could afford to buy things from time to time. I would pick up cables and connectors and any other parts that I could one day use to assemble something great.

My brothers and I loved music. Some of my friends had record players but there was no way we could afford one. But Anwar had left behind the gramophone radio that was in the hallway. It was too big to be portable so if we wanted to listen to music, we would sit by it on the floor. That was where you would find Khal, Bas and I every Sunday at 5 p.m. as we listened to the official chart countdown on BBC Radio 1. When we knew a song we liked would be featured, we'd sit next to the radio with our cassette player poised, ready to push the play and record buttons simultaneously as soon as Tony Blackburn had finished with his introduction. Then we would have to sit silently so that the mic only picked up the song. Sometimes Mum would shout, 'Roti! Dinner's ready!' eliciting a frantic response as we tried to silence her. All of this would be documented on the tape and meant we'd have to wait till next week to get a full, undisturbed version. I lived for years with a tape of Blondie's 'Atomic' with Tariq shouting for Mum over the top of the second verse followed by exaggerated shushes from me and Bas. But on the whole the technique served us well. My back catalogue of taped singles includes 'Imagine', 'Woman in Love' and 'Baggy Trousers'.

With our music being so restricted, I was delighted when a local market stall owner told me he was getting in a record player, and he would let me have it for £5. It was twenty years old, an HMV released in 1961, so wasn't the most up-to-date technology but I didn't care. Finally, a record player of my own and I would be able to get together the money to buy it.

The day it arrived I rushed down to the Easton market to collect it. It was bulky with big glass valves that looked like light bulbs encased in a light-green plastic box. Bas and I had to carry it back home together, stopping to take breaths. It wouldn't just play automatically; it needed to be turned on in advance to give it time to warm up. The record players of the time were automatically set to spin at 45 rpm for a single or 33 rpm for an album. But this one had been made before the industry had settled on these two standard speeds and was a law unto itself. It had two settings, one that sped the track up and gave it a comical high-pitched tone as the lyrics whizzed by; the other slowed down the song and dragged through with deep, sluggish lyrics.

I was told all of this upfront, but it didn't put me off. I just wanted my first ever record player. I installed it on a shelf in my dad's office. As I didn't have any records, the stall keeper threw in one for free. It was the 1967 single of 'Cry Softly Lonely One' by Roy Orbison, only the A-side was scratched so all I could play was the B-side, a far lesser known song called 'Pistolero'. I alternated playing it very fast and very slowly, delighted with the variety the settings provided me. I preferred it fast.

Owning my own record player opened me up to the idea that there were more opportunities out there. At Dad's warehouse, the local radio would be on all day, playing music for the customers and flooding them with adverts in the commercial breaks. With my new musical equipment, I decided we didn't need to be reliant on these public radio stations any more. We could create our own for the shop and we could advertise our own products on it.

I picked my time carefully. It was a Sunday, the busiest day in the warehouse, but Dad was out all day, presumably either buying more stock or cleaning the shop in Bedminster. But with Mum and Zia, the shop assistant, the only two in the warehouse, it was my chance.

My record player had detachable speakers on long cables. I kept one with me in Dad's office so I could hear the new radio station I would be creating, and then pulled the other one out of the door, down the corridor and positioned it just on the other side of a second door that led into the warehouse. After hours of dismantling and reassembling electronics, I had worked out that if you take a regular speaker, you could reverse it and create a makeshift microphone. I had a box packed full of old wires and parts that I had accumulated. I pulled it out from the back of a cupboard and dug out a cheap old speaker. After fiddling around with the electronics, I had my own microphone, although it had to be held just a few centimetres from my mouth in order to get it to register my voice at all and it soon became moist with my breath. Hearing my own voice come through the speaker was exciting.

As we listened to the charts on BBC Radio 1, I had a good understanding of the component parts of a professional radio station. I knew we needed a jingle. Using the same tape recorder that had helped me record John Lennon and Madness from the chart show, I made my own jingle. I adopted the deepest voice I could possibly muster as a pre-pubescent nine-year-old and said: 'You're listening to K-A-I-Z-A, Kaiza Radiooooooo.'

With my microphone, record player, jingle and speakers all in place, I was ready to broadcast. By now it was the afternoon. I sent Bas down into the warehouse to turn off the radio that was already playing. When he returned to the office and gave me the thumbs up, I hit play on the jingle. My voice echoed around the warehouse at an alarming volume given the size of the small speaker. We were on air.

As the 'o's of 'Radio' faded out, I kicked in with my most official-sounding radio presenter voice: 'This is Saj Jav, I hope you're having a great day. You're shopping with Kaiza Fashion Radio. Now, here's our first track and it's Roy Orbison with "Pistolero".' I hit play on the record player, opting for my favourite, the fast speed setting.

From my position in the office and away from the shopfloor I had no insight into the reactions of the customers. I imagine that the frenetic sound of Roy Orbison's helium-filled rendition of 'Pistolero' would have created a tense shopping environment. Mum's English was too limited to know exactly what was going on, but she knew that what she was hearing sounded bad. She sent a message with Basit for me to stop but, confident that I was on to a winner, I ploughed on. As the song screeched to an end, I positioned myself just an inch away from the DIY microphone to say: 'That was "Pistolero" by Roy Orbison and you're listening to Kaiza Radio.' I hit play once again on my jingle.

And continued with: 'Now it's time for some music again and next up we have Roy Orbison with a special slow version of "Pistolero".'

I managed to get through the track twice more, once on each speed setting before my dad burst through the office door. He was back, and unimpressed. He spoke over the low, heavy tones of a slowed-down Roy Orbison, 'What are you doing now?'

I explained about the vision behind the radio station and the advertising potential as quickly as possible in the hope that he would allow me to continue. He grew increasingly amused. 'I admire that you boys have managed to do this and I don't know how you've done it, but you must turn it off now.' I tried once again to implore him to see the potential but he was unmoved.

'Why is it the same song over and over again? And why doesn't it sound right?' Again, this was a valid question. I told him that the record player was to blame and talked him through the dodgy settings, but as Roy came to the end of his song, I knew we were also coming to the end of Kaiza Radio. Dad pulled the plug on the speaker and my career as a disc jockey was over.

One of the greatest treats as a child was when my parents agreed to rent a VHS video cassette player. We couldn't afford to have one of our own, but every now and again they would agree that we could hire one along with a video or two for a Saturday night. Us boys would be in charge of collecting the machine and the film, and in exchange we could watch it all afternoon until Mum and Dad got back from work, when they would curl up in the evening to watch a Bollywood film. One summer Rozina and Tes were in Bristol staying with us and as a special treat to celebrate our cousins joining us, Dad said that as well as renting the Bollywood film he wanted, we could pick a Western film (a film made in the West, rather than a cowboy film!) for us to watch too.

I was given the honour of going with Tariq to the shop to choose the film. We walked the ten minutes up Stapleton Road to Azad Videos. The shop was run by an Indian refugee family that were forced out of Uganda in 1972. We got on well with them and they stocked a substantial number of Bollywood films. While Tariq arranged the VHS player rental and searched for the video my dad had requested, I browsed the racks to find the perfect film for the rest of us.

I knew Bas would want Bond and Rozina would want *Superman*. Khalid would always prefer *Wonder Woman*. But it was rare that I got my choice, I wanted to take my time and get something *I* really wanted. On a shelf of family films at the back of the store, I found a video that stood out from the others. It was *The Rise and Fall of Idi Amin*. I didn't know then that Idi Amin was the brutal despot who had forced the video-shop owners out of their Ugandan home. I just knew that it looked interesting. I settled on the film as my choice, receiving a quizzical look as I handed it over to the shop owner. I was still chuffed.

I got home, excited to show everyone what I had picked. Rozina, Khalid and Bas were waiting in the living room, ready for the afternoon film.

'What did you get then?' Bas pounced on me as soon as I got in, unable to contain his excitement.

'I got . . .' I paused for dramatic effect before whipping the cassette out from my coat, '*The Rise and Fall of Idi Amin*.'

'You got what?' Bas scrunched up his face and snatched the case off me to examine it further. In its blank rental shop packaging, the case was giving nothing away other than the title. 'You idiot!' he said, throwing it on to the floor.

'Well, what is it about?' Rozina asked.

'It's a film about an African dictator who killed lots of people,' I said having gleaned only the very basics from the blurb.

'What is wrong with you?' Bas was furious and even Rozina was starting to side with him.

'We could have got *Superman*, Saj!' she said, throwing her hand up in the air as if she were giving up on me.

The living room cleared as all three of them decided they could better entertain themselves outside. None of them wanted to watch a film about ethnic cleansing with me. I was engrossed in the film, plus it was also one of the only times I got an afternoon in front of the telly on my own.

Those intermittent weekend VHS rentals were always a highlight of our childhood. When we moved towards our teenage years we looked forward to them for a different reason. When I was twelve, Tariq managed to get his hands on a grainy bootleg copy of a porn film called *Debbie Does Dallas*. The four of us, Tariq, Khal and Bas and I, would all gather round to watch it. Mum and Dad would be working away in the shop, utterly oblivious to how the boys were making full use of the rented VHS player.

On Sundays there would be an open market in the car park of the Bristol Rovers football ground. Me and Bas loved to walk around the market. My dad often had a stall to help supplement his retail business. We'd always stop by the stall and say hi to whoever Dad had roped in to man it for him. Then we would wander, often sharing a cone of chips and in search of a bargain.

The rows of stalls covered in sheets of tatty tarpaulin created a treasure trove ripe for the hagglers of the city. There were rails of handbags and trestle tables piled high with cut-price household essentials like tea towels, cling film and Tupperware. My brothers used to trawl through the vendors, with an eye out for anyone selling Levi's or Lee jeans at a hefty discount, and they made sure never to ask questions when they found them. But I was most interested in the electronics stalls.

These stands looked like someone had upturned their unidentified-cable drawer on to the counter, but I saw the chaos as a personal challenge. I would sort through the jumble searching for any hidden gems the stall owner had failed to recognise. On one of these treasure hunts I found a handheld transistor radio. The tiny Chinese-made device was green and had a speaker panel and a couple of dials on the main box with a comically long extendable aerial. As ours was so chunky and completely static in the hallway, the idea of taking the radio into my room to listen to the charts on my bed was a complete luxury. I had visions of taping it to the handlebars of my bike and riding around town blasting out music.

I didn't have the money immediately but scraped together what I could and went back to get it a couple of weeks later. Bas loved it too. He said he was going to save up to get the same type so he could have his own.

A couple of weeks after this, Dad announced that Bas would be moving to Pakistan. He had decided that one of his boys should be raised in his home country and Bas was the 'lucky' recipient of this privilege. His reasoning was unclear but, as with many Punjabi parents, he didn't feel the need to explain his logic to his children.

On the day Dad told us about the move, he walked into the living room while we were huddled over the coffee table eating breakfast before school. He told us like he was handing over an award. Bas should be honoured that he would be sent to Pakistan to live with Dad's brother Majeed and his family. He would play and learn and eat amazing Pakistani food.

Bas, too young to understand the full implications of a one-way ticket, was easily swept up in Dad's enthusiasm. He even started to taunt me that he was the one who would be going on the adventure, and I would have to stay at home. He was particularly excited about the prospect of flying on a plane and eating aeroplane food.

I tried to tell him that he should resist and say that he didn't want to go. Panicking, I explained that he wouldn't be coming back. That we wouldn't play cricket on the green any more, that there would be no more Freddos after school on a Friday and, worst of all, we wouldn't be in the same school.

One evening when Dad was prepping Bas for the big trip,

I made a last-ditch attempt to intervene. I urged Dad to reconsider. It wasn't a tactic that had worked before; if anything, imploring Dad not to do something just made him dig his heels in more, but I was desperate. 'You can't send Bas away,' I said, straining to keep my voice steady. But I got nowhere.

'Stay out of it,' he snapped back. 'This is nothing to do with you, it's your brother's trip.' I didn't try again, but as the day came closer, I felt increasingly low at the prospect of life without Bas, my best friend.

I went into my room and dug out that small, green transistor radio. I put in fresh batteries and then handed it to Bas. 'This is for you. It's that radio I bought at the market. I put batteries in it and it works.'

He looked excited, taking it from me with wide eyes. I continued, 'When you miss England, you can put on the radio on Sunday afternoon and you can listen to the charts. And I'll be listening too back home in England and we'll both know we're listening at the same time.'

As an eleven-year-old, I had little concept of how radio frequencies worked and didn't realise that he would be well out of range of UK radio. Later Bas would tell me that, on a particularly sad day, he had tried to tune into UK radio but had only found a handful of local stations playing rubbish Pakistani music, so eventually gave up.

9

Punches and canes

With Bas in Pakistan, I started secondary school without my usual comrade. He would have been in the year below me anyway but not having him around for the transition was a new and isolating feeling for me. Stockwell Hill School was predominantly white. In fact, the only other non-white kids were my two elder brothers, Khalid and Tariq. There was nothing grand about the building, just a 1960s block built for purpose – all concrete and no creativity.

It was the first time I wore a uniform to school. Previously, I would watch my brothers going off in their shirts and ties. Tariq had started wearing the tie the wrong way around so that the thin edge was on display. I thought he looked ridiculous but within a week of joining the school I was copying him.

Stockwell Hill wasn't one of the schools that my primary school fed into, so none of my old friends came with me. With the exception of my brothers, I knew no one. It wasn't close to our flat – it was in Downend, where we had lived when we first arrived in Bristol, and I needed to take a bus ride every day to get there from Stapleton Road. But the schools in our area were rough and got terrible grades.

For the first week that I went, my dad drove us there and back. From then on, we would be left to do the thirty-five-minute bus ride on the number 48 on our own.

Secondary school was the first time I found myself in laboratories. There were no facilities for complicated science in primary school but at Stockwell we had chemistry classes with Bunsen burners, conical flasks and boiling tubes. It was in one of these classes that, in my first week, I felt a sharp slap to the back of my head. It came completely unprovoked. Caught off guard, I jolted forward before turning round to see that it was a kid called Adam who I had hardly spoken to. He was smiling with another boy in our class.

My delayed response was to shout: 'What are you doing?' I lifted my hand up to the back of my head as if to check for damage.

His response was loud and clear: 'You're a Paki bastard. We don't like Pakis.'

'Don't call me that!' I said back. I wasn't shouting, I felt hot and embarrassed and didn't want to attract additional attention. We already had a handful of spectators from those who happened to be standing by my workbench.

'What are you going to do about it? Fight?' he challenged me, making deep, unswerving eye contact.

'Yeah, all right, I'll fight you.'

I was out of my depth. At that time I didn't do fighting. That was Bas's territory. I preferred to pummel people with my words or, let's be honest, run away. But I knew, from watching *Grange Hill* on the telly, that if I didn't nip this in the bud now, I could be subject to this kind of racism all the time I was at the school and I wasn't willing to take the risk. I was afraid of getting hurt, though. I was afraid of being embarrassed. And mostly, I was afraid that I would lose.

The time and location for the bout was set: after classes at the back of the drama hall. I was so new to the school that I didn't even know where the drama hall was but I wasn't going to tell him that.

By the time I arrived Adam was already there with some of his cronies and a crowd gathering. Word of the fight got around school quickly. They had formed a neat ring with a space in the middle for Adam and me to do battle. Khal was among the onlookers, and he was unimpressed. Bas was always up for a scrap, Tariq could be persuaded if necessary but Khalid would never hit back. He didn't try to stop me from fighting but he stood nearby on guard, ready to pull me out if the need arose. The others started chanting: 'Fight, fight, fight, fight!'

I stepped forward, doing my best not to let my legs shake as I did so. There was no backing out now. Adam did the same. We stood a metre away from each other, neither of us moving towards the other. How do you start a fight? Who goes first? The stalemate continued for another ten seconds, which felt far longer under the bloodthirsty baying of the crowd. I stepped forward and jabbed a hand in his direction. I made no contact but at least we were moving now. He stepped his foot in too, leaning his weight forward and hit me on my side with a weak, open-palmed slap. It was the kind I would have given Rozina in a playfight so as not to cause any actual damage. I reciprocated with a lacklustre kick.

The exchanging of mild physical violence continued until we got into a wrestling lock that allowed us to both take a break. We theatrically tussled around pretending to be aggressive before breaking up and pushing each other away. From that distance I shouted: 'That's it!' and he replied with the same forcefulness: 'Yeah! That's it!'

As we walked away in opposite directions I maintained my look of menace. Khal grabbed me and reminded me that Dad was picking us up so would be waiting outside. When we got to the car, Dad demanded to know why we'd kept him waiting. 'Where were you? Why were you late?'

'I just got lost,' I said.

Khal cut in, 'No he didn't, he got in a fight.'

'You got in a fight?' Dad said, craning round from the driver's seat to look at me and survey any damage. There wasn't any. 'Why are you having a fight with someone? You just got to this school, you shouldn't be fighting.'

'He called me "Paki" in the class and hit me on the head. He was the one who asked for the fight,' I said.

'And you said yes?'

'Yeah.'

'Who won?'

'I did.'

'Good. That's the last I want to hear of it.'

Dad didn't tell Mum or ever bring it up again. After a cooling-off period, Adam and I became friends. I suppose that in the first week of school, he felt he had something to prove and to him I was an easy person to prove it to.

Sadly for me, Adam wasn't the only person who had something to prove but the second time, they wouldn't settle for stage fighting. Tony was in my year but his family, including three older brothers, were infamous. One of his brothers had already been kicked out of the school for violence. Tony was short and stocky. He was shorter than me but far broader. He was solid. His hair was buzzcut and he wore Doc Martens with red laces. Tony did not like me.

At first, I could ignore him. He would barge past me in the hallways or shout a racial slur. Sometimes that was 'Paki', but sometimes 'nigger' or 'coon'. An ironic lack of discrimination within his discrimination. The intensity of his hatred and our close proximity in school was new to me, but the content of the insults and the actual jostling were old hat. It was in my second term when he decided to kick things up a notch and came up behind me in the playground. Before I knew he was there, he shoved me to the ground. I slammed face first into the tarmac, rolling over with just enough time to see Tony's sneering face before his Doc Marten boot made contact with my side. I recoiled and instinctively put my hands up to cover my face. A crowd had formed around us, not to help, just to watch.

Empowered by the audience and their lack of intervention, he continued kicking me in the side shouting that I should 'go home'. One of the other schoolkids ran to get a teacher and, eventually, they broke through the throng and pulled Tony away from me. I was bleeding from my mouth and covered in bruises. I didn't care that I was being watched. I was in such pain and shock that I cried. Tony was marched away by a teacher. But I was still there, on the ground.

It was Tariq that pulled me up. Someone must have gone to get him too. He was furious. He sat me on a bench and hugged me while I cried. After I tearfully relayed the situation to him and gathered myself, he insisted we go to the headteacher's office.

He went straight up to the door but was stopped by a receptionist. He said, 'I need to speak to the head right now.'

'Well you can't, Tariq,' the spectacled woman replied, adjusting her cardigan.

But Tariq was unconvinced. With more authority than is usually allocated to a sixteen-year-old, he said: 'I don't care. I need to speak to him now.' He pushed past the woman and into the office.

From behind the desk the headteacher stood up, first shocked and then affronted, 'What is this?' he barked.

'My brother Sajid has been hurt in a racist attack and you need to do something about it.'

He was fierce in his resolution. I sat silently while Tariq explained what had happened and said that we needed to be assured that Tony would be dealt with. His insistence that the matter be taken seriously led to the suspension and eventual expulsion of Tony.

With a five-year age gap between us, Tariq and I weren't close but I remember my feeling of pride as I sat mute, listening to him stand up for me in that office. I remember feeling that we were a unit that stood together. Mum would always say that us five boys were like the five fingers on her hand. She would ball her hand up into a fist and say, look how much stronger you are when you stick together. Then she showed us how weak we would be apart by splaying her hand and spreading her fingers. That day I felt that we were a fist, sticking together to fight for what was right.

I didn't see Tony again. I was told he'd gone off to a school for bad kids, and I was comforted knowing that I wouldn't have to watch my back in the corridors. Years later, when I was in my thirties, I drove Mum to Marks and Spencer in the Mall at Cribbs Causeway. She'd been given a gift that she wanted to return, which is what she did with every gift. I left her browsing the knitwear while I went to find a coffee from the food court. I jumped in the lift and just as the doors went to close a hand shot through, tripping the mechanism so they started the steady process of reopening. A man stepped in and positioned himself beside me.

It was Tony. Twenty years may have passed but there are some people you don't forget. His hair was longer, he was wearing trainers where his Doc Martens used to be and there was a new tattoo covering the entirety of one of his arms. But there was no doubt in my mind that it was Tony. I didn't move or say anything. When the doors opened on the top floor, I gestured with my hand that he should go out before me. He did the same and added an 'After you.' I smiled, thanked him and walked out of the lift. When my back was turned, he said, 'Excuse me, but did you go to Stockwell Hill School?'

I turned around, and said, 'Yes.'

'Are you Sajid?'

'Yes . . . are you Tony?' I asked.

'Yes,' he said. He paused. 'I just want to say sorry. I'm really sorry for what I did to you. I was an idiot when I was younger. Those days were bad days but I'm a different person now. I'm glad I bumped into you so I could say that. I never thought I'd see you again.'

He held out a hand. For a split second I considered not shaking it. I considered just walking away. But I reached out and shook his hand. I didn't stay to discuss it. I just said, 'Thank you for that and don't worry about it.' I meant both. I didn't need the apology, I didn't need any kind of release. But at the same time, it meant an awful lot.

I believe in forgiveness. I think there is power in apologising and power in truly accepting an apology. I think in that interaction we both showed real strength that neither of us would have been able to muster when we were younger. The lift interaction made me feel more positive about life for myself and, by that time, for my children. I didn't tell my mum about the conversation when I went back to M & S to collect her but I did call Tariq to tell him. His response was less forgiving but I appreciated that, all these years on, he was still protective.

It didn't take long for me to accumulate a close group of friends. Larry, Johnny, Hector and Bob were all white and middle class but we bonded over a dislike of Miss Cheryl's music class. Later we added Adam to our band, who never formally apologised for the chemistry class bullying and subsequent 'fight' but he did eventually announce that I was 'actually a nice guy'.

We weren't the naughtiest kids in class by any stretch, but we were cheeky and would take opportunities to mess around. During one English class held in the library, the librarian was running late. While we were left unattended, Hector dared me to set off the fire extinguisher. Never one to back away from a dare, I obliged, soaking a rack of books, two chairs and a table with water before shutting it back off again. The whole class stared open mouthed at the mess I had created. It had made a far greater impact than I anticipated. I was certainly about to get in a lot of trouble.

Thinking on my feet, I left the library and stood in the hall by the entrance. A minute later, when the teacher arrived, I explained that a strange boy in a big coat burst into the library and set off the fire extinguisher. I told her that he'd sprayed the room, then dumped the extinguisher and run back out of the door. She was shocked and dismayed at the damage the water had done. But she was also pleased with me for coming directly to tell her what had happened. She thanked me profusely. Hector and the others watched on, equal parts aghast and impressed.

My friends had houses with dinner tables and back gardens with makeshift football goals and cricket stumps, and I was welcome on the weekend. Once, in order to try and fit in with the others, I invited Johnny over after school. I asked my mum first as it was so unusual for us to host non-Pakistani guests. She agreed and bought in fish fingers and frozen chips for the occasion.

I showed him around my dad's warehouse and we played a few games before coming up for tea. The two of us ate in Dad's office rather than going up into the cramped flat. He seemed to enjoy himself and went off home with a full stomach. A few days later in school it got back to me that he told everyone my house was messy and it smelled of curry. I never invited anyone around again.

*

Despite the unpleasant incident in my first chemistry class, I started to really enjoy science. I liked working out how things were made and how I could make things happen for myself. I started reading books for young scientists at the library and it dawned on me that chemistry class had inadvertently taught us how to set off bangers remotely.

According to my research, if I could gather bangers, which I could get from any fireworks shop, magnesium, which was available in class, and an old clock, I would be set. All I needed to do was set the clock so that, when the hands met, they closed an electrical circuit. This could then be wired up to the bangers and bang! You had a remote explosion.

The idea of knowing that I may be able to build my own little explosive device was too thrilling. I'd watched plenty of films where the likes of Sean Connery avoided explosions and got the girls – perhaps this would be my very own Bond moment. It was over the summer holidays after my first year that I told the lads about my new skill. I hadn't actually tested it yet but I was pretty confident I had the science right. They were just as excited as I was and we set about gathering all we needed. Larry bought the bangers from a shop that stocked fireworks. Hector dug out an old clock from his mum's garage and I had already pocketed the magnesium while school was still in session. We went to Johnny's house to test it out. He had the biggest garden and both his parents worked so they wouldn't be home to hear the ruckus. After much trial and error, we managed to make a pretty loud bang, but compared to the 007 explosions, it was lacking. We wanted the biggest noise and sparks possible. We decided to remove the gunpowder from the bangers and use it raw instead, to create more impact.

When we were convinced we had the ratios right, Hector suggested that we take the contraption into school on the teachers' inset day before the students came back. We would give them a shock. The other three of us loved the idea and saw no problems with it whatsoever. We waited a week or so until the end of summer when the teacher training day was on and took the makeshift device into school.

We decided the target would be the bike sheds. As no pupils had cycled in, it was completely empty, so we wouldn't hurt anyone or damage any possessions. It felt like a generous concession. We snuck in and assembled our equipment, setting the hands of the clock to meet ten minutes later at midday, the time we assumed the teachers would be stopping for lunch. We crouched behind a wall with a good vantage point and waited for the clock to tick on.

A few minutes later, the device went off. There was a flash and a deafening bang. There was no fire and no discernible damage to the outside of the shed but the noise had been more than enough to get the full attention of the faculty. They streamed out of the building, keeping a distance as they tried to work out what had happened in the shed. We were delighted. Knowing that we were pushing our luck, we snuck out before we could watch any further fallout.

When school was back in session there was an announcement in assembly, demanding that anyone who knew anything about an incident in the bike shed should come forward immediately. The device had been far more bark than bite, and the shed was still standing and functional with little to no damage. Even so, we swore each other to secrecy and never told anyone outside of the group.

The same summer I was experimenting with bangers was the year Lady Diana married Prince Charles. My family didn't seem to know much about our future king. If his name was brought up, it was only ever with indifference or as a supporting character in their conversation about Lady Diana – whom they adored. My mum, in particular, fawned over the soon-to-be princess, praising her humanitarian work, gentleness and hairstyle.

When the wedding was announced, it was a big deal. We had a commemorative tea towel and a mug, both with drawings of the couple that looked like the artist had done them from memory. Mum and Dad sent Tariq down to Azad Video in the morning to hire a VHS player. The wedding was on a Wednesday and the shops needed to stay open, so while my parents worked, Khal recorded the wedding on a blank tape he got from the Eastville market. When the shops were closed everyone gathered around to watch the wedding back. I remember my mum explaining that they were having an arranged marriage, just like we would have when we were older. She pointed out how happy they were.

My secondary school years were busier than those before. I was now old enough to help out in the shop so weekends were often passed stacking shelves and manning the till. I was enticed to help out by Dad who always promised that I would be paid for my time. In reality, he may have slipped me a few pounds here and there but I was never paid a wage. At the end of the day, when we had locked up, I'd ask for the money and he would always explain that the 'toe-taal' was too low and he couldn't pay me. Sometimes I'd push back, reminding him of his promises from that morning, but it never made a difference. He'd just look downcast and say that he didn't have the money, often handing me the 'toe-taal' receipt to prove it. I carried on helping though. I knew my parents needed me to contribute so I didn't stop. I always held out hope that I would get a pay cheque that sadly never came.

Every day after school for an hour and for the whole morning on a Saturday, we were sent to the mosque on St Mark's Road to learn Arabic and, ultimately, to read the Qur'an. It took up a huge amount of my time, but Tariq and Khal had both done the same. The lessons taught us how to recognise the Arabic characters and associate them with the right sounds. So, even if we didn't understand the meaning of a word, we could read it and correctly pronounce it after seeing it written on a page.

All of the Pakistani boys, and some girls, from our area went to the same mosque to complete this rite of passage. It was the first time in my life that I was in a space that was entirely Pakistani. There were no white boys, or even Muslim boys from any other ethnicity. On the corner by the mosque was a small Indian-run convenience store. The owners were Sikhs and their kids would hang around outside getting up to much the same mischief we did outside our shop. Sometimes as we walked past they would shout insults, sometimes related to being Pakistani, others related to being Muslim. We would shout back equally childish insults and then continue walking. There was one day when I left the mosque to see that a fight had broken out between a group of Muslim boys on their way in and the Sikh kids from the corner shop. A man came running out of the shop shouting in Punjabi, the common language of both sides, 'Stop! Stop!' He pulled the two groups apart, both from the Punjab region, so visually indistinguishable, other than the Sikh kids had topknots and the Muslims didn't. As he marched his clan back towards the shop, he could be heard saying, 'Why are you doing that? Why are you fighting with them? They're customers!'

While we weren't allowed to speak during the classes, there was a sense of camaraderie with the boys in the mosque. In the summer months, when it got darker later, we would finish our class and go to the nearby green to play cricket together.

The mosque itself wasn't grand or ornate. It was just a basic space that had been converted from someone's living room into a place of worship. Walking through the door, you were greeted by an image of Muhammad Ali Jinnah, the founder of

Pakistan. It's a picture that is familiar to anyone who grew up in a Pakistani household. Everyone has at least one in their home. In a smart suit with a slim tie and wearing a Karakul hat, his eyes follow you no matter where you are in the room, like the *Mona Lisa*. He watched on as we walked in for our daily Arabic lesson.

Girls attended the mosque too but we were kept completely separate. The eight or so boys sat cross-legged lining the wall on one side of the room and the girls did the same on the other. The imam, or 'Maulvi-Saab', who was teaching us strode up and down in front of us as we read through the holy text. He was never far away from his sticks, which he kept in three sizes. The first was long enough that, when he was seated on the floor in the middle of the room, he could reach any of us to hit us without having to stand up. The second, slightly shorter, was the right length for him to be able to hit us as he walked past without needing to bend down. And the third, the shortest of all, was the perfect length for when we were standing in front of him. He would demand we place our hand palm up to receive our punishment. It was the deadliest.

There wasn't a session that went by when most children weren't hit multiple times. From his seated position, Maulvi-Saab would summon a child up to stand in front of him. They would have to recite the passage they were currently reading. Any slight mispronunciation or other mistake resulted in a smack. It was painful. If he caught you dipping in your concentration or even taking a break from the monotonous recitation, you would feel the impact of the long stick on your back or side.

We all got into the habit of rocking back and forwards as we read. No one ever discussed the practice but it was what the boys before us had done, so we did the same. The rocking was seen as an indication of commitment and concentration. When I was concerned I was about to take a hit, I would rock with more vigour, visibly demonstrating my interest in the passage.

The holy Qur'an is made up of six thousand verses and almost seventy-eight thousand words. In the Islam tradition, it is important that everyone read the entire book through in its original language. There are a handful of distinguished people who have not only read the Qur'an all the way through but dedicate their lives to learning it by heart. These men are called Hafiz. In achieving this sacred feat, they are considered virtuous. One of these Hafiz came from Saudi Arabia for an extended stay at the mosque. We hated having him there as he was particularly violent. By the time he was finished running a session we were desperate for the milder beatings of the Maulvi-Saab. He invested heavily in a small number of boys, taking them back to Saudi Arabia with him and encouraging them that they too could become Hafiz one day. Years later, it would come out that he had been sexually abusing those young boys. I was grateful never to have been chosen.

Much like taking driving lessons, once I had passed the milestone of reading the Qur'an, I would never need to go back to the classes. I committed myself with enthusiasm to the task in hand, though, even racing Rozina to see who could finish first when I visited Rochdale one summer. She, being studious, won. But I was only a few minutes behind.

10

This is our house, you need to leave!

Word worked its way through the grapevine and came back to us that Anwar and his family were not enjoying their life in Pakistan. I wasn't privy to the details but I gathered that the big adventure had turned out to be disastrous, and they were heading back to England.

Neither of my parents was pleased to receive this news. My mum was merciless in her condemnation of his actions and while my dad managed to muster a smidgen more grace, he wasn't far behind her. His last words to his brother-in-law had been that he didn't ever want to hear from him again. He believed that the request would be respected.

Perhaps it shouldn't have come as a surprise, but the day Anwar, Khalila and their four children turned up unannounced at Stapleton Road knocked us for six. It was a Sunday afternoon when the group disembarked from their beaten-up car, no longer the Pakistan-bound hatchback, and marched into the Kaiza warehouse.

It wasn't obvious what they thought they would find on their arrival but it was clear what they intended to leave with. They wanted the business and the flat back. Anwar stormed up to my father, with no intention of allowing him time to process the ambush. The pair just started shouting. My father was outraged at his sheer cheek. Anwar was insistent that the warehouse and flat were rightfully his.

While my father was occupied in this row, Khalila and their children barged their way up the stairs at the back of the shop and into the flat. My mum was cooking in the kitchen and Khal, Atif and I were in the living room. They came through the door and by the time I had looked up to see what was going on two of my cousins were standing in the living room. I got up to greet them, having not seen them in three years. I was stopped in my tracks by my mum, who started screaming from the kitchen.

My cousins, all older than me, had solemn faces. They weren't there for a reunion. Khalila turned to my mum and shouted, 'This is our house, you need to leave.'

'What? What's going on?' I said, as I moved towards my mum.

'It's our house, you have to get out,' Khalila said again.

It was too much for my mum to bear. The injustice of it just overwhelmed her. She didn't even respond with words, just a scream.

'You can't do this, it's our home,' I shouted over the din.

'We're back to reclaim our things and our flat,' she said again.

'We're not leaving,' my mum's eyes were inflamed and she spat each word, thickening her Punjabi accent for effect.

Taken aback by the sternness, Khalila started to back away. My mum was so angry, she was starting to look unhinged. My aunt grabbed a balled up plastic bag and threw it to one of her sons who was waiting in the hallway.

'Fill it up,' she said as she sent another one flying to her second son. 'This stuff, all the furniture, it's ours. Pack it up boys, now.'

Her sons smiled as they pillaged the house collecting items they recognised and probably some that they didn't.

'No!' my mum shouted. 'Stop! When you left, you left these things. These are ours now, these are not yours.'

She tried to grab the back of one of the boys as he pushed his way into the kitchen and emptied the cutlery drawer into his carrier bag. He shrugged her off and moved back out to the hallway.

'You stole our money, and now you steal our things!' my mum shouted. They ignored her.

Khalila marched through the house pointing at everything she felt she had a claim to, including the mahogany 'gramophone' radio that I had planned to crouch by later that afternoon to listen to the Radio 1 charts.

Her two daughters, the older of the four children, stayed by the door. They didn't step over the threshold and didn't partake in the raid. Their mum looked at them and threw the eldest a bag.

'Take that clock. That's ours,' she said, pointing to a plain wall-mounted clock above the door.

'Really, Mum?' the girl lifted an arm to catch the bag but otherwise remained static.

'Yes, really, we put that clock there. Take it.'

'No.' She refused to blink as her mother stared her down.

'What do you mean?'

'I mean no,' she said. 'Why are we doing this? This is stupid. Why are we taking this clock? This isn't our stuff, this is their stuff.'

'You stupid girl, you wait till I tell your dad. He's going to hit you so hard. Take that clock down now.'

She remained steady and unmoved, 'No, I'm not doing it.'

The tension in the hallway was broken as her youngest son pushed past her and said, 'I'll take it, Mum.' He reached up and lifted the clock off the doorframe and added it to his bag of swag.

Realising that she didn't have the full support of her team, my aunt swept out, calling the boys to follow her with their collections. She pushed past her daughters and walked down the stairs. Before following, the eldest daughter stopped and turned to me and Mum, 'I'm sorry. My parents have messed up and I'm sorry.'

She shut the door behind her and Mum walked to the living room and dropped on to the sofa. She was inconsolable. That's when she told us what had happened with Anwar, the business, the loan and the trip. She explained that it took them years to come out of the debt he left them in. She couldn't believe that even after the kindness Abdul-Ghani had shown them, they still came back to keep taking from us. She said they thought we were weak. They had got away with too much and now we were paying the price. We did what we could to calm her down but the sadness of her brother's actions was all consuming.

Dad came up from the shop and explained what Anwar had said downstairs. He said they had all left and he believed they wouldn't be coming back. He was right, they didn't. We heard through the family that they set up a grocery shop in Scotland. It was three decades later that Anwar contacted my mother. He had stage-four cancer and, after attempting treatment, they had said that all they could do was make him comfortable. He wanted to see his little sister Zubaida. My mum agreed and got the train to Scotland. He apologised for what he had done. He asked for *maffi*, the Punjabi word for mercy. When she said that she forgave him, he asked if Abdul-Ghani would come to see him too, so two weeks later my mum made the trip a second time with my dad. They both forgave him.

My mum was pleased that she got to see him and that he made things right before he died. It gave her the peace she needed.

Just nine months after he was sent over to Pakistan, Bas came back to the UK. There had been plenty about his time there he enjoyed, but his homesickness had become overwhelming, and when our relatives refused to let him return, he started playing up. I was relieved to have Bas back and as soon as the summer holidays hit, it meant that we could get up to our usual games around the neighbourhood.

One day that summer, Dad came home with a bike for me. I'd consistently asked for one, hassling my dad and begging him to buy me one ever since Khalid had written off my first one when he crashed into a car. Bas had a bike that he'd been given by a friend who was no longer using it. It was too small for him but at least it was something.

So, when Dad came home and said there was a bike waiting for me in the garage, I was over the moon. Bas and I rushed downstairs to see what it looked like. Waiting in the cold, concrete garage was a bike. A girl's bike. The bar at the top was slanted, rather than going straight across, and more than that, it was pink with a wicker basket mounted to the handlebars.

Wary of showing my disappointment, I tentatively thanked my father. 'Where did it come from?' I asked.

'It's Katharine's.' Katharine was almost my cousin, the stepdaughter of Dad's youngest brother, Hamid. She was kind and fun, but older than me so had far more time for Tariq, who was closer to her in age.

But now, I had her bike and for that I was grateful.

'So, it's mine?'

'It's yours for the summer. You can ride it,' he said.

'Great. Thanks, Dad!' I said, giving him a big hug, while

thinking how I could adapt this bike to make it suitable for a twelve-year-old boy.

When Dad left, Bas and I circled the new toy, trying to work out what was to be done. We decided it needed a full transformation. The first thing to go was the basket. I ripped it off and discarded it in the corner of the garage. Next was the front brake. Now, when I reflect on it, that was an odd choice and nothing to do with the aesthetics. I think, at some point in my school life, someone had said that it was cooler to have only a back brake on a bike and I had taken it to heart.

Next, we walked down to the bike shop and asked if they had any spray paint. I left with a small can of metallic silver. We hung the bike upside down in the garage, removed the wheels and I covered the pink paintwork and floral motif with a pure, solid metallic silver. The bike finally looked like something a respectable boy would ride, but I wanted more.

I went back down to the bike shop, haggled on the price of some used cow-horn handlebars and brought them back. Once they had been sprayed the same silver, I assembled the bike and stood back to survey my handiwork.

Bas and I had created a completely different bike and I couldn't have been prouder of it. The two of us rode around the area all summer. Now that I finally had a proper set of wheels I was able to experiment in ways I'd only dreamed of before. I took a load of the black bin liners that Dad would use to bag up particularly large purchases at the warehouse. I cut them along the edges to open them out and then stuck four or five together to create a parachute. I put Bas on the back of the bike and cycled as fast as I could. When I shouted 'deploy' his job was to unleash the chute. My hope was that it would slow us to a stop and render the final brake completely redundant. It didn't work as well as we hoped but that didn't stop us trying it out on the main road, surrounded by traffic. The adjacent cars were furious that their vision was being impaired by my bin-liner parachute. After receiving some robust feedback from other road users, we decided to stick with the brake. But I still kept the parachute with me on rides from time to time, in case we decided we wanted to use it.

I couldn't afford a bike lock, so wasn't able to secure the bike when we went in somewhere. Instead, I started turning it upside-down and resting it on its cow-horn handlebars when I went into a shop instead. The logic went that it would take someone extra time to steal it as they would have to turn it the right way up. By the time they'd managed this, I would have spotted them.

This is what I did the day Bas and I went to a local greasy spoon, the Rover's Café, to play on the pinball machine in the back. It was 10p per play and we had 40p between us. Two goes each. We had just lost our final ball on our third go when one of the customers in the café looked up from their mug of tea and said, 'Boys, was that your bike outside?'

Startled, we turned our heads to the door and, sure enough, the bike was gone. We ran to the street in time to see three Black kids pelting away, one on the bike and two either side. They were bigger than us, almost certainly fifteen or sixteen. Bas didn't skip a beat and started running after them, 'Oi! Bastards!' he shouted as he ran. I followed him and he pushed me back, 'You go home. Wait for me at home – I'll get the bike!'

'What? On your own?'

'Just leave it to me, Saj, I'll get it back!' He waved me away and rounded the corner we'd just seen them turn down. I stopped running. There wasn't time for my mind to catch up with the events. Of course, I shouldn't have left Bas to get the bike. He was younger than me, and I was younger than them. And there were three of them. And he was my younger brother.

And it wasn't even his bike. I had made a mistake, but it was too late. They were all long gone.

I started walking around the block to see if I could see my brother, my bike or the boys who nicked it. Bas had got into a number of fights, far more than me. He was capable but he wasn't big. He'd also taken a fair number of kickings. He was just fearless. He refused to stand down and his stubbornness sometimes paid off and sometimes cost dearly.

I took another corner and came out by a chicken shop. The bike was leaning up against a lamppost just outside, but in clear view of the large glass shop front, where the three lads were ordering food. But two doors up from the chicken shop was Bas, crouching behind a car, like a prowling lion in an Attenborough documentary. He was going to go for it.

I got a pang of guilt that I had left my baby brother to fight this battle for me and decided that I would go ahead of him and retrieve the bike myself. I sprinted past him with no regard for the attention the sudden burst of activity would attract. I got level with the shop only to slip and flop straight into the glass window. It didn't break but the thump did alert the boys to the operation. Bas, seeing me stumble past him and straight into the glass, overtook me, grabbed the bike and started cycling. I picked myself up and ran alongside him, trying to ignore his cries of 'You idiot, you fucking idiot! I told you to go home.'

We hurtled down Stapleton Road, with all three of the older boys in pursuit. Thankfully one of the men who worked for Dad in the warehouse was outside on a cigarette break. First, he saw the two of us coming towards him at full speed, and then he clocked the kids behind. 'Open the door!' I shouted to him. He held open the door to the warehouse as we pushed our way through it and then stood between us and the boys. Racial slurs were extended by both sides, but they gave up and walked away.

After the excitement of almost losing the bike, riding it round became all the more enjoyable. First, I had refurbished it myself, then I had to stage a rescue mission for it.

It was towards the end of summer that Dad's younger brother Hamid, his wife Lucy and their daughters Katharine and Ruby came to visit us. As I got home from a Saturday morning at the mosque, my dad called to me, 'Saj, look, it's Uncle Hamid and Auntie Lucy! And Katharine's here to collect her bike.'

Caught up with his businesses and work, Dad had no idea that I had customised the bike. Just as I had no idea that I would be expected to return it at the end of summer. Their family had been away on holiday in Europe. With just two children to care for and a bit more money, they were able to go to France or Spain, rather than just a week in Rochdale. But now they were back from sunnier climes and needed to collect the pink, basketed bike they had lent me for the month.

My initial reaction was one of incredulity. I didn't feel bad for updating the bike: I thought it was mine. Dad hadn't explicitly said that I would have to give it back and I had spent my own money on refitting it. I'd given it cow-horn handlebars and even designed a parachute to go with it. Dad asked me to take them to collect it from the garage. I decided to let the bike do the talking. So, with no explanation, I gestured to the now slightly scuffed metallic silver bike, with its garish handlebars and just the one brake.

'This isn't the bike, Sajid. Where's the bike?' said Lucy.

'Yes it is. This is the bike. I made some changes.'

'Some changes!' she said. 'It's a totally different bike!'

She was right. It was. It was mine now. I had toiled over it because the one my dad gave me was not up to scratch. But before I could explain all of that, Katharine started crying. That's when I knew that explanations wouldn't matter, I was just in trouble. When my dad came into the garage and saw the bike, he was furious. He insisted that he had said the word 'borrow'. I, to this day, insist that he did not. Dad now had to buy Katharine a whole new bike. He let her pick any she wanted from Halfords and it wasn't even second-hand.

Bas and I spent much of that summer roaming, sometimes with and sometimes without our bikes. But the expectation to attend mosque for lessons on a Saturday didn't let up because of the school holidays. We had taken to using a shortcut to get there by going through Stapleton Road railway station. The station itself was grim. It had only two facing platforms and you could cross the track by using a footbridge. There weren't many trains that passed through and on the whole the station felt sinister and abandoned. Our parents warned us not to use it as a cut-through but having not had any trouble ourselves, we continued to make use of the five-minute time saver.

On one Saturday, we were on our way back from the mosque, cutting through the station, when we were interrupted by a group of traveller kids hanging out under the stairwell. They were a few years older than us, maybe fifteen or sixteen. Their ringleader, Tommy, brandished a large stick. 'Hey, Paki, where you going?'

He stood blocking the pathway. Bas and I looked at each other, asking the silent question; 'Should we keep walking or turn back?' We seemed to collectively decide that we liked our chances and we continued to walk down the steps of the bridge and on to the path beyond it.

'You can't walk this way, Pakis,' Tommy said to a background of jeers from the rest of them. We gave him a wide berth, mounting the dirt verge to the side of the path. We continued past him without saying anything but he didn't like the intrusion. He leaped towards us and used the stick to hit us both on the legs. The rest of the boys laughed as he landed blow after blow on our knees. 'Stay away from here and stay away from my den,' he shouted, before taking a final swing as we scrambled back to the path and away.

By his den, he meant the space under the stairwell, where he and his friends had accumulated various things, like a shopping trolley and two chairs. We discussed walking through the station the following week but on balance decided to avoid the route altogether. We never walked that way again.

A couple of weeks later a family friend named Shanaz came to visit us for the day. It was still the summer holidays and it was particularly hot. In the afternoon, Mum was cooking dinner in the kitchen and, with an hour or so to kill, Bas suggested to Shanaz they go to a sweet shop to get a few treats. I decided to stay at home. An hour later, when Mum was putting the food on the table, Bas and Shanaz still weren't back. I walked over to the sweet shop but when there was no sign of them, we started to get worried. Another hour after that, the pair were returned home by a disgruntled-looking police officer.

'Are these your kids?' he asked my mum.

'Yes, they are,' she said, alarmed. I came downstairs and stood with Mum so I could translate. While her English was far better than in her early days, it was still helpful to have one of us on hand.

The policeman said, 'We caught these two in Stapleton Road train station where they were seen lighting a fire.'

My mum glared at Basit. 'It was an accident, Mum!' he whined.

The officer continued, 'Someone saw them starting the fire with matches, but we managed to contain it and no one was hurt.'

'Mum! It really was an accident,' Bas said. 'We were playing with the matches and then something caught fire.'

'Why were you playing with matches? Where did you get these from?' she asked.

'I had some matches from the kitchen and I just wanted to show them to Shanaz and then it caught fire.'

She accepted the explanation and thanked the policeman. As the pair rushed up the stairs to get their dinner, I caught up with Bas. 'Hey, what happened?' I asked.

Bas smirked at me. 'I burned down that gypsy fucker's den, didn't I?!'

11

Strimming by the sea

Bas's transition back to the UK wasn't smooth as his behaviour descended further, from cheeky into illegal. He started stealing. He would take small items that he knew he could easily sell on in school. But it wasn't just the money, he enjoyed the adrenaline of it. I knew what he was doing but refused to get involved. He was arrested after getting caught by a store detective in Boots taking a pocket full of fancy rollerball gel pens that he intended to sell on for 50p each. After that incident he swore he would stay out of trouble.

We shared our street with four amusement machine arcades. Not the fun kind, designed for children, but the ones with darkened windows that made it impossible to know the time of day once you were inside. The gloom and large 'no under 18s' signs would have made the spaces more intriguing to me as a thirteen-year-old boy, if Bas and I hadn't been able to stroll in and out unchallenged whenever we wanted. The proprietors respected age restrictions enough to hang the signs but not enough to enforce them.

Our favourite was Regal Amusements, two doors down

from my dad's shop. Once inside, the darkness was accompanied by a fog of cigarette smoke. It was heavy enough to give the once-white wallpaper a yellowy nicotine tinge. Babs, the manager, sat in a booth in the centre of the arcade, watching the comings and goings. She would chain smoke all day from inside her little cabin and dish out stacks of ten-pence coins in exchange for pound notes. Her skin was grey and her teeth had the same yellow staining as the wallpaper but she was kind to us, even as kids.

The more time we spent there, the more familiar we became with the regulars who sat in front of the fruit machines, day in and day out, ultimately losing money. The machines paid out just often enough to keep you interested but never enough to leave you in profit. We didn't stop to think about their lives and the sadness that was inevitably behind the decision to sit in there all day. Every now and again we would see someone break down. After losing more money than they could afford, they would start kicking and punching the machines. Babs would haul herself out of her booth, shouting that they should get out or she'd call the police.

Bas and I rarely had any money to stake ourselves. Occasionally we managed to get a fifty-pence piece from my mum, but that went straight to penny sweets from the corner shop. Tariq, the eldest of the five of us, would play from time to time. He was seventeen, still not legal, but passed as an adult in the dim lighting, especially with his George Michael-inspired goatee.

We were there on one cool evening in spring 1982 when I noticed a new group of kids. They were a couple of years older than Bas and me, maybe fourteen or fifteen. Tariq was trying, and failing, to hit the £3 jackpot on his favourite machine, 'The Big One'.

The new kids were playing on one of the flashing neon

machines. They huddled around it so that passersby, and crucially Babs, wouldn't have a clear view. I couldn't work out what they were doing but to me it felt suspicious. I said as much to Bas, who agreed, but neither of us got any closer. A jingle went off on their machine, along with frenetic flashing lights signalling a win. The lads crouched down to grab the coins that had been dispensed by the machine before calmly heading out of the door. I went over to check if they had dropped a coin or accidentally missed one at the back of the shoot but they'd been too thorough for that.

The following day Bas and I wandered the streets once again. We had found a small nook round the back of a row of houses that was surrounded by garden walls on three sides, so protected from the wind. Someone had dumped a shopping trolley there that we pushed each other around in and there was an old mattress that we jumped on like a trampoline. We called it the Batcave. I took on the role of Batman and Bas, being the younger brother, was Robin. As we walked down the road to the hideout, we saw the same group of boys on East Street heading out of Futurama, a rival arcade. Once again, they had plenty of coins and they started to share them out between the group.

Convinced that something was going on, Bas and I approached them and asked what they were doing. The ringleader of the crew, a tall Black boy with a high top, had no problem sharing their trick. He explained that they were cheating the machine into thinking they had put money into it and then playing for free. I found out later that the term for this is 'strimming'.

The boy showed us the tool the group was using: a thick piece of nylon fishing line that they had bent into a 'J' shape so it had a claw at the end. He described how they would stick the fishing tackle into the 10p coin slot and drop it down until they found the catch that would usually be activated by a coin. They would click it so that the machine registered credits they hadn't paid for. They would rack up twenty or thirty credits – £2 to £3 worth – within seconds. Having not paid anything, they knew they would be in profit because eventually the machine would pay out. It was genius.

Bas and I went home and started planning how we would be able to do the same. Our first task was to get our hands on the fishing line. This was a pastime we knew nothing about. Woolworths didn't have a fishing section and no one in our family had ever fished. In fact, the only fish I knew of was the one being advertised constantly on TV by Captain Birdseye. We used the source of all information at the time, the Yellow Pages, to find the address for a specialist store in the city centre.

The following Saturday morning, Bas and I walked forty minutes to Veals Fishing Tackle in Old Market. The owner's eyebrows raised when he saw the two of us browsing the shelves of the shop. His normal clientele was middle-class white and greying men rather than working-class Asian pre-teen lads. The shop held all its stock in the back room, with some cheaper and more common items on shelves and in boxes on the counter. This meant we couldn't just pick up some wire, pay and leave quickly. We had to actually speak to the kindly shop owner in order to get our hands on the fishing tackle. It was instantly clear that we didn't have a clue.

We asked for a metre of nylon wire, but the man explained that wouldn't be long enough for fishing. 'What bait will you be using?' he asked.

'What do you mean, bait?' I responded, completely oblivious to the process of catching fish.

He moved on, 'Where will you go to fish?'

Once again, we were stumped. I had replied to the last question, so it had to be Bas's turn. I stared at him until he said something. Inspiration finally came and Bas shouted the name of the only body of water he knew: 'The River Avon!'

Realising that he wasn't going to get any sensible answers from us, the man stopped asking questions. He sold us the short stretch of fishing wire we were after, and we were on our way back to East Street excited to try out the trick.

After school that week, we were finally ready to use the homemade device. Bas and I walked the two doors down to Regal Amusements and chose a machine, 'Nudge Shuffle', as far as possible out of Babs's eyeline. She didn't pay us any attention and stayed in her booth puffing away. Bas started as the lookout. He stared into the middle distance, pretending not to be focused on anything in particular, but reported any movements to me in Punjabi. It was our secret language. One that, in our whites-only area of Bristol, wouldn't be understood by anyone else.

I heard no Punjabi. The coast was clear. I dropped the plastic hook into the slot. The boys told us we wouldn't have to go too far down, just a couple of inches before we hit the catch. I slowly moved it until I felt some resistance. I pushed and wiggled the fishing wire, trying to activate the mechanism. I heard a click and looked down to see the red counter had recorded one credit. It worked!

I gave a thumbs up to Bas. Buzzing from the news, he said, 'Click it more then. Get as many as you can!' I began moving the wire up and down adding to our credits. I kept going until we reached twenty-five and then removed the wire and stowed it in my pocket. For two young lads who never had any money, this was exciting.

Bas and I huddled over the machine and took it in turns to play with our stolen credits. We didn't win the £3 jackpot, but a few smaller wins left us with £2.20. We shared out the earnings, £2.20 of pure profit.

Standing in that backstreet, staring at the cash we had just made, Bas and I felt rich. We spent the full £1.10 each on sweets and visited the other three arcades on our street over the next few days. This became our routine. We didn't want to raise suspicion by concentrating our work on a single street so we started going further afield, walking to other high streets in Bristol. We started saving our money, depositing it in a Lloyds Young Saver account our mum had set up for each of us to teach us about managing our finances. It started as a few quid but soon we were dropping off tens of pounds at a time with the Lloyds cashier. It was more money than we'd ever had access to before. We couldn't spend it all without rousing suspicion, so we carried on buying too many sweets and depositing the rest in the bank.

The con was going so well that Bas and I set our sights on somewhere bigger, somewhere with so many arcades that we could spend a day raiding them and come back with hundreds of pounds. The seaside.

We'd been to Weston-super-Mare before on a rare family day out and we knew there were loads of gaming shops in the town. So one summer Saturday that same year, without telling our parents, we took the hour-long number 350 bus from Bristol to the west coast. We sat on the backseat of the upper deck and Bas pulled out a ten pack of Silk Cut cigarettes, purchased with his profits.

'I got these from a friend,' he pretended, smiling as he took one out of the packet and held it up towards me. I found the idea of smoking far more appealing than the taste of a cigarette. I lit one up and puffed on it, recreating the mannerisms of the smokers I'd seen but without ever actually inhaling. I coughed enough to put the cigarette out quickly.

It was a hot summer's day so Weston was crowded with people enjoying the sunshine. Just a two-minute walk from the bus terminus we found a street full of the fruit-machine arcades. We felt like we'd struck gold. We planned to spend the day hitting each gaming shop in turn and then taking the bus home in time for tea.

We each brought our fishing tackle. I tucked mine into the top pocket of my shirt, reasoning that if I was searched, they would go for my trouser pockets. We walked into the first place on the strip. By now we were familiar with the machines, how to play them and which paid out the biggest jackpots. Just like on East Street in Bristol, the venues were ill-lit and joyless, and they were more than happy, despite the law, to let kids in to play.

While I was on lookout duty, Bas racked up thirty spins on one of the fruit machines. The two of us took it in turns to spin. It was on our fourth go that the jingle sounded, we had hit the jackpot. It was £3 in the bank.

On the twelfth spin, we struck it lucky again and added another £3 to our prize pot. This was exciting, except that hitting the jackpot was loud. A bell rang and the jingle played again, and with two wins in quick succession, we were starting to get some attention. All in all, after our thirty spins, we had made £13. Our biggest prize from one machine. We joked that Lloyds probably wouldn't be a big enough bank for us with winnings like these.

As we gathered the money from the dispenser tray, the arcade manager came over to speak to us. He was a short, podgy bloke with a small moustache and a grey combover. He smiled at us and offered congratulations on our success. 'You obviously love this stuff, you boys, you're really good. I don't mind telling you that I've got a special machine at the back with a ten-pound jackpot, instead of these three-pound ones!' He lowered his voice. 'I'll let you both try it out if you like.'

I liked the idea. I'd never played on a machine with such a big prize. I spoke to Bas in Punjabi, 'We should go, imagine a ten-pound jackpot!'

'Yes!' Bas replied. 'And he can't watch the machine in the back and watch out here, so we can get as many goes as we like.'

Confident that we wanted to try the machine in the back, we agreed and followed the portly manager through a grotty white door next to his booth. The moment we stepped through, into a small stock room, with no machines, we knew we'd made a mistake. The manager blocked the door while he shut and locked it. Then he turned around to us, looking furious. 'Right, you little Paki bastards, I know you've been ripping me off,' he crouched to get as close to our faces as possible. 'You've been stealing from the machines. If you weren't kids I'd kick the shit out of you, but I've called the police instead. They're on their way and you're going to jail, you little fuckers.'

We immediately started protesting. 'What do you mean? We haven't done anything. Let us out!' But we knew we were trapped. We were locked in and there was nothing we could do.

'I saw you do something to the machine to get money on it. What was it? Hand it over!' he shouted at us. We stuck to our story and both of us denied the allegations.

It didn't take long for the police to arrive. They came into the small back room to speak to us. One of the two officers asked if we had been stealing. We both said 'No.' They told us that the manager was convinced and that he said he had CCTV.

'I'm afraid we're going to have to arrest you,' the officer said. 'We'll take you down to the station and interview you properly there.' He read us our rights. We were marched through the arcade in front of all the gamers who had seen us win multiple jackpots twenty minutes earlier. As we walked towards their waiting car, Bas said to me in Punjabi, 'Drop the wire on the pavement, Saj, so they won't see!' He must have already discreetly got rid of his.

I put my hand in my pocket and grabbed hold of the device, waiting for an opportunity to discard it. As I got into the car, I dropped it into the gutter. The police officers didn't notice.

At the police station we were put in a holding cell together.

During a pocket search they found the Silk Cut cigarettes. We were sure these would get us into even more trouble, but they didn't seem to care. Once we were left alone in the cell, the panic of being caught out set in. I thought through each decision I could have made differently. *Why did we leave Bristol? Why did we keep going? Why did we get so greedy?* The police officer who had driven us to the station came in to explain the next steps. 'We're going to contact your parents,' he said. 'They can either come here with a lawyer or we can assign a lawyer to you. But because you're so young, we're not able to ask you any questions until you have an adult with you. Does that all make sense?' We nodded, before being left alone again.

Convinced that the cell was bugged and that the police would be listening in, Bas and I only communicated in Punjabi. It was only a few months earlier that Bas had been cautioned by the police for stealing the pens from Boots. He knew that a second arrest would be taken more seriously. We discussed whether or not to stop lying and tell them what we'd done. Bas didn't want to. He said that the arcade owner was breaking the law by allowing us, and all the other under eighteens, to gamble. I disagreed. I didn't want the situation to get out of hand and, by coming clean, I thought we may be able to walk away with just a telling off.

A couple of hours later, we were presented with a cup of tea and a cheese sandwich each. As we were finishing the bland lunch, the officer came back into our cell. He said, 'We phoned your family and spoke to Mr Javid, is that your father?'

'Yes,' I said.

'He said he's not going to come and get you. He's refused.'

This was bad news for us. The idea of Dad's anger was as scary as criminal charges. 'What did he say?' I asked.

'Well, let's just say that he was very upset. But we can still question you as we've arranged for a court-appointed lawyer.'

He gestured a hand behind him towards a dowdy-looking woman in her mid-thirties. She wore a knitted cardigan over her blouse. But her drab appearance put us at ease. She was softly spoken and explained that she wasn't there to work for the police, but that she was there for our interests.

'Does that mean we can say anything to you? And you can't tell them?' Bas asked.

'That's right, I'm here for you, so you can tell me anything,' she replied.

I wasn't sure if I completely believed her, but at this point, Bas and I had run out of options. 'Yes, we did it,' I said. Bas, still hoping that the manager's crimes would clear us of our own, added, 'But why did he let us in? We're under eighteen, so he's breaking the law!'

The woman replied, 'He shouldn't have and he could be prosecuted for that. But that doesn't mean they won't prosecute you too. You should think carefully about what to do next.'

'We're going to tell the truth,' I said firmly. I knew I was the one who had the final say and Bas would follow what I had decided. I was the older brother, Batman and Robin, after all.

'I think that's a good strategy,' she said with a smile. 'Because you're young boys and the police will take a more favourable view of things if you're honest. They want to give people another chance. You're from a rough neighbourhood. They might see that things are tough for you and go easy.'

It took two hours for the police officers to interview us separately. Our stories were the same, because we both told the truth. They confiscated the money we had won and sent us on our way with two bus tickets for the 350 back home to Bristol.

That should have been the most intimidating part over, but we were dreading going home. We knew the moment we got back, Dad would absolutely lose it. We discussed going somewhere else, to a different home, but we didn't have any family near us in Bristol. When we got back to the shop, it was already closed and the lights were off for the day. We walked up the external metal staircase to our front door.

Mum was the first to see us. 'I can't believe you boys,' she said under her breath, ushering us inside. 'What were you thinking? Your dad is furious.' She didn't pause for breath before adding, 'You must be hungry, sit down and eat your dinner. Then we'll talk about it.'

We were relieved to have been offered something to eat before the inevitable beating. But as we walked through the lounge to get our food, we came face to face with Dad. He had been sitting in an armchair in the living room but leaped up when he saw us. I knew what was coming. I dived to the floor and threw my hands up to cover my face, clamping my arms together over my abdomen and tucking my legs up into my body as tight as I could. It would be his hard leather Báta slipper. That was always his weapon of choice. It was quick to hand.

Dad only slowed down to remove the house shoe from his foot before he whacked me on the thigh with it. Bas tried to run past him but took a hit on the back. Mum started shrieking telling him to stop, that we had endured enough. But he shouted back that we needed to learn. Both Bas and I cried out 'Maffi,' asking for forgiveness, over and over. After a few more hits, he lowered his arm and left the room to calm down, still holding the shoe in his hand.

It was two months later that the police got back in touch with my father. They asked him to come into Bridewell police station, in central Bristol, with the two of us to discuss our actions and the next steps.

There hadn't been any mention of the incident since the evening we came home. If we annoyed Dad he would usually have a big outburst and then refuse to bring it up again. That was the pattern this time too. That was OK by me and Bas, as we weren't in a hurry to talk about it again.

Neither of us knew if we would be charged for the offence. If the police did decide to take it further, we knew that would result in criminal records that would stay with us. At thirteen and eleven, we hadn't spent much time thinking about our futures, but even so, we knew that having a criminal record would be disastrous. With Bas's previous caution for shoplifting, he was most worried. At the time of his first caution, he was warned that if he was arrested again, he would get convicted of both crimes. Dad was well aware of this.

We were shown into an interview room in the station and an officer we hadn't met before greeted us. The three of us sat down in front of his desk, Dad in the middle, and me and Bas on either side. The police officer had various papers arranged in front of him. He said: 'Thank you for coming in today, Mr Javid. We're going to make a decision about how to proceed with your boys. I just wanted to talk to you first. How have things been at home? Can you tell me a bit about your home life?'

I looked down at my lap. I was too ashamed to make eye contact with my dad or the police officer. Dad took a deep breath and began talking. He started by saying how disappointed he was that this had all happened and how upset he had been to hear that we had been stealing. He explained to the officer that he had moved to the UK from Pakistan for a better life for his wife and his children. That he had experienced some awful things when he was young. He wanted better for his boys and he thought the UK would offer that. He said that he worked long hours at the shop and that he was lucky to be a business owner. He said that he didn't get to spend as much time at home as he wanted because of his work and that maybe that's why this had happened. He suggested that if he had been able to give us more time and attention, we wouldn't have got into trouble. 'I feel like I've failed as a father. I am so disappointed in them and in myself, because this is not the future I want for my boys.' He had tears in his eyes. I had never seen my dad cry.

'My wife and I can't afford to stay home to watch the boys or to pay someone else to watch them. They know stealing is bad, I told them all after Basit was arrested that they must never steal. But I haven't been around enough to make sure.'

He turned to Bas, gesturing at his fourth son. 'This is all wrong. Basit is a good boy and he's really smart. He's so clever, he could be someone one day.' Then he turned in my direction. 'And Sajid has never been in trouble before. Everything is going wrong. Please, officer, is there any way you can give them a second chance?'

The officer was listening. He sat forward, taking in every word. He handed my dad a box of tissues from a drawer in his desk. I felt awful. I felt so guilty about what we'd done, but mostly about what we'd done to my dad. I felt like I was watching his dreams slip away and it was my fault. I had so utterly disappointed him. Bas was clinging on to Dad's arm and I turned to him and spoke in Punjabi, 'Please don't cry, Dad,' I said. 'We won't disappoint you. We won't disappoint you any more. I'll do something to make you proud to make up for this.'

He replied, 'I hope you do, son. But we have to hear from the police officer.'

The policeman spoke directly to me and Basit, 'Do you realise what you've done, boys, and how bad it is?' We both said that we did. He took the sheet of paper in front of him and turned directly to me. 'Sajid. This is a serious offence that you've committed. You did admit to it, and that's good. I know that there are circumstances that have made your life challenging. Are you prepared to turn your life around?'

'Yes, yes I will,' I said. I really meant it. I wanted to do better and to make something great of my life. I was going to do something special and make my dad proud.

The man pointed to my name on his sheet, 'You see your name here? Underneath it, I'm going to write "Caution". That means that we will keep a record of what happened, but if you never do anything again, that record will disappear when you turn eighteen and no one will ever know. But if you do something else, you'll be charged for that crime and this one.' I was too grateful to consider the possibility. I thanked the man over and over, and agreed that I would never break the law again.

Next, he turned to Bas. He said, 'Now Basit, your situation is a little different. You've been in trouble with the law before?' Bas nodded. 'So what we should do is convict you.' He pushed a piece of paper across the desk.

'You see here?' He pointed at my name on the sheet with the nib of his pen. 'It says "Sajid – Caution" and it says "Basit – Charge", right?' Bas nodded again.

The officer continued, 'I've just listened to your dad. I shouldn't do this.' He touched the nib of his pen on the word 'Charge' and, after a brief pause, drew a line through it and wrote 'Caution' in its place. 'Boys, you've just heard what your dad said. He and your mum have sacrificed everything for you children. Now it's up to you: make your parents proud.'

Dad wiped his damp face and insisted on giving the man a hug. As we walked out of the station, I felt lucky. I would never do anything like that again. I decided I would do something that would make up for my behaviour. I would do really well at school, not just OK. I would sit my O levels, maybe even be the first in my family to do A levels and, who knows, university. I would make lots of money in a job and I would buy my mum and dad a house so they didn't have to live above a shop. That's how I would prove that I had learned my lesson.

12

Back to Bedminster

My dad's businesses were never going well but with the recession of the early eighties, coupled with Anwar's theft, he took the decision to close Kaiza Fashions. He sold the remainder of the lease, flogged most of the stock cheap in the market, and kept the best items for the shop on East Street, Bedminster. He used the money he managed to recoup to secure the lease on 109 East Street, directly next door to our original shop. My parents now had leases on two premises next to each other and the new shop had a slightly bigger flat above it, so this is the one we moved into.

The previous owner had run a women's clothes shop as well. It was called Scallywags. My parents liked the name so decided to keep it. There were many perks to the move. They were no longer in the wholesale business, so could concentrate on retail. They still had two premises but now they were right next door to each other.

We were pleased to be back in Bedminster. The area was lively, we knew it well and a KFC had opened up since the last time we lived there. Of course, we weren't allowed KFC as it wasn't halal, but every now and again we'd buy a two-piece chicken and chips with coleslaw after school, sit on a bench and devour it before going in for dinner. What my mum didn't know couldn't hurt her, or us for that matter.

It was around this time that my parents sent Bas up to Rochdale to live with Phopo Salima and my cousins Rozina and Tes. Exasperated by his bad behaviour and conscious that the stint in Pakistan had done nothing to slow down his rebellious streak, they hoped that time in Rochdale would help. Salima didn't work so would be more available for the children than my parents could be. She also ran a tight ship where studies were prized over all else. My parents hoped it would be good for him.

My commute into school had already been long with a thirty-minute bus ride, but now that we had moved back to Bedminster, even further away, my dad said it would be near impossible for me to get there. The route would take close to an hour and a half and involve two buses. My parents made arrangements for me to go to a local secondary school instead. It was known to be a rough school. I had heard stories of kids getting beaten up there and intensive bullying. As I was likely to be one of the only brown people there, I was already a walking target for bullies. I didn't like the sound of the school at all.

My mum didn't understand my protestations: a school was a school and the distance made it impossible to continue at my last place. It made perfect sense to her that I would go somewhere nearer by. Compared to her upbringing, with no access to schooling whatsoever, she saw me as lucky and any complaining as ungrateful.

My dad's main motivations were finances and convenience. Not only would it be an inconvenience for me to travel across town every day to school, it would also be an inconvenience for him when he needed to go in for school meetings and other such appointments. He didn't want to have to pay for the bus pass that I would need in order to get there. Had I been attending a feeder school for the area we lived in, the council would have covered the cost of the travel. Better still, he could send me to a school within walking distance to save himself either the financial burden or the paperwork of applying for the travel costs.

Despite all their logic and reasoning, I flat out refused. I liked my school and I knew I would do better there. I would not move. The summer was littered with arguments over my education. My refusal didn't mean much to my dad, who continued with his plans and put in the transfer application for me. It was accepted and, as far as he was concerned, I would be starting at the new school that September. But I still stood firm in my refusal. My stubbornness frustrated him but, ultimately, he knew he had the upper hand. I didn't have any money for the four daily bus rides I would need and it would have taken two and a half hours to walk. Even so, my resolve didn't slip.

The end of summer rolled around and it was the start of the new term. Both schools, the local one I was now enrolled in and my previous school, started on the same day. My dad had already bought me the new uniform with its blazer and tie. But I still had the uniform I had been wearing the year before. The blazer was snug on the arms as I needed a bigger size, but there was nothing I could do about that now.

Despite all my stubbornness, my parents assumed that I would be going to the new school. On that first day, Dad had already left to go to the wholesalers to buy stock for the shops. Mum was making breakfast for all of us boys. I came down to the kitchen early wearing my old school blazer, testing the strength of the seams at the shoulders.

'What are you doing?' she asked. 'You're not wearing the right clothes!'

'I am,' I said. 'I told you, I'm going back to Stockwell.'

'Sajid, no! You can't just turn up at school. They're not expecting you, we've pulled you out. They will send you home!'

'Fine, they can send me home if they want. But I'm going.'

I refused the breakfast and headed for the door.

'You can't, Sajid! How are you going to get there?'

That was the salient point, but I had a plan. I didn't have money for the bus, but I still had my bike. I decided that the mix-and-match cow-horn handlebar bike would be the answer to all my problems. I would cycle the 6.3-mile journey. My mum looked alarmed at the news.

'No! It's dangerous!' I kept walking, set on executing my new plan. 'Please, Sajid. I'll give you the fare for today but you can't ride your bike all that way!'

Again, I ignored her. I needed my plan to have longevity. I needed to work out how I would get there every day and, to me, that meant cycling. I didn't have a route planner or Google Maps to help me work out how to get there. I had sat down with a piece of paper and mapped it myself. I knew how to get from Bedminster to Easton and from Easton to school so, regardless of efficiency, that would be my route. From Bedminster to the centre of town there was a flyover that was designed to help people skip the traffic of the city centre. It was strictly for cars only, but having never got a driving licence or cycling proficiency certificate, I didn't know that. As far as I was concerned, a road was a road and roads were for cycling. I got a lot of beeps on that first journey.

I set off on the treacherous trip but, having allowed extra time, I arrived with ten minutes to spare. Without an official form-group allocation, I tagged along with Bob and joined his class. The form teacher was bemused at seeing me. I insisted that it was all a mistake and I hadn't left. I said that I would be in class as normal. She left me to attend the first session, but halfway through the second, the deputy head called me into his office. I sat in the clinical-looking room on a felt sofa with a chrome armrest. He sat on a small chair opposite me.

'What's going on, Sajid? We weren't expecting you this year.' He was gentle in his approach.

'Yeah, I know,' I said. 'But I didn't want to leave. I want to keep coming here.'

'But, Sajid, if your parents want you to go to a different school, it is up to your parents.'

'No! It's not! It's up to me, it's my education. It's my future and I want to stay at this school.'

'Sajid, we shouldn't really be teaching you here when your parents have pulled you out.' He stood up and took a few pensive steps. 'Let me think about this. Can you give me ten minutes?' I nodded, appreciating that he was giving my situation some serious thought. 'OK, I'm going to speak about it to the head and then I'll come back.'

I sat on that hard-cushioned chair for another fifteen minutes before he walked back in.

'OK, Sajid,' he said as he shut the door and placed himself back on the same chair. 'I've had a chat with the head and we both agree that you're a great student. We all like you here and we'd be happy to have you back. But you can't decide this without your parents. We'll teach you for the rest of the week, but if by then they haven't agreed, you won't be able to come here any more.'

I was over the moon. It was one big hurdle cleared. I had bought myself some time. It took an hour for me to cycle home, and even though it was the end of the summer, it was blazing hot. I stopped on the way to treat myself to a celebratory blackcurrant-flavour ice popsicle. It felt like a glorious afternoon to be crossing Bristol.

When I got home, my dad was furious. 'You've got to stop

this,' he said as I pleaded for him to give his permission for me to stay at the school.

'No, Sajid, you're not listening to me!'

'No, I'm not. If you want me to go to school, this is the only school I'm going to go to,' I replied.

It took three days for me to break him down and finally he relented. 'Do what you like, but I'm not paying for anything.'

For the next two weeks, I triumphantly rode my bike on the precarious route across town to school. I would often turn up sweaty, crammed into a uniform that was too small for me. My mum was worried every time I left the house. She knew it wasn't safe for me to be making the trip and Khal, 'her little birdie', had told her that I was cycling on the flyover. She was desperate for my dad to pay for the bus so that I could get to school safely. Suddenly she was joining the petition, asking Dad daily to give me the money for a bus pass. After that first fortnight, Dad finally agreed. They couldn't afford to get me an annual pass, which would have worked out cheaper, so they arranged for me to have a monthly one.

From then on, I took two buses into school every day. The number 52 brought me into the city centre and the number 75 onward to Downend. The journey was no quicker, it took an hour and a half in total, but I was safe and warm on the upper decks.

I would often use the bus rides as time to do my homework, having ignored it the night before. But I preferred to read the paper. Each day, as I mounted the number 75, I would sit in the same seat at the back on the top deck. On that seat, someone would have left a copy of the *Financial Times*. I never crossed paths with my benefactor, but the paper was there, day in and day out, without fail.

It was a funny-looking newspaper, bigger than those I had come across before and with far fewer pictures. Also, it was pink. At first, I flicked through it, in case something caught my eye or to see if there was a cartoon, but in time I started reading it. I got used to the language and the terms the journalists used. I started to follow specific political stories and would update my friends on what was going on. I learned about the miners' strike, the Falklands War and the Big Bang in the City of London.

At the start of my second year, Stockwell Hill merged with a neighbouring girls' school to become Downend School. There were suddenly more girls around, which meant that, along with the lads I hung around with, I had more need to show off.

That first term back, there was a lot of conversation about where everyone had been and what they'd done with their summers. The usually ghostly white faces of my compatriots were suddenly rosy and freckled, with the occasional fleck of a tan. Bob and his family had driven down to France for a few weeks, taking a ferry to get them across the Channel. Johnny spoke about a trip to Italy with a bunch of his cousins. I had nothing to contribute. Conscious that I was the odd one out, the next time we came back from a holiday I decided I would just lie. I invented a trip to the south of France after the Christmas holidays and laughed along as they joked about eating frog legs. I was smart enough to never say I'd gone skiing, as I didn't know enough of the technique or terminology. But after a quick flick through a reference book in the library, I was armed with enough place names that I was confident I could fake a driving holiday. I started making a habit of this, reading up just enough about Spain to say I'd been over the summer, or Italy the following year. I was just pleased that my lack of tan couldn't give me away.

Another clear difference between my school friends and me was the games we played with. By this time action figures and trucks were well out and we were focused on computer games. The era of the personal computer was upon us and I was falling behind the trend. Plenty of my friends had the Sinclair ZX81 and when the next model, the ZX Spectrum, was released with colour and enough memory to play decent games, it was a big day for teenage boys everywhere. It took me a couple of years of Eid money to save up to buy myself one, and even then it was a second-hand model that I plugged into an old telly to use as the monitor. By this time, I was also picking up a copy of *Your Spectrum* for 35p an issue, so that I could keep up with the developments in the fast-moving new territory.

The computer was painfully slow by modern standards but, crucially, I could play games on it, which was a huge improvement on the rudimentary version before it. With the release of this new model, software companies started producing primitive games that could be downloaded on to the computers. These games, with their series of massive pixels, may look ridiculous by modern standards but they were the most exciting thing my friends and I had ever seen. The first to capture our attention was called *Manic Miner*, where Miner Willy had to explore caverns and collect glowing objects before his oxygen ran out. This was followed quickly by the sequel *Jet Set Willy*, where this time Miner Willy had to clean up a mansion after a party in order to get some sleep.

The manufacturers recorded the games on to tapes that you put into a cassette player that was linked to the computer. Hitting play would start a droll robotic sound like that of a fax machine. This would signal that the game was loading on to the computer. Even after this, a good game would need ten minutes or so to load up before play could start.

Each of these games cost £7 to £8 new from the shop, the equivalent of spending £30 to £35 on a game today, so I was completely priced out. I would borrow them from friends or play the occasional game that Tariq brought home, but there was no way I would be able to build up a catalogue of my own.

In school, people started coordinating so they would each buy a different game and then swap and rotate. I saved up to get one of my own so I could join the exchange programme and try out many more.

It was while I was borrowing a game – *The Hobbit* – for the first time that I realised I could just make a copy of it. I went to the market and bought a pack of six blank TDK cassette tapes for 50p and, using two tape decks, I recorded the game on to the blank cassettes. After doing this a couple of times, the operation became more sophisticated and I started also photocopying the cover of the game so as to package it as closely to the original as possible. My catalogue began to grow and it was then that I decided to start making copies of the copies. I made a few extra of each game and then brought them into school to sell for just £1 each. I did a booming trade.

With the more popular games now widely available through my bootleg service, when one of the kids at school got a new release, they made a big fuss about it. People would often bring in the new acquisition. Not so they could play it in school, but just so they could show that they had it. Getting used to this process of grandstanding, I brought my cassette decks and a big battery in and stashed them in my locker. The next time someone brought in a new game to show people I asked to see it and then snuck away. I loaded it into the tape deck and left it running in my locker for the five minutes it took to copy. While that was happening, I went into the art room and made a photocopy of the cover. Once the process was complete, I went back to the common room just in time to see the owner of the game having a fit, shouting at everyone, trying to work out who had stolen the game. I'd settle in and then casually ask if they were 'looking for this?' I would hand them the game and nonchalantly say it was on a table on the other side of the room. I only did this process three times or so, so as not to push my luck.

Two days later, when word got round that that same game was now in stock and cost only £1, I made a killing all over again. When the holidays hit, I went up to Rochdale and taught Tes and Bas to do the same thing. Between us we made over £100.

13

Reading my way out

There was never a time when money wasn't tight at home. It wasn't a case of feast and famine. All I remember was famine. Dad's businesses were only ever doing OK or badly. More than once, bailiffs came into the shop to collect for debts that had gone unpaid. Sometimes there was enough in the till to give them their minimum payment of £50. When there wasn't, they would take rails of stock, bagging it up and loading it into their van, along with anything else of any value, including the shop radio and a floor-standing fan.

The modest takings were always dented by shoplifters. We were plagued with people stealing. Sometimes the stock would just disappear, others we would catch someone slipping something under their shirt and attempting a hasty exit. There's no way to know for sure but, at an estimate, I would say the former happened daily, while I do know that the latter was a weekly occurrence.

I would help in the shop on weekends and sometimes during the school holidays. My favourite job was manning the till. I liked ringing up the purchases, taking the money, handing back the change, and then folding and bagging the items.

There was one Saturday afternoon when Mum and I were together. It was our busiest day and we had a handful of customers milling about, including a woman and her teenage daughter. They were pawing at the rails and speaking in whispers. Mum clocked them, always alert to people worthy of suspicion. She told me in Punjabi to watch out for them. I walked to the rack of jeans that they were browsing and stood, visible, watching them. Then, without trying to conceal her actions at all, the woman bundled up a pair of jeans and put them under her jumper. I continued watching as the daughter copied her mum and did the same. The mum looked up, made direct eye contact with me and scowled, as if daring me to kick up a fuss.

They started to move quickly to the door. I paused, frozen by the challenging stare. Then I shouted. In Punjabi I told my mum that they had stolen jeans and we both ran to the door, stopping them just as they made it out on to the street. Mum shouted at them in broken English, 'You thief, you thief. You take. Give to me!'

The woman stopped where she stood, eyes narrowing. A crowd formed as the other shoppers followed us out to watch the commotion and other passersby waited to see the scene unfold. 'No, we haven't taken anything,' the woman said.

'Yes they did, Mum!' I told her. 'They've got jeans under their coats.'

The woman continued with her protestations but as my shouts became louder the younger girl gave up. She opened up her jacket and removed the jeans bundled under her arm. 'Sorry,' she said remorselessly.

Her mum was incredulous, 'What are you doing? Put that back! Put that back!'

The girl ignored her shouts and dropped the jeans on the ground. Realising that she wasn't walking away with her cargo, the mum also removed the pair of jeans from her coat and added them to the pavement pile.

'Stupid fucking Paki idiots,' she said as she marched her daughter away. 'Your shop smells anyway, I don't want your jeans.' As always, we didn't call the police. It would involve a long wait followed by inaction.

Dad felt the weight of the lack of success his businesses experienced. His mood was dependent on the takings, which were never as high as he hoped. On reflection he was never built for business. He was kind, and wanted to see the best in people. He refused to drive hard bargains, thinking that we could all look out for each other. He hoped that there would be enough business to go around and, particularly in the Pakistani community, we would all naturally find success together. That's not how enterprise works and he was constantly ripped off and taken for granted.

He had started a business because of the immense pressure to provide and send money back to Pakistan. He had seen limitations in every avenue of employment; racism and a lack of Western education meant there was only so far he could rise up the ladder. But if he started his own business, to his mind, the sky was the limit. In reality, his chosen profession caused nothing but sleepless nights.

My father cared about people. He cared about advocating for his community. He wanted to bring Pakistani and white people together. He wanted to give them opportunities that could have been stripped from them and their families in India during partition, or denied them in Britain by some who were racist. When I think of my dad first arriving in Rochdale and campaigning and fundraising for a mosque, that's when I see his skills coming into their own. His passion for people and social change would have carried him further in life than his business acumen in women's clothes shops.

Dad took an active interest in current affairs. Once he'd shut up the shop, counted the takings and eaten some dinner, he would always sit down in the living room to catch the *Nine O'Clock News* on BBC One. For my brothers, this was often a nightmare. They might have started an episode of *Knight Rider* or *The A-team* on another channel and wanted to finish it. But there was no negotiating when it came to the news: Dad would be watching it and that was that. I felt less affronted by the interruption, because I started to watch it with him. The sound of the *Nine O'Clock News* theme tune cleared out the living room leaving only me and Dad. I enjoyed the rare one-on-one time.

At first, I enjoyed the jaunty opening jingle and then zoned out through most of the news. But in time I started to gain an interest, particularly as I was now reading the *FT* newspaper on my bus ride to school. I would ask Dad what trade unions were and why people were striking. He took pleasure in explaining the concepts to me. He didn't brush off my questions, but bedded in, ready to discuss the ins and outs for as long as it took for me to understand. He explained about the role of the Prime Minister and why it was so momentous that, in 1979, Margaret Thatcher, the first woman PM, had been voted in. At first, my dad didn't like her. He had always voted Labour but, sick of power cuts and strikes causing rubbish to pile up on the streets, he switched his allegiance to Thatcher, who vowed to stop the strikes if elected. I remember watching the news on the day the election results were announced and seeing my dad's delighted expression that Thatcher had made it. What struck me most about the coverage was not her remarks outside Downing Street, but watching James Callahan leaving just minutes before. To me, as a child, the outgoing Prime Minister looked sad. I wondered why they needed to film his retreat. I felt sorry for him.

14

The big one

Any time there was an issue at the shops, Dad would try and get it sorted as cheaply as possible. Mum always wanted an officially accredited contractor to come in and fix the electrics or plumbing. But instead, regardless of the issue, Dad called Joe and Moses. The duo were immigrants from Barbados and had set themselves up in Bristol. There was nothing they wouldn't turn their hand to, no handyman service they wouldn't try, and for a fraction of the price of any of the tradesmen in the Yellow Pages. Plus, and most importantly for Dad, they would allow him to pay with an IOU. Joe was chatty and always stopped to ask about our day or to see how school was going. Moses was the quieter of the two and, true to his name, he was very religious. He would quote the Bible in conversation and wore a rosary around his neck. He also demonstrated great patience with me when I would insist on seeing into any electronic equipment he was fixing, particularly the TV when the back came off.

Dad liked them but Mum was always wary. Racism between minorities was still rife and there was a lot of distrust. On one occasion my dad told Mum that he had asked the pair to join us for dinner and she tried to stop it happening. She said, 'What will I do with the plates after they've eaten off them?'

My dad was furious. It was rare to hear Dad tell Mum off but on this occasion he didn't hold back. He told her he never wanted to hear her speak like that again. Joe and Moses ended up joining us for dinner, and my dad made a point of getting the best plates out of the cupboards and using as many as possible. Years later, my mum would realise just how wrong she was and come to deeply regret it.

Dad always refused to conform to the expectations of others, particularly if he felt those expectations were steeped in prejudice. It was around this time, while we were at secondary school, that Khalid's class were going on a trip to Israel. He brought the information and consent form for Dad. Khalid loved studying religious education. He was the only one of us to fully devote himself to his studies at the mosque and invested far more in understanding Islam than the other brothers. The trip was expensive and, while our education was the one thing Dad could be convinced to spend money on, he thought that this would be too much of a stretch.

Word of the school trip got around the local neighbourhood and Mr Qureshi, a man Dad knew from the local halal butcher's, came into the shop to ask if Dad intended to send Khalid to Israel.

'I don't know yet, it depends on all the costs,' Dad told him.

'He can't go there,' Mr Qureshi responded.

'Why not?'

'It's the Jews. It's the land of the Jews. He can't travel there now. If he wants to go you'll have to wait until it's in the hands of the Muslims.'

'Do I?'

'Yes, Abdul-Ghani. You can't have him go there. He'll be surrounded by Jews.' The man grimaced as he said it.

'Why are you talking about Jews like that?' my dad asked.

The man pulled the same disgusted face once again, as if the question didn't need an answer. 'Because . . . they're Jews.'

My dad considered and after a pause said, 'Haven't you heard about the Second World War? Didn't you hear how the Jews were treated? If you're going to talk like that, you don't need to come into my shop.'

When Dad came back up into the flat that evening he had made his mind up and signed the consent form on the spot. He decided he would find the money. He wanted news to spread around the community that his son would be going to Israel.

On one weekend, Dad shut up shop on a Saturday night and Joe and Moses came in ready to dismantle the store, redecorate it and then put it all back together again ready to open on the Tuesday. As they worked, I saw that they had taken the CCTV camera off the wall and added it to the pile of shelving and clothes rails that would later be reinstalled. I saw my opportunity and I took the camera, smuggling it upstairs into my bedroom.

It was one of the weekends when we had rented a VHS player and I thought that if I could connect them together properly, I would be able to record from the CCTV camera on to a VHS tape. I had an old TV that I used as a monitor for my ZX Spectrum computer. I gathered all the elements I needed and set about trying to link them up. All the connections were different so I had to dig out my odds and ends electrical box to see if I could get the right connectors on the right wires. After hours of trial and error, I managed to plug it all in and there it was, the grainy image of my bedroom, complete with stacks of clothes, on the TV screen.

I got Bas, who was visiting from Rochdale, and showed him that we were on the telly. At the time, this wasn't technology anyone owned in their homes. To see yourself on your TV screen at home was a novelty. I hit record on the tape recorder to see if I would be able to write on the blank tape. Bas jumped around in front of the camera for a few seconds. I hit stop, rewound the tape and watched it back. The same Bas, same wild arm movements, fuzzy picture.

The final piece of the puzzle was to work out how to include sound. Without a proper microphone, I couldn't get our voices on the tape but I did have a cassette player that I could connect so that a pop song played along with the recording. What we had designed was the most primitive version of TikTok. We could dance around and lip sync to songs, and then watch the music videos back. I propped the camera up on a shelf, and Bas and I filmed ourselves strutting around and miming to Falco's 'Rock Me Amadeus'. I make sure to hit every beat with my imaginary drumsticks.

Tariq was enamoured with the set-up and took the opportunity to record his own version of Wham!'s 'Freedom'. By this point, he had already grown a George Michael-esque beard so he assumed the position of the lead singer while Bas took on the role of Andrew Ridgeley. For this one, I kept the camera moving between Tariq singing passionately into a hairbrush and Bas making exaggerated guitar strums on a tennis racket. Tes and Atif also got in on the action, singing along to Chris de Burgh's 'Lady in Red'. Tes whacked felt-tip marker pens on a Puma trainer box while Atif imitated the crooner into an upturned hammer.

We showed my parents the videos and they were both amused and impressed by the set-up, although Dad still told me off for taking the shop's CCTV equipment. Three decades later, when my father was in his final days, I found those videos and replayed them to him. The only moving images he had of his five sons as young boys. His response was: 'Thank goodness you stole that camera, God bless you.'

*

Bas was sent back to Bristol from Rochdale. The move hadn't helped with his behaviour. Resourceful as he was, he'd just found another group of rebellious teenagers to hang out with up north. The drinking, smoking, girls and petty theft all continued. On top of that, Bas was constantly fighting with his cousins. It was too much for Salima to manage so, after a year, Bas came back down to Bristol. As teenage boys we fought each other a lot. There was always a reason to wrestle or punch each other, and the constant fighting infuriated our mother. As we grew, she was increasingly unable to intervene and the risks grew exponentially.

Khal liked his stuff clean and tidy. He was the only one of the five of us who would help Mum around the house and in the kitchen. Everything had a place and he looked after his things carefully. Sadly for Khalid, we lived in a cramped flat with seven people, so it was rare for anything to stay in the exact place that you left it. When one of us took something of Khalid's, he would be furious. He couldn't stand the idea of losing control of his possessions. When you have so little, you protect what you have fiercely. On one occasion, I was in the firing line for moving his stapler and rather than opt for the usual punch, he picked up a hammer and launched it in my direction. The tool went flying through the air and knocked me on the side of the head. The resulting injury had me in Bristol Royal Infirmary's A & E getting a CAT scan. Thankfully there was no permanent injury, just a pool of blood left on Mum's carpet.

Khalid's punishment that night was a beating from Dad. Getting hit was the usual punishment for bad behaviour at home. It didn't happen often, probably only once a month or so, but we dreaded Dad finishing work when we'd been naughty that day. He had been hit by his father and his father would have experienced the same. To him, it was how to exact loving discipline. He was, he thought, providing a vital deterrent to prevent us from doing that bad and/or dangerous thing again. He would sometimes use his hand, but often opted for an implement like his leather slipper or a wooden spoon from the kitchen. It had been known for him to hit us so hard that the handle of the spoon snapped.

As soon as you knew you were going to get hit, signalled by him reaching for his slipper or going into the kitchen to get a spoon, you ran. In our small flat there weren't many places to run to, so you often ended up in the living room. Just like I had done when I came back from the police station, I would crouch down and cover my face with my hands, curling over my stomach to protect it. I would always prefer to take a hit on the arms or legs. Usually he would whack you two or three times and then stop. He wanted to see that he had hurt you, that you were crying and sorry, and then he would be satisfied that you had understood. Mum didn't like the hitting; she would tell him to stop but he would push her aside. Sometimes after a couple of blows, she would shout at him that that was enough, which usually prompted him to walk away.

Tariq moved out of the flat when he was sixteen years old. Sharing a bedroom with three of your younger brothers was never going to appeal to a teenager. He had always got on well with Hamid, Dad's youngest brother, and his wife Lucy in the semi-detached house where they would serve us tea and jam sandwiches. When Hamid asked if he would like to move in with them, he agreed. He was two years older than Lucy's daughter Katharine, and the pair got on well. With more money than Mum and Dad, they were able to offer him his own bedroom. Dad wasn't pleased; he wanted Tariq to stay but felt he couldn't force him.

As he moved out, my parents were worried that he was increasingly distancing himself from the family. He took an apprenticeship at Tesco after leaving school and, in an attempt to keep him close, Dad encouraged him to leave the job and come and work for him instead. Dad said he could manage the original shop on East Street and sell what he liked. Enticed by the idea of running a business, Tariq agreed and said he would sell children's clothes. They named the shop Little Things and Tariq took charge while Dad continued to run Scallywags, the women's clothes store directly next door.

At the time, much like the rest of the UK, Tariq would go into work wearing a George Michael-inspired blazer and tight jeans. While Tariq was excited by the job title, the actual tasks didn't interest him at all. As a teenager he was a bit lazy and not at all prepared for the responsibility of running a shop. Each day he completed the same circuit. The shop was supposed to open at 9 a.m., but he was often late, usually arriving at around 9.30 a.m. to let in the assistant, who was always a young woman or student who needed some extra cash. He would hang around until 11 a.m. or so and then open the till, take a tenner and go next door but one to Regal Amusements. He would lose most of the £10, but keep back a couple of quid to go to KFC. He'd buy some fried chicken, plus a Mars bar from the newsagent's, before heading back to the shop for the afternoon.

On one Saturday, Bas and I had nothing to do so decided to go and watch Tariq take his chances on 'The Big One' slot machine. 'The Big One', our favourite game, was 10p a spin and if you achieved the £3 jackpot, you were given the option to try and double it by hitting a button that alternated between 'double' or 'lose', which wiped out your winnings. If you managed to hit 'double', you could try again to double your £6 and again with your £12 until you hit the maximum of £24. We'd never seen anyone make £24. On this day Tariq didn't get anywhere near. He started with £20 to spend but within half-an-hour he'd spent and lost the lot. He hadn't even held back a pound for his fried chicken. Furious with the loss and convinced that the machine must be about to pay out, he stormed back to Little Things, took another £20 from the till and came back to the machine.

Half an hour later, he had lost that second £20 too. He hit the jackpot twice but he never knew when to walk away, always risking one more 'double or nothing'. He held back 40p, stormed across the road, got a Mars bar, Coke and a copy of the *Sun*, and went back to the shop to get more money. Bas and I had watched on in shock as he continued to lose more and more money. But every frustrated pound spent on the 'double or nothing' button made the spectacle more entertaining for us. Incidentally, Babs, who watched on from her booth, cigarette in hand, seemed delighted. With the show over, we needed to find something else to do. I had 20p so we agreed to go and buy some sweets and take them back to the Batcave. Until it occurred to me: 'Why don't we go back in and put the twenty pence in "The Big One"? He's lost so much money, it'll probably be ready to pay out!'

With a mischievous grin Bas agreed and we turned back and took the hot seat in front of the machine. I put in my first 10p piece, took a spin and got nothing. Put the second into the slot and, all of a sudden, the lights started running up and down the screen and the machine let out a jingle of delight. I had hit the £3 jackpot. I could take my winnings, a good return on a 20p investment, or I could go double or nothing. I was always going to gamble it. I put my hand on the big red flashing button, closed my eyes, planted my palm firmly down on to its convex surface and then looked up. 'Whoo whoo!' the machine blared. I had doubled my money: £6. Having learned nothing from Tariq's consistent failures over the previous hour, I decided to go again. With Bas egging me on, I hit the button for a second time and, again, the siren alerted me, 'Whoo whoo!', that I had just won £12. This was a huge amount of money for me, particularly when I had started the day with just 20p. The screen lit up and once again I was given the choice, cash out or hit the 'double or nothing' button. Wide eyed, Bas started chanting, 'Do it, do it!' I'd never seen anyone actually reach £24. It was the stuff of legends.

I hovered my finger over the button once again. A countdown was ticking in the corner telling me I had ten seconds to make my choice or lose the winnings entirely. This time I was tentative. I allowed my fingers to brush over the button and swallowed down the clump of phlegm at the back of my throat. The machine rang out, 'Whoo whoo!' I had won. I had just reached the previously only fabled £24 jackpot. Bas and I bent down to collect our winnings. Babs had a face like thunder.

I pocketed the money and, after we left, Bas ran ahead and burst through the door of Little Things where Tariq was lamenting his loss to Sue, the young female shop assistant, over the remnants of a bag of chips.

'Saj just won the jackpot!' he gloated. 'He won twenty-four pounds!'

Tariq stood up from his stool by the counter. 'What do you mean? Where did you win it?'

'Just now on the machine!'

I walked in behind Bas in time for Tariq to lunge towards me.

'That's my money. Give me my money.'

'It's not,' I insisted. 'I put my own money in!'

'Give it,' he said, thrusting his hand out.

'No,' I replied.

He moved around me and stood, blocking the doorway. 'Give me that money now.'

'No! I'm not giving it to you, it's my money!'

He punched me in the stomach. A firm and solid blow. I folded over with the impact and he pushed me down to the ground. He plunged his hand into my pocket and coins scattered everywhere. I felt the pain in my stomach and, as the injustice of the demand swelled inside me, I cried angry and hurt tears. I scrambled around trying to collect the money and return it to my pocket. Tariq began kicking me to stop me. I grabbed a last handful and ran out of the shop, leaving Tariq to gather the rest of my winnings from the floor.

I stomped through to the shop next door where my dad was sitting behind the counter. 'What's the matter?' he asked as he saw me, roughed up and red from the encounter.

'I'll tell you what the matter is. It's that fucking idiot,' I shouted at him.

'What are you talking about?'

'That fucking fat bastard of a son of yours. Do you know that every day he takes money from *your* till and loses it in the gaming shop? He doesn't do any work. He makes other people do his work for him. He takes the money, spends it on fried chicken and chocolate and sits there all day reading the *Sun*, and now he's nicked my money.'

My dad did not approve of swearing and far from inducing sympathy from him, he was getting increasingly angry with me at every word. I stormed past him and went up into the flat to nurse my wounds and work out how much of the money I was actually left with, muttering expletives as I went.

Next through the door was Tariq, followed closely by Bas. Tariq knew I would have told Dad what had happened so he was ready with his counterattack. He told Dad that he had won money on the slot machine and that I had tried to grab it from him then run off.

'You're lying!' Bas interjected. 'Saj won the money and you stole it!'

Tariq was furious. 'You know, Dad, this is why I left home in the first place. They behave like this and then they gang up against me. That's why I can't come back into this family and can't live with you. You let your sons get away with calling me these names and behaving like this. Now I'm being called a liar. I'm telling you he stole from me, so what are you going to do about it?'

That was all Dad needed to hear. He was desperate for his oldest son to come back home and spend more time with his family. Now he knew why he was staying away. In that moment, it was all my fault.

Dad charged upstairs and burst through the front door. 'Where is he?' he boomed through the small flat. I was sitting in the living room with Khal and Atif, in the middle of telling them exactly how Tariq had wronged me. Mum was tucked away in the kitchen, assuming that there was some trivial bickering going on. But as soon as she heard Dad's shout, she came out into the hallway. He was in a rage like none she'd ever seen. At that moment she was scared.

'What's the matter?'

'Where is Sajid? I am going to get him.'

She gripped on to his arm and tried to slow his progress to the living room. 'You must calm down, just tell me what happened.'

He turned back to face her, 'Our eldest son won't live here and it's his fault. Sajid has stolen from Tariq. He can't behave like this. Where is he?'

Mum released his arm and left him to muscle his way into the living room. I heard the shouting and assumed my safety position on the sofa, in the hope that he wouldn't actually hit me or at least it would only be one or two blows. He removed his leather shoe, raised it above his head and started whacking it down on me. There was no holding back, no restraint at all. I felt the entire blow of each swing as it landed on my body. He hit my arms and legs, and when I moved to try and protect myself he landed a blow on my stomach and face too. The heel caught just above my eye and I started to bleed.

I could hear my mum shouting increasingly frantically behind him. 'Enough! That's enough!' Her intervention would usually signal the end, but he didn't stop and didn't slow.

'I haven't even started yet,' he snarled as he landed another blow on my side. This was unlike any other incident. Usually if Dad was going to hit one of us the other brothers would leave the room, knowing it would be over quickly and not wanting to get caught up in it. But I could hear Khal shouting too, telling him to stop.

I squirmed out from under him, off the sofa and ran into the hallway. He continued to follow me. By the door for the living room was a standing vacuum cleaner, one with a long plastic handle that stood up and a sturdy base with rollers covered by a grate. I bolted past it and went to fumble with the front door to get outside. Dad picked up the vacuum cleaner as he pursued me. He clumsily swung it in my direction, sending the base crashing into the wall. I opened the door and got outside on to the metal platform attached to the fire-escape stairs. The vacuum cleaner came swinging out behind me. I cowered in the corner of the railings as it clattered down next to me. And then I ran. I hurtled myself down the stairs, out of the small yard door and on to the street, where I kept running.

I went and hid in the Batcave Bas and I would play in. It only took only a few minutes for Bas to follow behind me. I was physically hurt. The cut on my eye had clotted so there was no longer blood running down my face but I was bruised. My legs ached and my ribs hurt when I twisted my torso. I swore I would never forgive him.

I stayed out for hours. Even when Bas insisted he was too hungry to stay out, I refused to go home with him. Eventually I walked back into the flat at 9 p.m., terrified of what I could be coming back to. Tariq was long gone, having shut up the shop and gone back to Uncle Hamid's house. Dad was also nowhere to be seen. Mum was waiting for me. Sitting on a chair in the kitchen, eyes trained on the front door. 'Are you all right?' she said gently as I walked in.

'I don't want to see Dad,' I replied.

'You don't have to, he's not here. Will you eat something?' She had a plate of food prepared and waiting for me. I sat at the table and told her what had happened from start to finish. She nodded and listened, encouraging me to keep spooning food into my mouth as I spoke.

'I know my boy,' she said as she examined the cut above my eye. 'Basit told me what happened. I believe you. I will explain to your father when everyone has calmed down.'

I don't know if she did explain to Dad what had really happened. I assume she did, but he didn't address the incident with me back then. For the next few weeks I avoided being home when I thought he would be there. When we were in the same room I didn't look at him. I didn't want to make eye contact. After a while he started to make small talk with me again; he would ask me to pass something at dinner or ask how school was. The anger I felt faded, as did the bruises. That was the last time my dad ever hit me.

15

TV repairman

The education system in the UK has completely changed since I was fourteen and making choices for my secondary school exams. Back in 1986, when I would be taking my exams – just before the days of GCSEs – there were two types of qualification that sixteen-year-olds sat; O levels and CSEs. The CSEs were designed for the more practical and less academic students. The idea was that they gave a basic overview of the subject and set you up with a foundational knowledge that you could take forward into a trade or a diploma in a practical skill. O levels were for students who intended to move forward with more academic pursuits. At our school, in order to do an A level in a subject, you needed to have completed the O level first. The highest grade in a CSE, Grade 1, was equivalent to a 'C' grade in an O level.

Pupils could take a combination of CSEs and O levels depending on their aptitude in the subject, but this wasn't their choice. It was decided by their teachers based on their grades, potential and also the field of work they were likely to enter after school. My school was more heavily geared towards offering

CSEs. The teaching for O levels was more complex so it was usually capped at one class per subject.

Before the CSEs and O levels were announced, the school hosted a term of careers sessions. This was to give children a vision for their future, inspire them to work hard in their studies and also direct the teachers' thinking when it came to the qualifications the pupils would need.

In these sessions people from different professions came in and talked about what their jobs entailed. Then, towards the end of the term, we each sat a multiple-choice quiz about our interests and skills. The careers counsellor then took the completed quiz, along with your most recent school report, and came back with the grand answer: your future job.

The day that everyone's recommended careers were revealed was an exciting one. We were called one by one into a meeting with our form tutor and the careers counsellor for the big news. As a 'Javid' I was about halfway through the register, so had already seen a wide range of jobs suggested to the pupils before me, from veterinary nurse to brickie. I sat down ready to get the news. 'We've discussed your test scores and your work here at the school,' said the careers advisor. 'We've got a really good idea for you for a career. We think you would make an excellent television repairman.'

I found the result anticlimactic and it showed on my face. 'Really?' I asked.

'Yes,' the woman continued. 'You have an interest in electronics and everyone needs their TVs repaired. There are plenty of apprenticeship schemes for TV repairmen. Have you heard of Radio Rentals? You could enquire there?'

I had heard of Radio Rentals. It was the shop most people used to rent televisions if they weren't able to afford to buy one. The rentals came with a service guarantee, so if it broke down, someone would come over to your house to take a look.

I supposed they would be big employers of TV mechanics. The counsellor handed me a flyer with details of the apprenticeship scheme. It required five CSEs for entry. It wasn't a very high bar.

I took the flyer and the report home with me that evening. My dad was wholly unimpressed at the career advisor's lack of ambition for me. Unsure if I should just resign myself to my fate, I walked down to Radio Rentals that weekend. I started moseying around the shop, trying to work out if I was looking into the static screens of my future. The shop assistant came over with an encouraging smile. 'Can I help you?'

Well that's good, at least I'd have one nice colleague, I thought. I said, 'Can you tell me, how often do the tellies break down?'

The man looked a little surprised at the question.

'Take your most expensive one,' I gestured to the largest screen TV on a mid-height shelf. 'How often does that break down and need fixing?'

'Hardly ever,' the man said. 'Particularly the newer models, they're getting better and better. It's very rare for it to break.'

'OK, thanks,' I replied.

There I had it. Straight from the horse's mouth. Not only was this an uninspiring job, there was no market for it. I decided then and there, I would not be a TV repairman.

Despite this, my teachers now had me earmarked as a student who only needed CSEs in order to progress. I found out I would be doing four O levels and five CSEs. This was more O levels than many of my classmates, but I was still unhappy. Particularly as I wasn't doing O-level maths. I knew by this point that I wanted to continue on to A levels. To keep studying maths, I had to do the O level, and with only a CSE, I wouldn't be able to. I went to see Miss Williams, my maths teacher, to explain the predicament but she was adamant that the CSE was the right choice for me. She encouraged me to work hard and get a grade

1 in the CSE, saying that was the same as a C grade at O level and it would be very impressive. But it wouldn't be impressive enough, and I knew it. In the end, she explained that only a handful of students would be doing O level, and I wasn't going to be one of them.

I refused to be beaten. The school offered an option where, if you paid the exam board fee, you could still be put in for an exam they hadn't selected you for. They wouldn't teach you the material or help you get up to scratch for it, but they would allow you to sit the exam on the premises with the other students who were enrolled in that class.

I managed to persuade my dad to cover the cost of the test. I went into the library and found the syllabus, and made a list of everything I needed to know for the O level that the school wouldn't teach me. It was then that I realised I would need some help. I looked through the *Bristol Evening Post* to see if I could find a tutor. There were a number advertising their services, but virtually all of them cost £20 per hour.

I went back to my dad and explained that I needed more money in order to pass the test. 'Can't you teach yourself in the library?' was his, perhaps inevitable, response.

'No, Dad, I don't think I can,' I said. 'I've looked through the topics and I will not understand them without some help. I can teach some of it to myself but I don't understand it all.'

'How much is that going to cost?'

'There are people who teach maths to kids for their O levels and I can get one of them.'

'How much?'

'It's twenty pounds a session.'

'I can't afford it,' he said.

'Dad, I know it's a lot to ask, but I can't do it without this money.'

He stood his ground and said no but I was stubborn. Over

the next three days I pestered him constantly. I called each of the tutors in the paper and found one who offered sessions for just £10 a class. And finally Dad gave in.

'Can you learn it all in five sessions?'

'Yes,' I said with a confidence I didn't feel.

'OK. I'll give you fifty pounds and you have to get it done in five sessions.'

I knew it would be tight. I called the tutor back. His name was Wilson and he was a PhD student from Ghana studying at Bristol University. I explained that I was taking O-level maths but the school had refused to enrol me into the class. I said that I just needed him to cover the extra topics.

'So they've not put you in for the O level?' he asked, with a thick West African accent.

'No, they haven't,' I replied.

'Does that mean your teachers don't think you are able to do it?'

'I suppose so, but I am. I can do it. The only problem is, I've only got fifty pounds. I can only do five lessons. Can you teach me all of the information in that time?'

He paused. 'Look, I can't answer that question because it depends on you. Can I relay all this information to you in five classes? Yes. Will you understand it? And will you be good enough for the O level? That's up to you and how hard you work.'

'That's fine,' I said. 'I'm going to work hard.'

The sessions were held in his student accommodation in the university part of Bristol, an area called Clifton. To get to him I had to cycle up a massive hill. The area was worlds apart from Stapleton Road and Bedminster. It was where the wealthy slave traders first settled in Bristol, with the advantage of the port being at the bottom of the hill. The homes were grand, made with Bath stone, and set back from the road to allow for front gardens that were bigger than our entire flat. I would avoid buying a sandwich for lunch while I was in the area as it was far more expensive than a bun from Mountstevens bakery by my home – which was the Gregg's of its day.

Wilson's flat was small as it was part of the mature student accommodation. When I first arrived, his girlfriend was just leaving, and she gave him a kiss on the lips as she walked out the door. She was white. I remember thinking I'd never seen a Black person and a white person together like that before – as a couple.

Wilson was softly spoken and polite. He was tall and wore glasses that were befitting of a mathematics post-grad student. He pulled out a few basic books from his shelf and invited me to sit at a blue Formica table. The session went well, and by the time we were finished, we'd gone on for an hour and twenty minutes instead of just the hour we agreed. This was the pattern with all our sessions. He would set me exercises for homework and then run through them the next week, picking me up on any mistakes. In our last session, we'd covered all the material, but it still wasn't enough.

'We need to do some more. You should take these questions and do them at home so I can see,' Wilson said.

'I will work on it, but this is our last session so I can't come back again,' I replied.

'Don't worry, just do this homework and then come back.'

'I can't, I don't have any more money,' I told him.

'Don't worry about the money, just do the work and then come back.'

'Really? Are you serious?' I felt bad. He clearly wasn't wealthy, and he'd already given me more time than I'd paid for and at half the price of his fellow tutors.

'Just go and do the work.'

I saw him for another two sessions after that and he didn't

ask for another penny. By the end of our final session, he gave me a warm slap on the back and said, 'You've got it, you've completely got it. You're really good at this. You'll go far, Sajid.'

I felt so encouraged by him. What Wilson taught me wasn't just the basics of sin, cos and tan, he also introduced me to general exam technique. He explained how to pace myself and why it was so important I read the questions multiple times. He showed me how best to present my working so that it would be understood by the examiner and explained that having a tidy exam paper could even help me get higher grades. I brought these practices with me into every exam I sat in 1986. It gave me a leg up I never would have experienced otherwise.

Of the five CSEs I sat, I got grade 1 in almost all of them. And in my maths O level, I got a B. I was over the moon. I called Wilson to tell him the good news and we celebrated down the phone. We said we would see each other again soon, but we never did.

Straight after my O levels, we moved once again. This time back into a house. Khalid now had a full-time job, at Sun Life, and he and Dad went in on the house together. Even for the time, it was pretty cheap, costing £55,000 for five bedrooms. It was further out of the centre in an area called Stockwood. But that didn't matter, because it was the first time since Downend that Mum got the house she so desperately wanted. And it was the first time in my life, aged sixteen, that I had a bedroom to myself.

Tariq didn't make the move with us as by now he had started renting his own flat in Clifton, and had a job flipping burgers at a new American burger bar that had just opened near him. Tension between him and my parents grew as Tariq came over one day and told them that he would be marrying Katharine. My parents were not happy. They had intended for him to have an arranged marriage with a cousin in Pakistan but he flat-out refused. In our culture, to marry outside of the community was frowned upon. To add insult to injury, he had sprung it on them just a fortnight before the ceremony would take place. My parents refused to bless the marriage or attend the wedding.

Tariq wasn't put off and he married Katharine in a local church near to their home. Before the wedding, Mum and Dad sat the rest of us boys down and told us in no uncertain terms that we were not to attend. The three of us, Khal, Bas and I, discussed it and decided we would go anyway. Atif also wanted to come to the wedding but, as he was so much younger, we knew we would have a job getting him out of the house without raising the alarm. On the day, we snuck out. We didn't have fancy clothes so we just wore the smartest things we could find in our wardrobes with our school shoes. Our parents found out later and they were upset, but by then it was done. Tariq was really pleased that we had shown up. For months after, my parents would agree to see Tariq but refuse for him to bring Katharine over to the house. Eventually they relented, and came to see Katharine as the warm and kind-hearted daughter-in-law she was.

Having already 'lost' one son to an unwanted marriage, our parents were determined not to let it happen again. Fearing that Khalid might resist an arranged match, they moved quickly. He was bewildered when they first suggested he should marry someone from Pakistan he had never met – and that it should all be done in a rush. To ease his concerns, my dad made him a promise: once Fouzia, the daughter of my mother's younger sister, arrived in England, they would have two years to get to know each other – to court properly, and marry when they both felt ready. Khalid agreed on that basis. But that promise was quietly set aside. To Khalid's shock, just six weeks after Fouzia landed in the UK, the wedding took place.

*

Having previously stopped at year five, at O levels, my cohort was the first that was invited to attend Downend's new sixth form. I knew I wanted to do A levels so I was set on staying on to continue my studies. It was Rozina who first told me about university. No one in our family had gone before. I hadn't considered it until one summer when she was staying with us in Bristol. She was set on going and told me that I should go too. We went to Bristol City Library on College Green, where they had a collection of prospectuses from all the biggest universities in the country. I remember sitting at a table poring over pictures of Manchester and Reading. Rozina handed me a fancy-looking pack saying, 'Look, this one is Cambridge. That's one of the best to go to!'

When Rozina had left, I kept going back. I looked through the brochures several times, trying to get a feel for each and work out where I wanted to apply to go. I got to know the librarian, who was used to seeing me drop in. She helped me narrow down the most suitable choices and, having gone to university herself, talked me through the application process. A key piece of advice from her stuck with me: 'You want to go to a university Sajid, not a polytechnic.'

She told me to concentrate on getting high grades in my A levels and that I would need three to go to a good university, especially if I wanted to do an academic subject like maths or science.

With that in mind, I decided to do maths, chemistry and computer science for A level. The only problem was that, once again, my school wouldn't let me. On requesting my A levels, the newly appointed head of sixth form told me that no one in the school would be doing three subjects. I had to choose two. I went in during the start of the summer holidays to speak to the teacher directly and appeal to his better nature. It was no improvement on his worst. He continued to dig his heels in. I would just have to accept that I could do two A levels.

By this point, we were only a couple of weeks away from the start of the new year and he was right, I had very little in the way of options. With no desire to do A levels, both Tariq and Khalid had gone on to do diplomas at a further education college called Filton Technical. I was discussing the dilemma with Tariq one morning when he told me that I should call them up, because they offered A levels too.

I took his advice and phoned the college, announcing that I was Tariq Javid's younger brother and I wanted to speak to the head. Remarkably the name did seem to open doors and five minutes later I had brought Mr Huntsford up to date with my problem. He listened with the occasional sympathetic hum on the other end of the line. He explained that applications were now closed but that they did have a little space in their A-level classes so they may be able to accommodate me.

'However,' he said, 'your school has been clear that you shouldn't be doing more than two A levels, and you would think they know you best.' I had been prepared for this and went to launch into my rehearsed rebuttal. But Mr Huntsford raised his voice and carried on talking to silence me: 'But, I must say, I admire your spirit and determination. Honestly, I don't know if you can do three A levels, I don't know you well enough. And it's hard work. It's a lot harder than what your brothers are doing. But if you want to try then you can try. If you fail, you fail. It would be your failure.'

I couldn't believe that I had managed to persuade him. I went straight into the college that day to hand in my application and settle on my subjects. Of the three I wanted to study, I could take maths and computer science, but chemistry clashed with my other choices. I had to choose between English and economics. I wasn't entirely sure what economics was. It had come up a lot when I was reading the *Financial Times* but even so, I couldn't quite pin down the meaning. After being reassured it was suitable for those who liked maths, I decided to take a punt on it. It was a punt that changed my life.

After securing my place at the college, I called the head of sixth form at Downend and took pleasure in telling them that I wouldn't be coming back.

'What do you mean?' he said, clearly having not considered my dropping out a possibility.

'I'm going to Filton,' I said. 'They're going to let me do three A levels and they said I could do maths as well.'

'Saj, why are you doing this? You know you can't succeed. You're setting yourself up for failure.'

'I don't agree,' I said.

'OK, well, Sajid, you do what you want!'

After two years at the college, I left with the top grades of A in both maths and economics and B in computer science. These were the grades I needed to get into my first-choice university, Exeter, to study economics and politics. My Filton economics teacher, Dr Charles Stambolieh, was so impressed with me and Philip Cowley, another boy he taught, that he put us in for the prestigious S level, or Special-level exam. He was proudly Greek. His real first name was Charalampos, but he went by Charles for the sake of his English-speaking colleagues and friends. He was short, with a paunchy tummy that wouldn't have been notable on a taller man, and gestured wildly as he spoke with a distinct Greek accent.

S level was a test that was reserved for the most gifted A-level students. He tutored us privately for it, giving his time freely, at his home in Clifton, sitting round his kitchen table on Saturday mornings. I recall his young son playing with toy cars around us, sometimes running them up my leg making *brrrrm* sounds. Charles told me that I had a gift and, with some work, I would be able to do very well. This was the first time a teacher had encouraged me that, not only could I achieve what I wanted, but that I wasn't aiming high enough. He would announce that I was going to Cambridge to study economics. After one particularly positive class, in which we discussed Nigel Lawson's just-delivered famous Budget, he slammed his pen down with an eccentric flourish, pointed at me and said: 'Young man, I swear it, you are going to be Chancellor of the Exchequer!'

I remembered his enthusiasm and carried it with me in future years. Many years later, when I was Business Secretary and overseeing further and higher education, I tried tracking down Dr Stambolieh. I even asked the department to help, but had no luck.

Then, in 2019, soon after I was appointed Chancellor of the Exchequer, Dani, my parliamentary assistant, knocked on my office door and told me she had been sifting through my correspondence when she came across a letter I would probably want to read myself. I knew if Dani thought that, I'd better read it. I took it from her. It was from a man that said he knew me as a child as I used to visit his home in Clifton to see his dad. He said his dad used to be my economics teacher in Bristol, Dr Stambolieh, and that he recalled me getting extra tuition at his home. He was the boy with the toy cars. He wanted to write to me to congratulate me on becoming Chancellor and, specifically, wanted me to know that although his dad had died a few years earlier, he knew he would be so proud of me. He said I was his dad's favourite, that he often talked of me, and that he knew his dad would be smiling down on me from heaven right now. As I read the letter sitting in the Treasury, in the Chancellor's office – my office – I felt a flurry through my heart and wept.

It was while I was studying for my A levels that Bas came home one day and announced that he had joined the Royal Navy. He'd made no attempt to discuss the decision with anyone in the family beforehand. My parents were surprised but not displeased by the revelation. I think my dad felt that it would be a good way to keep him out of trouble and that, perhaps, the discipline and camaraderie could be the making of him. And he was right.

16

Trading games

Always on the lookout for new ways to make money, at sixteen years old I came up with a new scheme. This time it was both legitimate and had huge scope. Having now spent years sitting with Dad talking about current affairs, reading the *FT* at the back of the bus, and having started studying economics, I was getting very interested in business. I had followed the policies of Dad's favourite Prime Minister, Margaret Thatcher, and seen her decision to privatise government-owned businesses such as Cable & Wireless, British Aerospace and BT. While these aren't topics most teenagers are interested in, I saw an opportunity to make money and I didn't want to pass it up.

Thatcher sold off the first batch of government-owned businesses in the early 1980s as part of the government's policy of denationalisation. And when she did so, she priced the shares cheaply. Even with my limited knowledge of shares and finance from the news and the *FT*, I could see that the price had started low in order to gain interest and make the whole deal look successful. With that in mind, and with more privatisation deals on the horizon, I wanted to get in on the action and make some money for myself.

Given that the government wanted to reach the average Joe on the street with these shares, rather than big investment banks, it wasn't impossible that I would be able to get my hands on some, then sell them on and make a profit. The only snags were that I was under eighteen and I had no money to invest. I was sixteen when they announced that the next company to be sold off would be British Gas. A huge campaign was launched, promoting the opportunity to buy shares with the infamous slogan: 'If you see Sid, tell him.' Application forms to buy the shares were even printed in newspapers to make the process accessible and unintimidating.

I was convinced that if I put in £500, it would be worth £750 in a matter of days. A sweet £250 profit for almost no effort. I just needed to get my hands on cash for the initial investment. I started by asking my dad. He was clear that he didn't have anywhere near that amount to give me, despite my conviction that it was such a safe investment. I didn't know where else to turn. We didn't have rich relatives or family friends: every adult I knew was as poor as we were.

So, I called up my dad's bank, Barclay's on East Street, and asked for an appointment for 'Mr Javid' with the bank manager, putting on my deepest voice and a bit of a Punjabi accent. The request wasn't exactly a lie, I was technically Mr Javid, although I knew I wasn't the Mr Javid he would be expecting.

I wanted to put my best foot forward in my first meeting with the bank, so I put on a school shirt and tie and wore one of Khalid's blazers over the top. I looked as smart as my wardrobe allowed. On arrival, I announced to the desk clerk that I was Mr Javid and that I had a meeting with the manager. A little bemused, she sent me upstairs to sit outside his office. The smartly dressed branch manager, complete with lush moustache and a pocket square, came out eager to meet Mr Javid. 'Oh,' he said, when he saw me. 'Hello, are you here with your father?'

'No. It's just me,' I replied.

'I've got an appointment with your dad. Is he unwell?'

'No, I'm sorry, sir. That's actually me, I'm Mr Javid.'

'It was you who made the appointment?'

'Yes. I need to talk to you.'

'I see. About what?' he stood over me, making no indication that we would be taking the conversation into his office.

'I just need five minutes,' I asked.

'OK,' he relented, stepping to one side to allow me entry. 'Just five minutes.'

I walked into the office and sat down in front of the desk, taking the same seat my dad had sat in years earlier when he learned about Anwar's theft from the business. The manager left the door open and walked around to take his own seat.

'What's this about? Is there a problem with your dad's business?'

'No, there's no problem, I came to see you because I wonder if you can lend me five hundred pounds?' I proceeded to explain my deductions about the government's privatisations. I told him how I expected the shares to be cheap so it would be easy to make a profit quickly. As I continued talking his eyebrows rose with his smile.

'Well, Mr Javid,' he said. 'I wasn't expecting that. I think your logic is sound and, to be honest, you're probably right, there probably is money to be made. It's obvious you've thought about this a lot. But I can't lend you five hundred pounds.'

'Oh please, I will pay you back,' I said.

'Even if I wanted to, the law says you have to be over eighteen to borrow money.'

I knew this to be the case but I was hoping for some loophole. 'Is there anything you can do?'

'I tell you what,' he lent forward in his chair conspiratorially, 'here's what I can do. You're very convincing. I will lend your dad the money. I'll give him a personal overdraft for five hundred pounds, and he can then give it to you to buy your shares. If it goes wrong, your dad will still have to pay me back the five hundred pounds. If it goes right, then you can pay it back with the money you made.'

I was delighted. I went back down the road to Dad's shop and explained what the bank manager had said. Far from being annoyed that I had made the appointment under his name, he was impressed. I think he was also relieved that this latest money-making idea didn't involve fraud or theft.

I took the £500, and made the application for the shares at 60p each. On the first day of trading, I flipped the shares at £1.05 each, making a 60 per cent profit of £300. I paid my dad back, and he ended up being overdrawn only for a single day.

When it was announced the British Airports Authority (BAA) was also being sold off, I did it again, this time recycling my £300 profit and the £500 overdraft. By the time Rolls-Royce and British Steel were up for sale, Khalid was doing the same. I ended up with more than £2,000 in profit. I used it to buy a new computer and a second-hand motorbike that meant I no longer needed to take the bus into college. I still had a few hundred left that I put into savings and would later prove vital in my first year of university.

In those days, university tuition fees were paid by the government. This meant that all I needed for the three years at uni was enough money to cover my general living expenses. For this, many people got support from their parents, some worked and others got grants. Avon County Council offered means-tested grants to those in the lowest income families and, with my dad's business doing typically badly, I qualified.

As my dad was self-employed, he didn't have a stash of

payslips he could hand over to prove his eligibility. Instead, the council requested the most recent year's audited statements from the company so they could review its income. Dad was always late handing everything in to the accountant and always incurring fines for paying his tax late. At times, his accountant Gordon would despair as he could be up to three years in arrears with his reporting. As a result, Dad put off sending in the grant application over and over again until we missed the deadline, and it began to look like I wouldn't have the money for the start of term in September 1988.

At the end of summer, it dawned on me that I would have no money to pay for food or travel while I was at university. By the time I was about to start, the application was in but the council had requested more information and Dad was still dragging his heels in providing it. I implored him to hurry up, but he found the paperwork so stressful that he just did nothing. The letters started to pile up and, with every new correspondence, Dad became more inert.

Dad paid for the first term's lodgings but nothing else would be covered. I had no idea how I was going to manage. Any time I brought it up with him, he assured me he'd give me something before I went. Eventually he handed me £50. It was a start but nowhere near what I needed to cover three months of living expenses, despite the fact that I had worked over the summer. He insisted that he would send more during the term. He never did.

A month and a half in, I was down to my last few pounds. I had exhausted the little savings I had left from the privatisation investments and I needed to eat. I went back to see Mum and explained that I needed money to live and Dad was ignoring me. She took £50 cash out of the till and said that for now I would have to make that stretch. She said that from then on, at the start of each term until I got my grant, she would give me £250.

Every now and again, when she really needed something but there was no money, Mum had a technique to get a little cash. When someone bought an item from the shop with the exact money, she would pocket it and not ring the purchase through the till. If she rung it up, it would have to go to Dad, but if she kept the money, she could build up an emergency fund for herself and for us. I knew that was how she was planning to help me. I was grateful.

I got the grant halfway through my second year, but with no back pay. Despite knowing that I had no income until the grant came through, Dad didn't give me any additional money and never asked how I was surviving. He preferred to stick his head in the sand and hope it would all work out without his intervention.

17

Laura

The summer of 1988, when I sat my A and S levels, was uncharacteristically hot. In typical British fashion, we complained that the warm weather was never coming and, when it did, we complained even more. It was a sticky heat that resulted in a drought in the UK and a national hosepipe ban. But for me, the sun just added to my great mood. I'd constantly listen to tunes that I had recorded from the radio while I was revising for my exams. Simply Red and Tina Turner were my favourites. From July, I was waiting for my grades, and I was feeling good about my chances.

The summer months lay ahead, and I knew I had to try and to make a bit of money before I went off to university, especially as I was worried about getting the grant on time. One of my best friends from school, Bob, had finished his BTEC in business studies at Filton, and had got a summer job at an insurance company called Commercial Union. Everyone knew about them, and their huge office in Victoria Street in the centre of Bristol. Each year they recruited a cohort of students to take on their mountain of paperwork and admin.

I had met Bob on the first day of secondary school when I was eleven years old. He looked fine when we were younger, but as we got older, he got taller, dressed smarter and became a really good-looking chap. He didn't have many girlfriends, but he was meticulous about his clothes. Chinos and nice shirts, always properly ironed. Everything had to be just tickety-boo. That attention to detail carried over into all aspects of his life; his handwriting was beautiful and his time keeping was impeccable. He was the perfect, reliable summer employee for a big firm.

We were speaking on the phone a couple of weeks after he started and he asked me, 'Saj, are you still looking for a summer job?' I confirmed that I was, and he continued, 'You should apply to work at Commercial Union with me. It seems pretty nice and the pay is decent. I know that they're looking, so I can put a word in for you. Maybe you can come and meet me at the office to take a look around?'

I was excited by the idea of it. I wanted a big name on my CV and Commercial Union would certainly provide that.

'Sounds great,' I said. 'What's the totty like?' I was half joking. But only half.

Bob started laughing, 'The totty is good, it's good. There's a lot of people and a lot of girls. But listen, if I get you this job, you have to promise me one thing. There's one girl here I really like, who I'm trying to bag, and it's hands off, OK?'

'Yeah sure, don't worry about it,' I said and I meant it. It wasn't as if I was some big womaniser who delighted in stealing other guys' girls. I was just pleased that there would be some fun young people to chat to and flirt with.

I applied for the job, was given a brief interview by the office manager, and started the following week. I turned up on Monday morning at 9 a.m. in a shirt that I had previously worn to school tucked into a pair of suit trousers. The office was completely open plan with banks of desks in rows, grey felt floor tiles and harsh strip lighting. My job was to open envelopes containing life insurance applications, check that the applicant had included all the required information, staple the sheets together and put the bundle on the next pile. There were fifteen or so students all assigned equally mundane tasks.

I was sitting at my desk on the end of a row, sorting through sheets of paper, when I was distracted by someone walking down the aisle past me. From behind, all I could see of her was her slim figure, toned legs and glossy long blonde hair. Two minutes later she walked back up the aisle, this time facing me with a coffee in her hand. She wore a fitted pencil skirt that sat just below her knee and a floaty cream blouse. I had known many girls, but she was different. She looked elegant, like a woman. I was convinced she was way too beautiful to be single, she would definitely have a boyfriend. I wanted to stare at her and take in each part of her one at a time but, at the same time, was mortified by the idea that she could catch me looking. I was totally, utterly captivated by her.

When my friends asked me about girls, I knew all the right things to say. I talked up dates that I'd had and girls that had been interested in me and dalliances over the school holidays. In reality, though, I'd had little to no experience with women. I was interested in them, but had never had a girlfriend and had only dated a few, and never romantically kissed.

I wasn't frozen by the idea of speaking to girls. I had a lot of female friends and was close with my cousins Amna and Rozina. I was confident that I could chat to them, but I didn't know how to navigate what came after. Even with my lack of experience, I knew what I liked. And I really liked this girl!

At the end of the first week, Bob and I went to get a tuna sandwich and a packet of crisps from my favourite deli. We sat on a bench stuffing them down before the lunch break was over. I asked Bob if he'd spotted the incredible blonde. 'What did I tell you?' he replied, suddenly very animated. 'I said hands off, didn't I?!'

'What? Is that her?' I asked.

'Yes. That's her!'

'What's her name?'

'That's Laura King. She's the girl I like – the one I told you to keep your hands off, right?'

'All right, all right. I haven't done anything, I haven't even spoken to her!' I said, gutted that I had singled out the one girl of the forty or so on our floor that I'd promised not to go near.

'I've been trying to get her attention for weeks now,' Bob explained. 'I've invited her out for after-work drinks a few times, she's very polite, but she's always got an excuse. I've asked if she wants to grab a sandwich for lunch but she said no to that too. She's not gone for it yet, but I'm going to keep getting to know her.'

A bit disappointed by this roadblock, I decided that a promise was a promise and agreed not to try and pursue her, giving him space to continue his attempts.

The following Monday, I came into the office to find that the layout of the desks had been completely restructured. The company had finished recruiting their students for the summer so now wanted each person to have an assigned desk. The chairs were labelled with our names. I found mine in the middle of a bank, took my seat and settled into my new working space for the summer. Then Laura walked over on the opposite side of the row. She had been assigned the seat directly opposite mine. We would be facing each other, eye-to-eye for the coming weeks. I was never going to get any work done.

I was over the moon. This was the best result I could have hoped for. I snuck a shifty look round at Bob, who was right on the other side of the group glaring at me. Tough break for him; dream scenario for me.

As the days plodded on, the mundane job of opening envelopes, sorting papers and stapling them didn't feel so boring. Laura and I made idle chit-chat about our friends, films we'd seen and what we'd done on the weekend.

I found her absolutely stunning. I relished every moment of conversation with her. I remember thinking she was posh, as her accent didn't have a hint of Bristolian. She sounded like a BBC newsreader. She'd gone to one of Bristol's top private schools, Colston's Girls School, while I had been at an average state school. Yet, this posh, beautiful white girl seemed interested in me, a working-class Asian lad.

We were getting on very well and I started to realise that she may actually like me. Any of the lads would have been pleased to have spoken to her, and many of them tried to get her attention. But she kept speaking to me.

I was hooked on her, but tried not to let it show. I would think about her day and night. I loved that she paid me attention. Progress was slow. There were no drunken office parties or secret snogs in the stationery cupboard. Instead, I enjoyed elongated eye contact and laughing a bit too hard at each other's jokes. Thanks to the office stationery shortage, the two of us shared a stapler, handing it back and forth across the desk as we worked. I started to lengthen my hold on it as I passed it to her, before releasing my grip. Slowly I inched my hand up so that eventually, as I passed the stapler over, our hands would touch. Feeling emboldened as she didn't pull away, I stretched out a finger to stroke her hand and, from then on, she started to do the same. A small innocently flirtatious gesture was by far and away the most exciting part of my day. I was in heaven! Meanwhile, Bob was sitting too far away to have any part in our conversations; he couldn't even hear them from his new position. But he still slogged away in the breaks and after work, trying to strike up a flirtation with Laura himself so that she would go out with him.

One Friday, Laura told me about a friend of hers from school called Esther. She lived just down the road from her and the pair intended to go out the following day after work for a Friday-night drink. When Bob asked her out for the umpteenth time, she asked, 'Why don't you and Saj come and join Esther and me for drinks?'

Bob was over the moon, and of course I wanted to spend time with her. Bob told me after work and he couldn't hide his delight either. 'Brilliant,' he said. 'That's perfect. She wants to go out with me but she needs a couple of gooseberries there to make it easier. You're the gooseberry! Hey, maybe you'll even like this Esther girl and we can double date!'

I knew that Bob had misjudged the gooseberry situation. But to be fair to him, I hadn't told him about the hand stroking over the stapler, and I would have felt stupid explaining it. I told him I was happy to help out, knowing full well that I wouldn't be operating as his wingman on the evening.

In the end, we settled on heading over to Laura's house as her parents were away and she said she would cook pizza for the four of us. I borrowed my dad's leased Isuzu Piazza and picked up Bob from his house in Downend.

The fact that Laura and I had very different upbringings was never more apparent than when I first saw her home. She lived in a small village called Frampton Cotterell. It was a half-hour drive north from the centre of Bristol, and was quaint with an English countryside feel. In order to get to her house, we drove over a stream via a small stone bridge and then up towards her drive. The huge, detached home had space for four or five cars to park at the front. The garden was sprawled around all sides of the house, with the nearest neighbours well out of earshot. I knew instantly that I could never take her to our cramped house in Stockwood.

She flung open the front door and went straight in to

hug me. She gave a quick greeting to Bob before leading us through to the living room. It was a large lofty space with sofas you could sink into and a big telly on a cabinet. There was a separate kitchen and dining room, all equally spacious. To me, it was the best house I'd ever been in. Laura and Esther were sharing a bottle of wine and Bob said he would have a glass too. I didn't drink so she poured me out a cranberry juice. I was a bit worried that me being teetotal would come across as unattractive, but fortunately she seemed to think it was actually quite cool.

Laura sat next to me on the sofa and directed all of her conversation towards me. Even Bob couldn't help but notice where her affections lay. He looked slightly crestfallen as he realised I was not chaperoning his date, but it was the other way around. I knew we'd have a conversation in the car on the drive back.

'I've got a pizza in the oven,' Laura announced cheerily. 'Saj, do you want to come and help me in the kitchen?' I threw an apologetic look at Bob as I got up to follow her into the next room.

Laura and I chatted for a minute or two in the kitchen before the timer went off on the oven letting out a shrill beep. She took the pizza out, laying the tray on top of the stove. 'I made this earlier,' she said, nodding at her creation. 'I hope you like ham and pineapple!' I recoiled inside, torn between impressing the girl I liked and telling her that I, as a Muslim, didn't eat ham. I opted for the latter and said, 'I'm sorry, I don't eat pork. And I don't like pineapple.' She looked at me very apologetically, as though somehow she had made a mistake.

'I'm sorry. I should have asked. I can take it off the top?'

'I actually can't eat it as the pork has touched it. I'm sorry,' I did like her, but I knew this was something I did not want to compromise on. She looked mortified. It was clear that after having taken the time to cook for us, she was hoping for a more enthusiastic response from me. She rushed about the kitchen putting together a sandwich, while I stood there worrying that I'd blown it. I hoped that she didn't think I was boring, for first turning down her wine and then her pizza. With the pizza in one hand and my substitute dinner in the other, we went back into the living room and played Monopoly with Bob and Esther. I played with the hat – I was always the hat. I was also the banker. I won.

I pulled up in Bob's drive later that evening as I was dropping him home. He paused with his hand on the inside of the car door and turned to me. 'Saj,' he said. 'It's obvious what that was about. She likes you, not me. You like her too, don't you?' I confirmed that I did. He paused and then said, 'Fine. Look, she's not going to date me, so she might as well date you. Over to you, if you want to have a go, you have a go.'

This was the release that I needed. Coming into the office on Monday, I felt empowered. As we continued our stapler routine, I decided I was going to ask her to join me for lunch. Not with everyone else, just the two of us. Thinking of that deli where I had my regular tuna sandwich order, I asked, 'Do you want to go and get a tuna sandwich at lunch?'

Laura laughed, 'Is that all I would be allowed to have?'

I clumsily explained that she would be able to order anything she wanted and she continued to smile at me through the fumbled explanation. She came to lunch with me and had a chicken sandwich. The two of us sat on a nearby green, Castle Park, bathed in sunshine, eating and chatting and, from then on, I thought of little else but Laura.

Over time, I sadly lost touch with my old friend Bob, without whom I would never have met the love of my life. I heard from mutual friends that he had gone on to be a delivery driver in Bristol. Then one day, out of the blue, in 2000, I got a letter from him at my parents' address, with no contact details. He wished me and Laura well, said he missed the good old days, and that he was now living in the US working as an actor – in hardcore porn films! Bob the Knob. It brought back memories of *Debbie Does Dallas*!

18

Exeter initiations

The first-year students were invited to come on to campus at Exeter University a week before classes officially started. This 'freshers' week' allowed people to get settled in and meet each other. Of course, for most it was just a chance to go out drinking.

I couldn't arrive until the Sunday after, as Khalid's wedding was scheduled for the Saturday. I considered going to university for the week and coming back just for the wedding but with Bas in the Navy and Tariq and Dad on bad terms, Khalid asked me to stay to help with the plans. Dad was in charge of the organisation and, true to form, nothing was arranged.

Fouzia was now in the country and the wedding was set for the first Saturday of September. For the event, we hired a hall above a warehouse on Stapleton Road called Millionaire's Club. The entrance was tucked behind the job centre and I suspected no millionaire had ever set foot within a mile of the place.

On the day, everything that could have gone wrong went wrong. In Pakistani culture, a wedding invite is considered an open invitation. One guest will bring their entire extended family. Dad didn't say no to anyone who asked to bring additional guests, and the majority didn't even ask, they just turned up. So what was an already large wedding of four hundred people exploded into six hundred guests. To top it off, the food, which my dad had ordered from a caterer in Birmingham because he thought it was cheap, arrived two hours late. When it did come, the caterers dropped off vats of curry and rice in the kitchen and then left, with no intention of serving them. What ensued was a dramatic scramble between my brothers and me to find the plates and cutlery required to distribute the food. We rolled up our sleeves and started a production line, all plating up. Without serving utensils, we used mugs, plastic cups and our hands to get the food on to the plates, which were then lined up on a table for guests to come and collect. Khalid and Fouzia were at least shielded from the drama as they sat at the top table, along with Dad who held court with his most esteemed guests.

The day after the wedding, Dad loaded up the van and dropped me and my things at Exeter. I was in Brendon House, an all-male student building. It was directly opposite Hendon House for girls, so we weren't starved of female company.

Having arrived a week after everyone else, I was on the back foot when I met the students with dorm rooms on the same corridor as me. They seemed to have already sunk into an easy rhythm with each other. They had already been on a number of nights out and had in-jokes as they laughed about people they'd met and things they'd done at the social events. I wondered if they'd known each other before, but on investigation, it was just the escalated bonding of a few nights' drinking. Here, I was also on the back foot, as growing up in a Muslim household, alcohol wasn't a part of our lives. I didn't want to start drinking either.

At the time, the vast majority of Exeter's students came from private schools; the figure that was commonly cited at the time – but I haven't been able to verify – was 90 per cent. It was known as the Oxbridge rejects university. Their accents were posh, their clothes were expensive, many of them had cars or flashy watches. On top of that, 99 per cent of the students were white. I felt like an outsider in many ways. And now without that first week, and without alcohol to galvanise relationships, I was worried I wouldn't make friends at all. One of the oddest concepts for me were the formal dinners held each term at Birks Halls – it was the first time ever I wore a dinner jacket (purchased from Burton for £99 using my bank overdraft).

The first people I met were those who shared my corridor in the halls of residence. Danny was two years older than the rest of us and was studying for a master's degree, which qualified him as a 'mature student'. In his undergraduate degree he'd also studied economics and politics, a remarkable coincidence as the course only took on fifteen students a year. We bonded over Margaret Thatcher and a mutual inability to eat pork, as he was Jewish. He was a British public schoolboy, raised in Hong Kong, and it didn't take long before he was giving me tips for my course and showing me the best non-pork alternatives in the cafeteria.

In the next room down was Ian. He was everything I imagined a British lad, let loose at university, to be. He routinely drank until he blacked out or vomited on the carpet. His main source of entertainment was drinking games. Occasionally he would deviate from the norm and suggest a game of truth or dare instead. He would boo if you chose a truth. He couldn't pass by a traffic cone on the street without stopping to put it on his head and once only ate Spam for an entire week for a £10 bet. I liked him, though I tried to limit our friendship to before 10 p.m. when the real messiness kicked in, but beneath all the bravado, he was a very kind friend.

Across the hall was David. Sadly for David, his entire personality was shaped by his love for his girlfriend. Andrea was studying in Reading and was his sole topic of conversation.

Their song was 'New Year's Day' by U2 and when he missed her he played it on repeat on his CD player at full blast, regardless of the time of day or night. I am now unable to hear it without thinking of Andrea and wondering what she's up to now.

The final person on my corridor was Marcus. Raised in Britain, but with a German mum and an Italian dad, he was trilingual. Despite this, he spoke with a plummy English accent that he'd presumably picked up from his public school in Kent. Marcus was relatively normal. He drank every now and again but didn't have Ian's drive to get obliterated. He had a girlfriend but kept his pining to a minimum. In freshers' week, he'd attended a ballroom dance social where he'd met another boy from our block, Binesh. He was an Indian Hindu lad who grew up in Wrexham. He was the only one of the bunch who, like me, went to a state school. To this day, Marcus and Bin are two of my closest friends.

In my first month at university, I also sought out and joined the university Conservative Association and made many friends that shared my interest in current affairs, especially Robert, Tim, David and Nickie. Some twenty-five years later, four of us would become MPs.

I grew into a friendship with each of them, but Marcus and Bin became my day-to-day guys. We would drop by each other's rooms and eat together at mealtimes. We'd talk a lot about politics. Marcus had travelled a lot, while Bin and I hadn't. Bin was the only one of us who was single and he was fearless in his approach to women, which Marcus and I enjoyed immensely from the sidelines. Bin was into music and was one of the first people I met (along with David) who owned a CD player. He introduced me to Simple Minds and Fleetwood Mac. He also had a U2 album, but I was already a fan. Marcus was passionate about food and was a surprisingly good cook. He introduced me to new dishes and I learned a lot from him about food.

In that first term, Laura came down to visit me twice and I went to London, where she was already studying before we met, to see her twice as well. I took the overnight coach as it was the cheapest option. When I knew I was about to see her, I would be excited for days beforehand. Then, when we were together, I would feel the weight of the build-up to the time I had to leave. I would try not to show how much it affected me and how much I didn't want to say goodbye. Taking a leaf out of David's book, I would play songs I knew she liked to help me feel closer to her when we weren't together. These were often by Tracy Chapman or Sade, but I had the decency to play them at a very low volume.

Laura and I wrote letters to each other once a week. Hers would often be twice the length of mine and she would seal the envelope with a lipstick kiss. I would call her on a Saturday between 6 and 7 p.m. from the payphone in my block. As she was a second year, she was already in a shared house that had a landline, so it was easier for her to receive calls. I would have to join the queue by the phone and wait for my turn.

It wasn't just Laura whom I missed while I was away. Up until that point, I had relied on my mum for everything. She was always there, cooking, cleaning and doing my washing. It was the first time that I was stripped of the comfort of being looked after by my mum. I wasn't able to write to Mum as she couldn't read or write back, but I phoned her every week at midday on a Sunday. That first Sunday when I called, she asked how I was and wanted to know what the food was like and if I'd made any friends. I choked back tears trying to make sure my voice didn't break on the phone. I felt like a wimp. When I hung up I wiped my eyes with my sleeve. I turned around to face the queue of people waiting, and one boy said, 'Are you all right, man?' To which I replied, 'Yes, we've just had a family loss,' following it up with a stoic, 'I'm OK though.' I went back to my room and cried.

My nineteenth birthday was the first week of December and, despite only knowing them for a couple of months, the boys on my corridor decided to throw me a party. That afternoon when I tried to come out of my room, they insisted that I stay in for another hour. They had set up the hallway and common room. Marcus had made a vat of punch with every type of alcohol he could get his hands on. David rolled the massive speakers of his CD player, usually reserved for U2, out into the hallway so we could have music. Ian had a 'Space Invaders' arcade game in his room and brought that out for the partygoers. Bin brought some lads from his corridor and a bunch of girls from Hendon House too. Plus they had secretly arranged for Laura to come down that day and surprise me. As they let me out of my room, David hit play on the music and the Beastie Boys began shouting that we had to fight for our right to party. The whole crowd sang along, jumping up and down and dancing about. I was blown away. I couldn't believe they'd made such an effort for me after such a short amount of time. And unexpectedly seeing Laura was the finishing touch.

As the night went on, Marcus and Bin came over with a drink for me. They insisted that they'd made a smaller batch of non-alcoholic punch and, as it was my birthday, I had to down it in one. After checking twice that it definitely wasn't the alcoholic version, I took a few huge glugs, almost completely finishing the mug. It didn't taste like any juice mix I had had before. Seeing the commotion, Laura came over and tasted what was left in the mug and confirmed that it very definitely was alcoholic.

That was my first taste of alcohol. I didn't continue drinking it so the effect wasn't huge, but I danced just a little bit harder that night and by 1 a.m. I had a headache. If that was drinking, I wasn't fussed.

The following day Marcus and Bin both came to knock on the door and apologise for the deception. I was unimpressed and made it clear, but forgave them after their admission of guilt and sincere apology. I didn't want it to ruin the memory of the party and the incredible communal gesture.

That weekend Laura stuck around. Being at university was the first time that we had the privacy that we weren't allowed at our parents' houses. We could sit around and chat and stay in bed all day if we wanted. It was that weekend that we first had sex. It was the first time for both of us, and it signalled a progression in our relationship. Laura was adamant that she wouldn't have casual sex and, if we were to sleep together, it would be because we saw each other as potential life partners. I knew how seriously she took the level of intimacy. So, in taking that step, we both made an unspoken commitment to each other.

That night, at one of the most intimate moments locked away in my room, Danny banged on my door and jokingly shouted, 'Put it away, Saj'! It was too late.

19

Son, you're already engaged

After that first term at university, Laura and I freely spoke about how our future would look. Like many infatuated young lovers before us, we discussed what our kids would look like and re-ran the moments when we first met, dissecting each with romanticised wonder. Laura knew she wanted children, and I knew I wanted a big family. When I spoke about my aspirations to work in finance and that my tutor had said I could be Chancellor of the Exchequer, she never allowed a flicker of doubt to cross her face. She believed in me, in us and in our future.

I hadn't got down on one knee, and nothing was guaranteed, but we were both committed to each other and made plans accordingly. Knowing that Laura wasn't just a casual fling, I became increasingly aware that I should talk to my parents about her. I had met Laura's parents, and they even invited me on their family holiday to stay in a gîte in France. Once I had looked up what a gîte was, I was excited. They were always kind and welcoming.

I came back home during a reading week and decided it would be the ideal time to tell Dad that I had met someone. I knew that it would be complicated. I was keenly aware of their hurt and anger when Tariq announced his engagement to Katharine juxtaposed with their jubilation at Khalid's arranged marriage. By this time, however, Bas was dating a young British woman called Donna. My parents didn't seem delighted with the match but tolerated it, presumably thinking it would be temporary.

I managed to catch Dad in the house when no one was around – it must have been a Sunday for him to be home in the daytime. I sat down in the living room and asked him to sit with me. He slowly lowered himself on to the sofa and made concerned eye contact.

'Dad, there's something I want to speak to you about,' I said. It occurred to me that he may have already assumed I would be dating and meeting people at university, but his face didn't show any sign that he'd anticipated what I had to say.

'I want you to know about a new friend of mine.'

'Oh yeah, a good friend?'

'I just want you to know because it's a girl.'

He paused. 'OK,' he said.

'Her name is Laura.'

'What? An English girl?'

'Yes.'

'She's from your university?'

'Well, not quite. I met her in the summer when we were both working as interns. She's from Bristol but she's studying in London, so she's there most of the time.'

'And she's a good friend?'

'Yes, Dad, she's a good friend.'

'How good?'

'We're really good friends. And I wanted to tell you because

I really like her and I think you would really like her. She's a nice girl and she likes me. And maybe one day this is the kind of girl I want to marry.'

He considered. 'Puttar,' he said, the Punjabi word for son. 'Are you sure? I'm not sure this is a good idea.'

'Why not?' I asked.

'When you want to get married, you want to make sure it's the right girl. There are certain things you want to look for. You want to make sure she is from a good family and that she's Muslim. You can't just think about yourself but also about *your* family and *her* family and how they will get on.'

'I have met her parents and she *is* from a good family. They're really nice.'

'But how do you know that? It is good to marry from a family we know, so we can be sure.'

I moved the conversation on, 'She's not Muslim but she's Christian. I read that Muslims can marry Christians and have an Islamic marriage, so it's fine.'

'Why are you talking about marriage already?'

'I'm not, well, not yet. But I wanted you to know.'

The conversation went on, with him explaining how important it was to stay within our community and wider family for marriage, and me trying to convince him that, if he gave Laura a chance, he would approve. It was amicable but emotional.

'Puttar, thanks for telling me. I'm pleased you told me. But I don't think this is a good idea. Don't make any commitments for now. Let's continue talking about it,' he said.

Then he stopped for a moment and added, 'I don't mind you enjoying yourself. If you want to have a relationship with this girl, you can have fun. I don't mind that. Honestly, I don't mind. Just don't tell your mum about how much fun you're having. But for your fun relationship, I don't have to get involved and your mum doesn't have to get involved. We don't have to meet her. There's a whole big difference between having fun with a girl and saying you want to marry her. I don't think it's a good idea. Let's talk about this again.'

We left it there and for a couple of months, he didn't bring it up.

I was back at university when I made my usual Sunday lunchtime call home. I would speak to whoever answered, but ultimately I was calling to talk to Mum. Usually it wouldn't be long before the phone was handed over to her so we could have our weekly catch-up. On this occasion Mum answered, but before asking how my week had been, she said, 'Your father wants to speak to you.' Before I had time to acknowledge how unusual this was, he was on the line.

'I'm going to come and have a chat with you,' he said.

'What do you mean?'

'I thought I'd come down to have a chat with you.'

'What, to Exeter?'

'Yes.'

'Why? What's wrong?'

He softened his voice, 'No, no, nothing, puttar. When I come there we'll have a chat.'

'All right,' I said, the anxiety of not knowing his intentions already rising up inside of me.

'How about next Saturday? At twelve o'clock?' he suggested.

'OK, but Dad, are you sure that you want to come all this way? Has something happened?'

'Nothing, nothing, I just want to chat with you.'

It would be the first time Dad had come on to campus since he had dropped me off with all my things after Khalid's wedding. I was worried. I didn't know what was serious enough to warrant such a visit. I considered that it could be related to our conversation about Laura and, if it was, he wouldn't be coming all that way to tell me he was ready to meet her.

It was a tense week waiting for the meeting. When he arrived he came into my room and sat on the bed. There was nowhere else for him to sit. He presented me with a Tupperware box of Mum's samosas and I made us both a cup of tea. I sat down ready to hear whatever news had brought him all that way.

'Son,' he said, starting in English this time, 'at Christmas you told me about your friend Laura. How is she?'

'She's great.'

'You're still boyfriend and girlfriend?'

'Yes.'

'OK, well, I wanted to speak to you about something. I wanted to tell you a while back but I was always waiting for the right time.' He took a sip of his tea. 'Because of what you told me, I think now is the right time.' Another sip of his tea. 'When I told you that you shouldn't turn this into a serious relationship, there was something really important I want to say.' He took another sip. I willed him to put down the mug. 'I know when I tell you, you will totally understand. And I thought I should tell you now before things get more complicated.'

'Dad, just tell me what's going on.'

'OK, you said you like this Laura and maybe one day you'd get married. But you can't marry her.'

'Dad, come on,' I sighed. 'I said that I'm not marrying her now. I'm just going to see how it goes.'

'No, no. You can't marry her. At all.'

'Why can't I?'

'You can't.'

'Yes, Dad, you said that. But you don't have any real reason. Just because you don't want me to isn't enough.'

He stared at me and took another long sip of his tea. I could have knocked the mug out of his hand and on to the floor.

'The reason you can't marry her is because you're already engaged.'

I let out a laugh like the cork popping off a shaken bottle. 'What?' I said. 'What do you mean, I'm already engaged? To who?'

'We'll get to that later,' he replied.

'What do you mean, we'll get to that later? Who am I engaged to? I haven't proposed to anyone. So when you say I'm engaged, you mean you've engaged me to someone. Who is it?'

'We don't need to talk about that now.'

It was infuriating. How could he turn up to deliver such momentous news and then refuse to tell me what was actually happening. He was drip-feeding me information like I was a child, presumably so he could manage the impact of the news, but in reality it was just making me angrier.

'Dad,' I shouted. 'You really think you're going to drive all the way down here to Exeter, tell me I'm engaged to someone and not even tell me who it is?'

'Yes, OK, OK, calm down, I will tell you. It's your cousin.'

'Cousin, which cousin? Amna, Rozina, Nazia?' I listed off the first few that came to my head. I had more. Many more.

'Amna.'

I had to take a moment to compute. Amna was the daughter of my dad's brother. My first cousin. My dad's brother had died years before, so his widow Fatima and daughter had moved to the UK from Pakistan to be nearer to some of her family. They lived in Leeds. Dad had always felt an obligation to his brother's widow, offering for Amna to come and visit on holidays and sending money from time to time, even though he didn't have it to spare. I knew Amna well enough, we probably saw her once a year at weddings or events along with the rest of our extended family. She was only a few months younger than me.

'What? What do you mean, I'm engaged to Amna? What happened? How did this happen?'

'We don't need to go through all the details now. But you

know your mum and I believe that the best marriages are arranged marriages. We believe it's best to keep marriage within the wider family; like Khalid and Fouzia. They were from the same family and she grew up in my village in Pakistan and now she's in Bristol and very happy.'

Trying to get just one of the many thoughts in my head to stay still for long enough to articulate it was proving my biggest battle. Shocked didn't even come close to how I was feeling.

'How? How can this happen? How can you commit me to someone without me knowing?'

'Because, puttar, we know you two get on. You laugh and chat every time you see her.'

He was right, we did, but because she was my cousin. She was funny and she was fun to be around. After seeing Rozina and I apply for university, she had decided to do the same. She was training to be a pharmacist. There was nothing wrong with her as a woman or as a match, apart from the fact she was my cousin.

'Does she know?' I asked.

'Yes.'

'How does she know?'

'I don't know, your Aunt Fatima told her, she's known for a while.'

'Does Mum know?'

'Yes, Mum knows and she is very happy and supportive of the match.'

'This is not right.'

'Puttar, why not? You can have all the fun you want at university; I know there's lots of girls here. I get it. But when it comes to marriage, this is different. You're engaged to your cousin. So, when you finish university, you'll marry her.'

'Dad,' I was stern in my delivery, 'I won't.'

'What do you mean, I won't?'

'I won't marry her.'

'Because of this Laura? You've just met her! How can you be so in love with her already?'

'No, Dad, it's not because of Laura. It's because she's family. It's like you asking me to marry a sister.'

'Stop, Sajid! You are only saying this because you've made promises to Laura.'

'No! Dad, you're not listening.' I was shouting again. 'Even if I'd never met Laura, I still wouldn't marry Amna.'

'Why not?'

'She's like a sister. It's like you're asking me to marry my sister.'

'It's not like that. You've grown up together, you know her mum and her family. You know everything about each other. There's no surprises. You'd have beautiful children together.' His sales pitch was only adding to my frustration. 'Look, I understand how you're reacting to this. You need to think about it. But deep down, you know this is the right thing. Just take some time.'

He had finished his tea well before the end of the conversation, so he set the mug down on my desk and got up to leave.

Left alone in my room, I replayed the entire conversation in my head. That summer Amna had come to Bristol. She'd spent time with the whole family but had singled me out to ask if I'd like to go into town with her to walk around the shops. I'd said yes, not thinking anything of it. Now I wondered if, to her, that was a date. Special time, wandering around a romantic and historic town. We hadn't just grabbed a sandwich from a shop, she'd wanted to sit somewhere where they take your order and bring the food to your table. Was it all part of us spending time together? Getting to know each other on a more grown-up level? Was I supposed to be falling in love while instead I was oblivious, walking around on a family day trip?

Life was different for girls. Amna wasn't given the same

freedoms as my brothers and me growing up. She stayed at home far more and had stricter curfews and restrictions on who she could hang out with and where she could go. While my parents didn't love the idea of their boys dating, they knew we would have 'a little fun' when we were young. The same was absolutely prohibited for Amna. She would not have been allowed to have a boyfriend or hang around with boys. She didn't challenge those rules either. She would have always assumed that she would have an arranged marriage. It just would have been more recently that she found out to whom.

I felt an anger that I only felt when it was paired with a loss of control. It was a dangerous helplessness. Promises had been made that affected every aspect of my life and future, and I hadn't been consulted. It felt cruel that no one ever tried to ask what I thought, or if I wanted an arranged marriage, or if I would have considered Amna as a potential wife. I was angry for Amna. As far as she was concerned, she was engaged. I felt that my parents and her mother had wronged her. They'd given her false hope. They'd promised her a future that was not theirs to offer. I cared for Amna, we did get on well, and I hated the idea that she was about to experience pain and disappointment because of me. I couldn't imagine how she would feel when they told her.

Then I thought about Laura. How would I tell Laura that the reason she wouldn't be able to meet my family was that, as far as they were concerned, she was the other woman? How could I tell her that they would never accept her as my wife because they had chosen one for me? If I told her, would she stay and stick it out? Or would she decide this was too much to deal with and leave? I wouldn't blame her.

I told my friends Bin and Marcus, but they didn't fully understand. They could appreciate the sense of injustice and the anger I felt, but their parents didn't have arranged marriages. They didn't understand the culture and tradition behind it. To them, it just sounded crazy. My brothers were fully supportive of me. Even Khalid, with his own arranged marriage, told me that I should marry for love and not to give in to our parents.

It wasn't until the next time I was home that I spoke to my mum about the situation.

'I know you're shocked,' she said. 'I know you're annoyed we didn't tell you. I did tell your dad to tell you sooner, he wanted to wait. But I think this is the right thing. Amna is an amazing young woman. She's well brought up, pretty, well educated. It's a marriage made in heaven.'

When it came to her boys, Mum was desperate that we would make good marriages. That didn't mean that they had to be financially advantageous or facilitate social climbing. She wanted us to be happy. As far as Mum was concerned, we were far more likely to achieve that happiness if we married within our community. Aside from that, she had built a negative opinion of most white British women. Having not spent a huge amount of time with white girls, she based a lot of this on the opinions of her friends and what she saw of white women on shows like *Dallas*.

'Also, you know,' she continued, 'these white girls, they all love you then they leave you. They all have affairs. They'll want your money.'

'What money, Mum?!' If there was one thing I was safe from, it was gold diggers.

'Don't get me wrong,' she continued, 'I'm not talking about your friend . . .' she gestured with her hand trying to summon up her name.

'Laura,' I helped.

'Yes, I'm not talking about Laura because I don't know her. I just know that all white girls are the same.'

'Mum! How can you say that? That's like saying all Pakistani girls are the same. You know they're not! Laura is really special, Mum.'

'I'm sure you mean that. I'm sure she's great.'

'Why don't you meet her? Then you can see for yourself.'

She shook her head. 'We're not interested, we're not going to meet her.'

These conversations carried on for the best part of the next year. I started to dread going home to Bristol because I didn't want to go around in the same circles. When I did come home, I spent as much time as possible out of the house, usually with Laura.

The pressure continued and my dad started to recruit others to apply it too. He asked my brothers to tell me what a mistake I was making. When they all flatly refused, he asked other people I trusted, including a close family friend, Reema. I was in the kitchen at our house, on a day that Reema was visiting, when she came to sit with me.

'What's this I hear about you and this English girl that you want to marry?' she asked.

'Well, it's just someone I've met,' I said. I had been avoiding talking to Mum and Dad about it so didn't want to get into it with anyone else.

'But Amna would be brilliant for you. Why don't you think about that? I know she wants to marry you.'

Again, I brushed her off, completely uninterested in having the conversation yet again.

'I just think you're making a mistake,' she continued. 'And also, you know if you had children with her, your children would be half-Pakistani and half-English. They'd be half-caste. I wouldn't touch them.'

She shocked me. I'd heard the mixed-race argument before from Mum and Dad but not with such strong sentiment. I couldn't believe she was saying that she wouldn't have contact with my children if they were mixed race.

'What do you mean?' I asked.

'I couldn't touch your children because they're just mixed race. I wouldn't want to touch them.'

I couldn't believe it. The words didn't sound like her, they were so unkind and vile. It was totally out of character.

'I can't believe you're saying that to me,' I said. 'Are you really saying that if I had children with a white girl, you wouldn't touch them because they're half white? They're still my children.'

'Yes, I wouldn't touch them.'

If I wasn't interested in having the conversation then, I definitely wasn't interested after that.

'Fine, Reema,' I said, walking out of the room.

I didn't have children yet. For all I knew, Laura and I never would but it felt like a new low in the battle against our relationship. The threats not to see my children didn't make me feel worse about Laura, they just made me want to put distance between me and my family. Years later, when Laura and I got married, Reema asked to speak to me before the wedding and apologised for what she'd said about my future children. She told me that she hadn't meant it at all but that she had been asked to say it to try and persuade me. I didn't doubt her and forgave her.

As a concept, I'm not against arranged marriages. The idea that parents can make introductions and suggestions is one that is fundamentally good. But ultimately, the choice must lie with the couple themselves. No one should be forced into a relationship that they don't want to be in. While my parents weren't forcing me, the amount of emotional pressure they put on my shoulders to agree to the engagement was not right.

My dad had made a commitment to his brother's widow;

a woman he cared for and respected, a woman that he felt an obligation towards. As far as he was concerned, I was embarrassing him. He told me regularly that it would kill her if I let him down. He said she was weak and she would have a heart attack with the heartbreak. He would list off everything the woman had gone through in her life, starting with her own childhood journey in partition. Then he'd end with me, the man crushing the hopes she had for her only child.

As well as feeling pushed into the union, I couldn't get past the idea of marrying a first cousin. I knew there was no way I would be able to be in a relationship with such a close family member; with or without Laura in my life, it wouldn't happen.

First cousin marriage is a common practice around the world, including in Pakistan. It helps to consolidate the assets of a family by not inviting in outsiders. Despite having been in Britain for years, my parents still felt like outsiders. Sticking together was important to them. The idea of bringing different races and cultures into our family scared them. They worried it opened them, and their sons, up to more racism and poor treatment.

Through all of this, I stuck to my guns. I would not be marrying Amna and I would continue my relationship with Laura. Deep down I thought that in time they would come around to the idea, but I also knew I was rolling the dice. If every threat was followed through, I would be an outcast from my family, which would be left in tatters. Laura and I would never be welcome and no one would want to meet our eventual children.

I told Laura about the arranged marriage and she knew a lot of what was going on, but there were many things I kept from her. Not least the suggestion that our kids wouldn't be touched by the family. I knew that there were some bridges that couldn't be uncrossed. I didn't want her to be in a situation where she wasn't able to like my family. I was also afraid that if she knew every detail, she would walk away. Perhaps out of exhaustion, perhaps out of care for me. I worried that she would valiantly fall on her sword, end the relationship and I would be left with a huge argument with my family and no Laura. The worst of both worlds.

Through all of this, every unwavering denouncement of the engagement, my dad always held out hope that I would change my mind. He wanted me eventually to give in. I think he thought it was possible that my young-love relationship with Laura would burn out and, without her on the scene, I'd be more open to the arranged marriage.

Partly out of this hope, and partly out of cowardice, Dad hadn't told Fatima and Amna that I had refused the match. After more than a year of these conversations, I finally insisted that Dad had to tell them. He refused. Still maintaining that she could die of a heart attack, he said that he would not be the one to tell Fatima. 'You tell her,' he said instead.

I was, once again, furious. I had not created the mess but I was expected to fix it. I knew it had to be done and I knew that, for Amna, it had to be soon. The longer she believed that she was engaged the more painful it would be for her to find out the truth. I planned to drive to Leeds to tell them myself. I reasoned that she was an adult; it would be disappointing, but she would come to terms with it in time. I thought that once she and I had found a way forward and she had processed her disappointment, we could tell her mother and hopefully soften the potentially fatal blow.

Mum agreed to drive with me and we arranged to go through Manchester so that she could stop at a few warehouses on the way to buy clothes for the shop. We agreed to stay with Fatima in Leeds. I would have a conversation with Amna after dinner and then I would head home the next morning.

After stocking up on clothes, we continued the drive for another hour on to Leeds. Fatima had prepared a dinner for us and once we were finished, I asked Amna if the two of us could chat. Her eyes lit up and she agreed, leading me into the living room and away from our parents. We sat on the sofa in front of the gas fire and I tried to formulate my first sentence.

'Look, Amna, I just wanted to have a chat about things,' I started, geeing myself up to become more specific. She beamed at me. I knew that she had pictured this moment over and over since she'd been told. She was probably expecting me to make a formal proposal and to solidify the arrangements.

'Yes?' she said.

'Look, you know our parents have made some plans?' I said, understanding why Dad had needed the cup of tea as a prop.

'Yes,' she said again.

'Some plans concerning us.'

'Yes, I do.'

'How do you know?' I asked.

'My mum told me.'

'Right, so you've known for a while?'

'Yes! And now they've told you! I feel like I've been waiting forever for you to find out.'

'Well, yes.'

'It's amazing! I've been waiting for the moment when we can talk about it.'

'Look, Amna. Stop, just slow down a second. That's not what we're going to talk about.'

'What do you mean?' She leaned back slightly but carried on smiling. I couldn't believe my parents were making me do this.

'I've got to tell you something. My parents did tell me about it, but it's not going to happen.'

'What?' She pulled even further back, this time her smile dropping into a look of horror.

'It's not going to happen,' I said again, convinced that firmness was the kindest way to communicate.

'What are you saying? Why are you saying that? What's the matter?'

'I've grown up with you. I love you but I love you like my sister. I can't marry a sister.'

'But, Saj, this happens all the time and I love you. I'm in love with you.'

This was the worst-case scenario. I assumed that she hadn't hated the idea, otherwise my parents wouldn't still have been pushing it, but I didn't realise she would be quite so invested.

'Stop,' I said, desperate for her not to keep talking for both our sakes. 'Don't make this any harder than it needs to be. It's not going to happen.'

Tears started streaming down her face and she began audibly crying. I was worried she would attract the attention of our mothers, but both had gone up to bed. 'Is there someone else?' she said through sobs.

'I don't want to get into this,' I replied. I thought it would complicate things to tell her about Laura.

'There is someone else,' Amna said. 'You've met someone, haven't you? You've met someone. I knew this was going to happen. They should have told you earlier. I knew when you went to university you'd meet someone.'

'Look, it's not that,' I said.

She started listing names of any female friend she heard me speak about over the last summer. I didn't realise she'd been paying such close attention but now I guess that made sense.

'Stop, Amna, no!' I urged her. 'It's none of them.'

'So it is someone else, just not them.'

'Yes, there is someone else, but I'm not going to get into it. Even if there wasn't, this isn't happening.'

She grew increasingly distraught, asking me to explain why it wouldn't work, insisting that I had to try.

'I don't want to try, Amna. I want you as my cousin. I love you like a sister and we'll always be friends.'

She was holding on to me, clinging on to my leg and talking through wails. I tried to get her to loosen her grip. I stood up and tried to move away but it only made things worse. I sat back down and hugged her.

I felt awful. I felt like I had just dumped someone after years of leading them on. As far as she was concerned, she had every reason to believe that I was going to marry her. I had just shattered that dream. I had to keep reminding myself that this wasn't my fault, that I wasn't a bad person, that I had been put into an impossible position and was just trying to do right by everyone. So why did I feel so evil?

Eventually Amna gathered herself and managed to stop crying. As she settled, I started to think ahead to the best way forward.

'We're grown-ups, right? Our parents haven't been grown-up about this. This is not how things are done and it's not how it's going to work. Do you agree?'

'Yes,' she said with a small nod.

'So, let's do this our way now. Let's do this like grown-ups.' I was so desperate not to rock the boat any further in the aftermath. 'Let's agree that the marriage is not going to happen. I know you will need some time to come to terms with that and you take all the time you need. Once you feel OK about it, then we'll tell your mother. My dad's really worried about telling your mum, he thinks it will make her unwell. So don't say anything yet. Let's wait until we've both calmed down and we can tell her in a more manageable way.'

'OK, you're right,' she agreed. 'I won't, I won't say.'

With a plan in place, the two of us went to our bedrooms. I was sharing the guest room with my mum, who was already curled up in her twin bed, pretending to be asleep. I climbed into mine and lay there, attempting to get a good night's sleep for the journey ahead.

The next morning I woke up and got dressed straight away. After the night before, I knew I didn't want to stay long. We would have a quick breakfast and then be on the road back to Bristol. I went downstairs and into the kitchen where only Fatima was already up and about. She had her back to me, making something over the stove.

I gathered myself and said in my chirpiest voice, 'Morning, Auntie Fatima, what are you making? Eggs?'

She continued bending over the stove. She didn't turn around or respond. I thought she must not have heard me. 'Auntie Fatima?' I said again, a little louder. Again there was no answer. 'Auntie?' I said, gently touching her on the back of the arm.

She turned around revealing a puffy, crimson face and swollen, bloodshot eyes. She'd been crying all night. 'Putter, what have you done?' she started beating her fists on my chest. 'What have you done? What have you done?' She pounded on me, not with enough force to cause pain but enough to make her point. I put my arms up to stop her and she fell back, collapsing on to the floor where she sat crying.

'Don't do this!' she said to me. 'Don't, don't do this.' She pulled on my trousers, clinging on to my leg.

'Please, Auntie Fatima, please stand up,' I reached out a hand that she ignored. 'I don't think we should talk about this now.'

Hearing the commotion, my mum came down the stairs and went to hug Fatima, who was still in a heap on the floor. 'See what you've done?' she hissed at me. The house was small. I heard the tears of Amna start up again from her room upstairs and then surveyed the scene on the kitchen floor. I needed to get out.

'Mum, let's go,' I said.

'What about breakfast?'

'No breakfast. I'll get you breakfast on the way. We're leaving, now.'

I took my bag from upstairs and grabbed hers at the same time. As I came down the stairs, I said one more time, 'Mum, we're going right now and if you don't come out to the car, I'm leaving without you.'

I could feel myself starting to lose it. I marched out the door and got into the driver's seat and started the engine. Mum followed a minute later and sat in the passenger seat. I screeched off before she even put on her seatbelt.

As we turned the corner at the bottom of the road, Mum started on me again. 'See what you've done? You've destroyed the family. Everyone is heartbroken and what for? You've done all of this for your own gratification. It's all for your own satisfaction. This is all about you. You don't care about anyone else.'

I couldn't handle it. I slammed on the brakes. 'Shut up,' I screamed. 'Mum, if you don't shut up, I will pull over, open that door and kick you out of the car. Shut up. I don't want to hear anything more about it. I haven't done anything wrong. You did this. You and dad. You didn't think about anyone else. You certainly didn't think about me or Amna. You didn't have the guts to consult me and then you didn't have the guts to tell her. I'm the one who had to deal with it and eat shit. So you need to shut up!'

We did the entire three-hour drive in silence. It was a horrible journey. I dropped Mum off at home and went straight out so I didn't need to be near her or anyone in the family.

It took Fatima two years to speak to me again after that visit. Amna didn't initially accept that the plans were over. For a while, she wrote to me, trying to persuade me that it was for the best. But when her letters went unanswered, she eventually stopped.

It took time for us to reconcile, but we made significant steps forward when Amna met the man who would eventually become her husband. It freed us up to resume the friendship that we'd had before the whole sorry incident. She's now happily married with three beautiful children and all of them are regularly in my life.

20

Savage Javage

For my second year of university, I moved into a shared house of five people, including my closest friends Bin and Marcus. My room was bigger in this house and I had more space for books. I had started to gather a serious collection. Eventually, the crowning glory was an entire thirty-two-volume *Encyclopædia Britannica*. I had entered a countrywide in-store Waterstones competition to win the chunky volumes and then completely forgot about it. I was stunned when a letter arrived at the house in Bristol saying that I'd won. I phoned the head office number as instructed and was told they could ship the set to me or I could take the financial value of the books, £2,000, instead. It was a no-brainer for me. I took the books. Having spent years going back and forward to the library, I now had a chance to have my own mini-library in my bedroom. They delivered the collection straight to my university house and I stacked the volumes proudly along the wall in my bedroom. I used them almost every day for my work, or just because there was something I wanted to look up. In the days before the internet, it was a luxury to have access to so much information.

Laura and I continued to get closer. We made the coach trips to see each other every few weeks. My parents still refused to meet her, hoping that the horrible fling would be over and I would make reparations with Amna.

Laura felt worried that they were never going to accept her or the relationship. She feared that, without their blessing, I would never actually propose. She had a few Asian friends at university but she didn't know much about Pakistani culture. It didn't help that one of the girls in her shared house was an Indian Hindu and insisted that all Muslim boys 'were the same'. She would often tell Laura that, regardless of what I told her, eventually I would do what my parents said and marry a Muslim girl. She would often wait until I'd left to remind Laura that even though I was a nice boy, I would eventually let her down. I found this infuriating so I encouraged her to ignore this friend.

It felt like there was some movement forwards with my family when my dad announced one day that he would meet Laura's parents. He insisted that it should be just her parents and that the four of them would go for dinner. I wasn't sure what this would achieve, but I wanted to show willing as it was the closest we'd come to any form of acceptance.

Her parents, Sue and Robin, thought it was a bizarre request but politely agreed. It was clear to them that the relationship was important to Laura. They were aware that my family disapproved, not of Laura directly, but of my marrying outside of the community and rejecting their arranged marriage.

When her parents came home from the dinner, I was waiting for them at Laura's house. They were polite about the meal and the company but vague about the actual conversation. Sue described it as 'lovely'. It's her trademark adjective.

Satisfied that we had inched closer to harmony, I left Laura's house to head home. We agreed to meet for breakfast the following day and when we did, it was clear she had been crying.

After I had left, her parents opened up about the dinner. It transpired that Dad's intention in setting up the meeting wasn't to get to know his potential in-laws, but rather to scare them off. He started by telling them what a terrible idea the relationship would be. He said that their daughter would never be accepted in the Pakistani community. He explained that the mixing of our two cultures would be a disaster and rounded it all off by saying that the most loving thing they could do would be to tell their daughter to leave me.

Laura was desperately disappointed and her parents were naturally concerned. She was now firmly convinced that we faced too many obstacles to get married. It took weeks of conversations, reassuring her that I loved her and that we could make the relationship work regardless of my parents, to get the two of us back on track.

Basit, who was stationed at Plymouth for his Royal Navy training, had a car by this point so drove along the coast to see me once or twice a term at Exeter. He had been thriving in the Navy but it was around this time that he wrote to tell me he'd been called up to the Gulf War. As part of Operation Desert Storm, he was joining the US in the attempt to liberate Kuwait from its Iraqi invaders. Donna was devastated and all of us were worried about him. I wrote to him every week, while Donna wrote twice a week.

My dad was proud that Bas was serving the country and that he was a valuable member of his vessel. We followed the reports on the news, and at university I had access to CNN, with its around-the-clock coverage of the war. Some people in our Pakistani community were unimpressed by Basit's involvement. They would complain to my dad that he had sent his son off to help the white people kill Muslims. But he didn't see it that way and defended Basit with pride.

It was in my second-year university house that I watched the footage of the Berlin Wall collapsing in November 1989 and then, a few months later, on 11 February, the release of Nelson Mandela. We all knew that he was supposed to be coming out of prison that morning. We gathered round to watch as he made his dignified walk, fist high in the air, from his years of incarceration. At that time, it felt like everything was happening all at once. The world was changing and we had a front-row seat.

I knew I wanted to work in the City when I graduated. I had my sights set on big banking firms but was aware the competition would be fierce. As I've mentioned, perhaps 90 per cent of the students at Exeter University came from a private school background. I came from a comprehensive. Anyone I knew who wanted to go into a similar industry already had contacts – their dad worked at one of the merchant banks or their uncle had arranged an internship for them. I was going in completely free of support or connections. I also didn't look or talk like any of them.

I wanted to fill my time as much as possible to prove I wasn't idle and was worthy of a job. I applied for work experience in the holidays at various different banks, and got nothing but a perfunctory letter of rejection, sometimes personalised to include my name, sometimes not.

I widened my search to big professional firms in other industries and focused on companies with easily recognisable brands so as to add credibility to my woefully nepotism-free CV. One company accepted me: Marks and Spencer. I was invited to do a two-week internship over the Easter break in their Cardiff store as part of their graduate management internship scheme.

Before I went to work there, I wanted to learn more about the company, so I bought a copy of the chairman Lord Marcus Sieff's memoirs. I pored over the pages, marking up anything that I found inspirational. It was one of the few autobiographies I had read. His story was one of a Jewish family who faced huge adversity, but he managed to build something amazing.

Each day I commuted from Bristol to the Welsh capital. I was introduced to the different departments and assigned a manager to shadow for the fortnight. The work was reasonably run-of-the-mill, checking in on rotas and making sure the shelves were fully stocked as expected. There was some lively debate about the placement of Easter eggs but that was about as exciting as the work got, until I spotted a poster on the staff notice board. The chairman himself, Lord Sieff, would be coming to the store to address the staff the following week.

I couldn't believe my luck that I would still be working at the store during the visit. I would get to meet the man I'd been reading about and admiring. I would get to hear him speak.

On our afternoon patrol of the shopfloor, I told my manager how excited I was about the visit. He furrowed his brow and said: 'You can't come.'

'Why not?' I asked.

'You're not staff.'

I was taken aback by his response but I swallowed my incredulity and tried to appear measured. 'Why does that matter?'

'It's an event for staff and you're not staff.'

'But I can stand at the back of the room if there isn't space. I just want to hear him talk.'

'No, you're not allowed.'

'Can you ask the store manager perhaps?'

'I don't need to ask the manager.'

He was unflinching and I knew I'd already pushed it. But I was resolved. I would meet Lord Sieff. I set about trying to find a way that I could make it happen. I asked around to see if I could work out the timings of his visit and found out that he would be coming into Cardiff Central train station from London Paddington, so I assumed he'd be going back the same way. There was some time for questions after his talk but it was due to wrap up at 5 p.m. and he, along with his entourage, would be on the train back to London shortly afterwards.

I decided I was going to leave a little early and run to the train station to try and catch him. I made an excuse to my manager and left the building just after 5.15 p.m., running for seven minutes or so before reaching the station. I didn't stop there. I found the platform for the Paddington train and bolted down it, hoping to spot the face of the man I had seen on the cover of his book.

He was easy to spot in a smart dark grey suit and surrounded by similarly dressed businessmen. I stopped running and hung back, mopping my brow and arranging my tie, so as to look just a little presentable after my sprint from the high street. I held his book with me in my hand.

I made a confident approach, striding forwards until I was adjacent to a man who turned out to be the CEO of Marks and Spencer, standing alongside his chairman.

'Lord Sieff?' I said, like I was walking up to a blind date and checking I had the right person.

'Hello,' he replied.

'I'm sorry to disturb you, my name's Sajid Javid and I'm an intern at Marks and Spencer.'

His companions had been gearing up to politely shuffle me along but I sensed a slacking of their jaws at the news that I was working for the company. I had bought myself another twenty seconds at least.

'Oh, you're at Marks and Spencer, are you?' he said jovially. 'Were you at the talk I just gave?'

'Actually, no. I wasn't'

'Why's that?' he asked.

'That's why I'm here. The management said I couldn't attend because I'm just an intern.'

At this point, the CEO interjected, 'What do you mean?'

'Well, yes – that's what they said.' I responded with a smile of resignation before turning back to Lord Sieff. 'I was just so keen to see you.' I pulled out the book and held it up demonstratively. 'Because I read your book and I think your story, your family, is fascinating. I wanted to meet you and shake your hand. And I wondered if you would . . .'

'Sign your book?' Lord Sieff finished my sentence. 'I would love to.' He turned to the CEO to ask for a pen. The man riffled through his pockets and obliged, handing a fountain pen over to him. Lord Sieff was the vision of politeness, and despite the ambush, spoke to me with a warmth that made me feel comfortable.

The train was pulling in so he quickly signed his name and handed the book back to me. As the group collected their belongings, he said, 'So glad you came to say hello.'

The CEO collected his pen, but before putting the cap back on, he made a note of my name in a little pocket book. 'So you said Savage Javage did you?' he asked as he wrote. 'And they told you not to come to the talk?'

'Yes, sir. And it's Sajid Javid.'

'But you were working in the store today?'

'Yes, sir.'

'But then how did you make it over to the station in time to see us?'

'Well, as soon as I finished work, I ran.'

'You ran? Just to see us?'

'No, sir,' I replied. 'I ran to see Lord Sieff.'

The group broke out into polite chuckles as they started to mount the train. Lord Sieff and the CEO boarded behind them with a few words of goodbye. I was delighted.

The next day I got into work at the usual time of 9.30 a.m. and was called straight into the store manager's office. Not my manager's office, but the whole-store manager. I went up to the top floor, convinced I was about to be reprimanded. Interns didn't have contact with the manager. It was unheard of. I was greeted enthusiastically, offered a pot of tea and some mini Easter eggs. He explained that he'd heard about my interaction with Lord Sieff last night and I should let him know if there was anything I needed during my final few days with the company.

A couple of weeks later, when I was back at university, I was on the phone to Mum on one of our Sunday calls when she said she had received a letter for me at the house. Unable to read it back to me, she got my dad to forward it on. It was from the head of graduate recruitment for Marks and Spencer, saying that she had had excellent feedback following my internship. She said that she understood I'd met the CEO and chairman and, despite it being very unusual at this stage, they wanted to offer me a full-time graduate position when I finished my degree in 1991. I was delighted. But I decided to turn down the offer, keeping my sights firmly set on banking as my career.

21

Boys, go and get your hockey sticks!

As the years went on at university I became increasingly firm in my conviction that banking was the right industry for me. Partly because I enjoyed studying maths and economics and partly because, having grown up with nothing, I wanted a job that paid well. I saw myself in a grand office in the City with a fancy suit and an engraved fountain pen. It was around this time that I also decided that, eventually, I would try and get into politics.

But despite my big dreams, I was a realist. I didn't know anyone who worked at the big prestigious firms and I didn't have the whole cultural capital that usually came with these high-powered jobs. Over the years at university, I collected a number of internships after Marks and Spencer, some in insurance and one in management consulting, but I was always rejected by the investment banks. Being in those other offices, though, even just for a week or two, gave me vital exposure to the unfamiliar customs and practices of professional work. They had their own language and hierarchy. I observed people doing presentations and mimicked their mannerisms and phrasing. They were completely foreign to me but I picked it all up quickly.

Exeter University hosted a job fair or 'milk round' for third-year students. When I went, I made a beeline for the British merchant banks. Each bank had a stand manned by a former Exeter student who now worked for the company. I got application forms for S. G. Warburg, Kleinwort Benson and Rothschild. But noticing a trend in the types of toffee-nosed former students manning the stands, I also decided to hedge my bets and apply to join the American banks Merrill Lynch and Chase Manhattan. Their representatives had a slightly warmer, less stuffy attitude; more of a 'can do!' spirit.

On sending off my applications, I heard back from four; Kleinwort Benson, Rothschild, Merrill Lynch and Chase Manhattan. The American banks invited me to their offices in London, while Rothschild invited me to a hotel in Bristol for the regional, southwest interviews. If I was successful, I would be invited to the next round in London.

Before these appointments, I knew I needed a suit. I had never owned a suit before. I had shirts and some formal Pakistani dress, but not a proper suit. I went to Next on Exeter High Street and opened up a store credit card account with them, with 34 per cent APR. I spent £150 on a suit, shirt, tie and shoes. I didn't care that it was on credit or that I would be forced to pay an extortionate interest rate, I was going to look the part.

The Rothschild interview took place in a five-star hotel in the Clifton area of Bristol, not too far from the university campus. It was called the Swallow Hotel and had an imposing entrance with big balustrades. I'd occasionally cycled past it, but I'd never been in before. At reception, I was directed to wait outside a meeting room and joined the other candidates seated on a row of chairs in the hallway. I rubbed my new shoes on the fluffy, patterned carpet and bit the nail on my right-hand index finger as I waited for my name to be called. No one in the waiting area spoke to each other.

When I was called in, I was led into a large wood-panelled function room. It had been stripped of all furniture other than one chair, positioned in the centre, and a platform that was raised a foot off the ground, showcasing a large table with five identikit men sitting behind it. All white, all in their fifties, all wearing pinstriped suits. It was an intimidating sight.

I considered for a moment whether I was supposed to approach the bench of judges and shake each one by the hand. I was issued the firm instruction to 'Take a seat', so thought better of it. I nodded to them and said hello as I settled into the chair. They each had a notepad and pen in front of them, as well as a photocopy of my CV. The questions began with much what you'd expect from a group interviewing a young man with no career to speak of. They asked about my studies and a little about the work experience I'd done. Then one of the indistinguishable men said, 'What does your father do?'

'He runs a shop,' I replied.

'What do you mean?'

'He owns a women's clothes shop in Bristol, so he works there. It's not too far from here.'

'Oh,' the man replied. 'Has he done that all his life?'

'No, he was a bus driver before that,' I said. I saw a grimace on one of the men's faces as he let out a sharp and nasal 'Oh.' They cast glances around at each other and I knew at that moment they would never hire me. They were never going to allow a boy with my background to speak with their clients. I didn't have experience of members' clubs and divot stomping at the polo, I had spent my winters sheltering from the cold in Regal Amusements. They weren't going to let me into their world and I wasn't convinced I wanted access.

I was right. They didn't offer me a job, nor did the other stuffy old British bank, Kleinwort Benson. I now had my sights firmly set on the American banks, where employees weren't from the establishment and there was more diversity and opportunity for those chasing 'the American dream'. I had felt far more comfortable speaking to the interviewers at Merrill Lynch and Chase Manhattan. The latter had hosted a full assessment day, where there were only two people from Exeter University, me and a French guy called Claude. The others were all Oxbridge students.

Some weeks later I received a letter from Chase Manhattan. I opened it and scanned over the words, barely taking them in, until I saw the key phrase 'delighted to make you an offer'. I had been invited to join their graduate scheme along with twenty other students from the assessment days. The starting salary was £20,000 per annum. A generous graduate salary at the time, equivalent to around £50,000 today, to me it was a colossal sum of money. I couldn't believe that there would be a time, in the not-too-distant future, when worrying about money and what I could afford wouldn't be an hourly reality. I would be able to pay off my debts, pay back Laura and clear my overdraft in that first year of working. The release of pressure I felt was phenomenal.

That same day on campus I bumped into Claude, the other Exeter student being considered. He was walking across the green, arm in arm with his girlfriend, when he saw me and shouted me over. 'Hey, Saj. Hey, come here, man.'

'Hi, you all right?' I said as I approached.

'Yes, I heard back from Chase Manhattan and I am pissed, man, they turned me down.'

'Oh, I'm sorry to hear that.'

'Have you heard from them yet?'

'Actually, yes I have. I got a letter today and they did make me an offer.' I felt sheepish saying it. His face dropped, he made no attempt to hide either his disappointment or surprise.

'But I don't understand,' he said. 'They rejected me and they take you. What the fuck is wrong with this country? They give you a job and they don't give me a job?!' His girlfriend's hand tightened on his arm, whitening her knuckles. And yet, he continued, 'No offence, man, nothing personal, but you're from a shop. You didn't go to a good school, you don't speak any languages, well, you don't speak European languages. I speak three. What's wrong with these fucking people?!' To her credit, his girlfriend looked alarmed at the tirade and marched him off, speaking in quiet but firm tones.

In order to enrol on to the graduate scheme, I needed to graduate with at least a 2:1 in my degree. That wasn't a problem for me as I had firmly set my sights on a first. For the third year, I moved back on to campus and cut down on my trips home and to see Laura. I wanted to concentrate on getting the best possible grades. Of the fifteen or so of us on the course, it was me and one other, Adrian, who were in line for the top spot. We were told that only one person in the class would be given a first and the competition between us was friendly but fierce. I needed to get at least 70 per cent in each exam in order to be in the running.

In the final weeks of the year, a teacher in the department pulled me to one side and said that I was doing really well. But, she told me, so was Adrian, and I should go and speak to the head of politics to talk about it. I went during his office hours and he confirmed what the other teacher had said. We'd both received very high grades.

He told me: 'You've done really well and Adrian has done really well, but Adrian has applied to stay at university to be a post grad.'

'So?' I asked. 'What's that got to do with anything?'

'Well, if he gets a first, he won't have to pay any tuition fees, that's the system. But if he gets a 2:1, he would have to pay and, in that case, he would probably have to leave as he couldn't afford it.'

'But that's not fair,' I said. 'It should be judged on merit. I've worked hard because I wanted a first. If I earned it, I should get it. Just as Adrian should get it if he earned it. Nothing else should be taken into account.'

The tutor sighed. 'That may be right, but we are in this system. I can't confirm or deny anything but I can say the two of you are very close.'

'So give out two firsts then! If we both deserve it!'

'I can't do that, I'm afraid, it's not the university's policy. Sajid, let me ask you this though — would it make a difference to you? Other than to say you got the grade?'

He was right, of course; it didn't affect my job offer. I liked Adrian and he hadn't come from a wealthy background. Like me, he had struggled and worked hard for what he had. But I couldn't help but feel that the whole thing was unfair. Adrian did indeed end up with a first and was able to continue with his studies without having to pay tuition fees. I got a 2:1, which affected nothing, other than my sense of justice and resentment towards the university systems. As time's gone on, I've spent little time mulling over my degree result, but reflecting on it now, I think I would have done the same: to prioritise one boy's chances of progression over my desire to be fully recognised for the work I put in was the right call. Although the resentment that we couldn't both be given a first still lingers.

I threw myself into the world of banking at Chase Manhattan, embracing the long hours and high stress without complaint. Within months, they asked if I would temporarily transfer to New York to join a training scheme and I agreed. Despite being in a very junior position, I still benefited from many of the lavish perks that were offered to bankers in the eighties and nineties. I ate in restaurants I never would have dreamed of going to before and even started having a glass of wine or two with dinner when I was entertaining clients.

The biggest surprise came to me in the December of my first year at the bank. It was annual review day, a day that in many industries is dreaded as it means feedback and potential challenges on your work and productivity. At Chase it was a highly exciting day, because, when they had finished reviewing your performance, they told you what you were getting for your annual bonus.

As a new employee on a graduate trainee scheme, who had been there for less than a year, I wasn't anticipating anything very much. Any additional money would be helpful for me and my parents but I knew I wasn't in for the heady amounts that were given to those on the top floors. My boss was called Cindy, a larger-than-life New Yorker with a wardrobe of expensive shoulder-padded suits and short blonde hair.

I walked into Cindy's glass-panelled office at my allotted time, the last to see her that day, and on seeing me she flung her arms in the air and said, 'It's bonus time!'

'Hi, Cindy,' I said. 'Yes, thank you!'

We ran through a little small talk, followed by feedback from senior people on the team that I'd worked with. Her review was positive and it was in that meeting that I was promoted to associate. At twenty-three, I was the youngest person to be given the job title at that bank.

'And we're going to give you a bonus,' she said.

'That's great, thank you.'

'Your bonus is going to be eighty thousand dollars.'

I thought she must be joking. It was three times my annual salary. 'What?' I said, stunned.

'It's eighty thousand!'

'Really?' A smile broke out across my face and I stood up with a little hop.

'Yes,' she said.

I whooped and threw my fist up into the air. 'Wow! I wasn't expecting that! Thank you, thank you so much!'

I leaned over the desk to frantically shake her hand. I would have hugged her if the desk hadn't been in the way.

'I'm glad you're happy. What are you going to do with it?'

'I've got no idea,' I said, rubbing my forehead at the prospect. 'I wasn't expecting that. I think I'm going to buy a bike.'

'Great, great. It'll be one hell of a bike!'

I sat back down, slapping my hands on my legs as I did. My brain was swimming with everything I could do with the money. Cindy theatrically cleared her throat to recentre me and get my attention.

'Right, I'm glad you're happy, Sajid, but now you need to listen to me. You've just started in banking and I think you're going to do really, really well. I know you are. But let me give you a tip. In this job you're going to get bonuses every year and they'll get bigger and bigger. But if you want them to be as big as possible, never react the way you just did again.'

I stared at her, my smile dropping.

'Tell me why I'm saying it's a bad idea for you to do that again,' she said.

'Because then they'll know I'm really happy?'

'Exactly! I'm not saying you should look sad, but don't look happy. Sajid – we're going to do this again.'

'What?'

'We're going to do this again and you're going to react differently. Come on, I'm serious. Get up, go to the door and come back in!'

A little taken aback, I stood up and walked back to the door,

I opened it and shut it again as if I'd just come in. As I walked over to the chair, she greeted me once again with exactly the same chirpy welcome, 'It's bonus time!'

I sat down and this time we didn't bother with the small talk and performance review. Cindy just leaned forward in her seat and said, 'Sajid, we're going to give you a bonus this year. It will be eighty thousand dollars.'

I paused, looked her dead in the eye and said, 'OK, thank you. Eighty thousand, you say? I was expecting a little more.'

Cindy raised an eyebrow, 'Oh, you were, were you?'

'I was, Cindy. I am grateful, but when I look at my performance over the last few months, I had considered that I could be more valuable to you than that. Thank you for this, but if it doesn't improve next year, I'll have to think about my options.'

'Brilliant!' she said, slapping both her hands down on the desk. 'That's what I'm talking about!'

I smiled and shook her hand one last time before turning to leave.

'Now go and call Laura and tell her about your new bike,' she said after me.

That bonus cleared my debts, dug Dad out of some of his and went towards a pot that, in a year or so's time, would finally buy Mum and Dad a house of their own. It was the first time in my life I was completely financially free.

Delighted with the financial freedom the bonus and regular pay cheques afforded me, I decided it was time to embrace adventure. Along with Binesh and Marcus, I planned to climb Mount Kilimanjaro. We met in Tanzania and completed the momentous feat, dishevelled and exhausted by the end. The other two decided that they would relax for a few days in Zanzibar before flying back. I, however, needed to get back to New York for work.

In order to get a flight into JFK I had an overnight stop in Nairobi. At the time, the guidebooks suggested that Kenya, and especially the cities, would be dangerous. Knowing I had ten hours to kill overnight, I decided the safest option would be to book into a decent hotel near the airport. The Yellow Pages suggested that the InterContinental would be a suitable place, so I had called up and booked myself a room.

As I arrived, I noticed a huge sign by the door with handwritten lettering: 'The InterCon welcomes the Pakistani hockey team!' Inside I chuckled, but didn't spend much time dwelling on it. At reception a Kenyan member of staff, who introduced himself as John, checked me into my room. Despite handing him my British passport, he asked if I was Pakistani. I confirmed that my parents were from Pakistan but said that I was born in the UK. To me, it was an inconsequential interaction that happens often when you're abroad and people take a polite interest in your background.

Up in my room, I dumped my bags and kicked off my shoes, slumping down on the bed to rest my aching muscles. Within five minutes, the phone by my bed started to ring. I begrudgingly rolled over and lifted the receiver.

'Hi there,' the cheerful voice said. 'It's John. I just wanted to check that the room is OK and everything's all right, Mr Javid.'

'Everything is fine, thank you,' I said, poised and ready to hang up again and resume my rest.

'Good, that's great. I just have a question,' he said. 'Do you know the exchange rate between Pakistani rupees and British pounds?'

It struck me as a strange question, but without the internet for to-the-penny conversion rates, we didn't have quick access to this information at the time. As it happened, I did have a rough idea. I said, 'Well, yes. It's about sixty rupees to the pound.'

'Would you like to buy any Pakistani rupees?' he asked.

'No,' I said.

'Are you sure? Because we can probably give you a better rate?'

After the physical exertion of the climb and the travelling, I didn't want to continue the nonsensical conversation. 'No, I don't want any Pakistani rupees.'

I could hear muttering in the background from some of John's companions who were presumably also listening to the conversation.

'What about one hundred rupees for every pound?'

'No, really no thank you.'

'One hundred and fifty?!' John spluttered in desperation.

'Please,' I said. 'I don't want any Pakistani rupees.'

Finally he conceded, thanked me anyway and we ended the call. Completely dumbfounded by the bizarre exchange, I decided to get some food from the hotel bar before going straight to bed.

I took the lift down to the lobby and turned left at the reception desk and into the bar. It seemed that the athletes had already had the same idea. I was greeted by a dozen or so fit young Pakistani men all clustered around tables loudly chatting. I grabbed a menu from the bar and tried to decide if I wanted a club sandwich or if I should just stop kidding myself and get a burger and fries, when I overheard some of the men's conversation, speaking in Punjabi.

One of the men was frantically asking the other to explain again where he 'put it'. The other replied, 'I put it in the safe.'

'How can money go missing from inside a safe then?' the other retorted.

'I don't know!' he said, gesturing wildly. 'I put it all together and put it in there as you said, that's all I know. Then when we got back from the reception, it was gone!'

'So you didn't shut the safe properly?'

'I don't know how that's possible, but I suppose maybe. I don't know! It's just all gone.'

The realisation landed with a sickening thud. Their money had disappeared, just as the hotel reception team were trying to flog a stack of Pakistani rupees. I was so tired and so hungry, and the last thing I wanted to do was get mixed up in uncovering criminal activity. But I froze, no longer hungry.

I had three choices. I could keep my mouth shut, sleep well and be on my plane the next morning. I could tell the hockey team who had their money, and ask them to keep me out of it so I could hide from the inevitable drama in my room. Or I could tell the hockey team, and then get out of there sharpish for fear of being punished for revealing the perpetrators of the crime.

My conscience would only allow me to do one of the last two and I knew which one it should be. I put the menu down on the bar, walked back to the lift and pressed the button to summon it. When it arrived, I stood in the door, my foot blocking it from closing, and gestured for one of the hockey players to come and speak to me.

'Hey, come over here,' I half hissed, in Punjabi.

Intrigued at finding another Punjabi speaker, I caught the attention of a few of them and three walked over to me at the lift.

'Did you call me?' one said.

'Yes,' I replied. 'Listen to me really carefully. I'm just going to tell you this one time and then leave.'

'What?' they replied.

'I know you've had some money stolen from your safe.'

'How do you know?' the man replied.

'I know because half an hour ago, that man John at the front desk and a few others called me and offered to sell me a load of Pakistani rupees and I said no.'

'The bastards!' he said. 'They've taken our money!'

'Listen,' I said. 'I'm going up to my room to get my bags and leave. Please give me five minutes before you do anything.'

He nodded and looked me directly in the eye. 'Thank you, sir,' he said in English. As the doors closed on the lift, I heard the same man shout, also in English, 'Boys, go and get your hockey sticks!'

I was out of the hotel just five minutes later. I took my bag and rode the lift down into the basement car park where I walked up to the street and caught a cab back to the airport. I never went back through the lobby. I don't know if they gave me the five minutes I requested or if they ever got their money back. That night, I slept on the floor of Kenyatta International Airport.

22

Who are you and what do you want?

My temporary stint in New York turned into five years, the last of which Laura came out to live with me. We moved back to London together in 1996 and that was when we started to plan our wedding. There was no formal proposal, I never got down on one knee. We just moved back to the UK, and started making arrangements.

In the eight years of our relationship, the first two she had spent completely away from my parents. But they had agreed to meet her after three years. It was after I told Amna and Fatima that the arranged marriage was off and their horrendous parents' meeting didn't work that they started to relent. My parents had exhausted all options and I knew that they were desperate not to repeat the distance and damage caused when they rejected Tariq's wedding to Katharine.

All my brothers came to Laura's twenty-first birthday party in Busby's nightclub in central Bristol. We even snuck in Atif, who was sixteen at the time. Laura had started to get on well with Bas's girlfriend Donna so we would all go to the pub or the cinema together from time to time. My brothers spoke highly of her and encouraged my parents to give her a chance. So finally, in 1990, Dad said he would like to meet her.

'No messing around this time?' I asked. 'You're not going to tell her she shouldn't be with me?'

My dad laughed, 'No, puttar, not this time. Bring her around and we'll meet her.'

On the day, I borrowed Dad's red Isuzu car to drive over to Laura's parents' house to collect her. She was nervous, and she'd asked several times what to wear but I had been no help. She opted for a cardigan and jeans. She'd asked if my brothers could be there too, just so that it would be less intimidating with a few familiar faces. She came over and both she and my parents were all politeness and smiles. There was no mention of previous tension or objections. They offered her tea and pakoras and asked after her parents. Dad spoke in English while she was there and even Mum made an effort to say what she could. When Mum broke into Punjabi, Dad translated for Laura to keep her up to speed. The whole encounter lasted for an hour and a half and I felt such a sense of relief knowing that it had happened without any incident or awkward silences.

From then on Laura would come around every now and again when we were both back in Bristol. My parents started to get used to her and the idea of having her around. It was the summer before Laura started her job as a trainee chartered accountant with Coopers & Lybrand and Dad was short of people in the shop. By this time, he had shut the two shops at 107 and 109 East Street and consolidated them into just one store further up East Street in St Catherine's Place shopping precinct. I wasn't able to help so he asked if Laura would consider it.

'Laura?' I said.

'Yes, if she is free.'

'I can ask her.'

'Tell her I will pay her, same as I do everyone.'

'Not the same as you do with me, but yes, Dad, I'll ask her.'

I phoned Laura at home to put the question to her.

'Are you free on Saturday?' I asked. 'Dad wants to know if you'd be able to help in the shop. He said he'd pay you for your time.'

'Oh,' she said, even on the phone I could tell she was reluctant. 'Who would I be there with?'

'You'd be there with him,' I said.

'What? Just me and your dad?'

'Yes.'

And then, to my surprise, she agreed.

Laura spent all day in the shop, serving customers, helping them with the changing room and working the tills. My dad came home raving about her. It was no small thing for him to have asked her for help. That she had been so attentive and diligent put her in high regard in his eyes.

He started asking more regularly and, when she could, she continued to help out. Every time she spent the day in the shop, he would come home telling Mum how polite she was and what great service she gave the customers. From then on, Dad became very pro Laura. He would talk about her and things she'd said. Even Mum started to catch up and I once overheard her boasting to a family friend that Sajid's girlfriend was going to be an accountant. In time, Mum agreed that Laura was 'very nice' and 'not like the others'.

With my parents increasingly on side and Amna now married, we started to plan our own wedding. We set the date for the summer of 1997. Having seen a number of weddings by then, Khalid's included, we discussed the format and decided we definitely didn't want a free-for-all of a guest list. We wanted to make sure we were in control of who attended. That would mean that we should pay for most of the wedding ourselves. To accept money from my parents would be to accept their unlimited guest list and demands. I explained to them that they didn't need to put money into the wedding, but that we would be planning it ourselves.

In the run up to the big day, Mum suggested that I go to Pakistan to have the wedding clothes made, including Laura's traditional Pakistani dress as it would be far cheaper in Lahore. After some discussion with Laura, we decided it would be a good idea. She wasn't able to join us so, with Rozina's help, she sent me off with strict instructions as to what she wanted, a lot of photos for reference and a list of her measurements for the seamstress. Dad and Bas decided to fly out with me to help with the shopping but also to see family.

When we arrived we went straight to the house of my dad's brother Majeed in Lahore. He had moved from their village into the city for work as a school teacher years before, so his daughters Shehla, Humera and Sadia were city girls. They were well educated and spoke fluent English. As they'd never come over to the UK before, while I'd heard about them and seen photos, I'd never actually met them. Shehla, the oldest of the three, was four years younger than Bas. As she came in to put a tray of tea down on the table, I could see immediately that she looked stunning. She had a sheer piece of fabric, a *dupatta*, draped over her head and deep brown eyes. I looked to Bas, intending to pull a subtle face of appreciation that we could discuss in private later, but he was completely gone. He wouldn't have noticed my subtle expression, or noticed if I'd smacked him over the head and shouted, 'She's pretty!' directly into his ear. He didn't take his eyes off her. Like a lovestruck teenager who has been subject to some sort of spell, he was mesmerised. They spoke a little over the tea. He did his best to make her laugh but she was coy and quiet in her responses.

From Majeed's house in Lahore, Dad, Bas and I went straight to Dad's village Lasuri, accompanied by Majeed himself. There we stayed for the night. Bas and I shared a bedroom and he sat up on his bed talking about Shehla for hours. He barely slept that night. I asked him about Donna, the woman he'd been dating for as long as I'd been with Laura. She was at home expecting her boyfriend to bring back gifts from his trip, thinking that she would be getting a proposal soon. But he didn't want to talk about her or to address any of the real-life practicalities of pursuing another woman. He was completely infatuated. He said he wanted to ask to spend more time with her and I warned him that if he did that, the parents would assume he wanted to marry her. He didn't care. He just wanted to be with her by any means necessary.

We had no plans to go back to Majeed's house for the rest of the trip. The following day, Bas approached Dad and asked if there would be a way to see Shehla again before we left. Mum and Dad had met Donna. They liked her, though she wasn't the choice they would have made for their son, as they, of course, wanted all their boys to marry in the Pakistani community. After the battle they faced with Tariq and me, and given the length of time Bas and Donna had been together, they had accepted the choice without much of a fight. But now Dad saw an opportunity to get one of his sons, whom he had previously assumed was a lost cause, married to someone in the community. He acted fast. He spoke to Majeed. The pair reworked the trip itinerary to travel back to Lahore to collect Shehla and her younger sister, Humera, to accompany her. The women joined us for the rest of the week. In a matter of days, Bas proposed to Shehla and she accepted. They decided that they would be married and Majeed set about making arrangements for a wedding on the last day of the trip.

Bas, a law unto himself, refused to talk to me about Donna,

only saying that he would meet up with her and explain it all when he got back. Dad called Mum to let her know that the wedding would be happening, but she was the only person back home who knew. We flew back with all of the outfits and landed in Heathrow; Bas now a married man; Shehla, a married woman awaiting the paperwork to join her husband in the UK; Dad delighted by a successful trip; and me, utterly dreading the fallout.

Dad continued straight on from Heathrow back to Bristol, while Bas and I went back to my flat in Dover Street in London. Laura had cooked up some pasta for us and wanted to hear all about the trip. We sat and ate, volunteering very little information, like teenagers back from a school outing. 'You tell her,' I said to Bas after half-an-hour of small talk.

'Tell me what?' Laura asked.

Bas shuffled uncomfortably in his chair.

I said again, 'I'm not telling her so you will have to.'

'OK, someone is going to have to tell me what's going on,' Laura said, putting down her knife and fork and sitting back in her seat, arms folded.

Bas relayed the whole story, from the tea in Lahore, to the trip and eventually to the wedding. Laura didn't pick her knife and fork back up. She couldn't eat. She was stunned.

It took days for Laura to calm down. She couldn't believe that Bas could have gone abroad and dropped his long-term girlfriend so quickly. She and Donna were friends. They had sat across the table from each other on countless double dates. Their relationship had been as long as ours and she'd had to endure his long periods of absence with the Navy. She was angry with my dad for encouraging the match and at me for not stopping him, although I argued that I didn't think there was much I could do.

When Bas made his mind up about something, there was

very little that could sway him. But Laura suddenly felt that she could be dropped at any moment for a Pakistani girl. It made her feel vulnerable and fragile in our relationship. And most of all, she felt devastated for Donna, a woman who believed she was in a happy relationship with the man she loved, but didn't know he was now someone else's husband. Bas went to Bristol to see Donna and told her the following day. He says it is the worst thing he's ever done to another person. She was heartbroken. In time she picked herself back up and married a man who happened to be Bas's best friend from the Navy. It took years, but eventually the two couples started to spend time together and regained a friendship.

When we started to plan the wedding, the first thing we had to discuss was religion and how we would handle the religious elements. Laura and her mum are Church of England Christian and proud to be so, while her dad is an atheist. They weren't particularly strict, but Laura's faith was just as important to her as my faith was to me. I didn't ask her to convert. I knew she wouldn't want to and I knew that wouldn't be right.

Even so, it was important to my parents that we had a Muslim wedding. The Qur'an says that a Muslim man can marry a Christian or Jewish woman as they are 'people of the book'. It would still be considered an Islamic marriage and would be blessed by Allah. So, we planned two services, a registry office one with just thirty close family members for the legal elements, and then a Nikkah, the Islamic ceremony and the main event. Our guest list ended up at 120 people, half of them my family and the other half a combination of Laura's family and our friends.

We had the civil ceremony at the Swallow, the same five-star hotel where I had appalled the Rothschild's interview panel by saying my dad was a bus driver all those years ago. Laura wore a traditional British white wedding dress, the same one her mum had worn on her wedding day. After the short ceremony with the exchanging of vows, we all had lunch in the hotel. I remember my mum making a face as the waiters served grilled salmon. She would have preferred Pakistani food.

The bigger event was set for 20 July 1997 at Ashton Court, a Grade II* listed former stately home in Bristol. In order for the service to be considered Islamic, it needed to be officiated by an imam. While an Islamic ceremony can be performed between a Christian woman and Muslim man, some imams refuse to conduct these services. Our imam, at my dad's mosque, politely declined, saying that he didn't approve of my marrying outside the faith. Dad was insistent that he would be able to find someone suitable so I left the job with him.

It took him a few weeks, but he found an imam who was willing to perform the ceremony for us. We didn't know the man and had no existing relationship with him, so he asked to meet the two of us before the big day. Laura, my dad and I went to his house in Fishponds, back near Stapleton Road.

The meeting was brief. He was sitting in his living room with another man he never introduced, and a few of his kids running around. His English was decent but he spoke with a strong Pakistani accent that meant it took some concentration to understand every word he said. We sat politely as he gave us a lecture on Islam and the importance of marriage. He confirmed that we could marry according to the Qur'an but stressed that it would be far better if Laura converted. He gave her an invitational look but I jumped in before the line of enquiry could go any further, 'We're not here to discuss that.'

'OK, OK,' he said. 'Your dad told me that so it's fine.'

We confirmed the dates and times and other details for the event and then left him.

*

The day was beautifully sunny. Everyone hopes for good weather if they book a summer wedding but, of course, nothing is guaranteed. The venue looked beautiful and Laura was tucked away with her bridesmaids – Sam and her younger sister Zoë – getting ready in one of the upstairs rooms. The day was a blend of British and Pakistani traditions. Laura wore her Pakistani lehenga (an ankle-length skirt) for the day. I would find out later that my mum went into her room before the ceremony to wish her well and give her some traditional gold jewellery to finish off the outfit. Her dad would walk her down the aisle to her favourite piece of classical music, Pachelbel's Canon, played by an elegant string quartet. All the food was from Pakistani caterers and we found a Sikh DJ from Birmingham who could play a mix of Western and Bhangra music.

The ceremony was due to start at midday. Laura was poised and ready in her room upstairs, waiting for the nod to come down. All the guests had taken their places and the stage was set with seats on one side for Laura, her mum and maid of honour Sam, and on the other with seats for me, my dad, Bas and Tariq. The string quartet was warmed up and ready to go. The only problem was that the imam was nowhere to be seen. Fifteen minutes passed, then half-an-hour and there was still no sign of him. Without mobile phones, there was nothing to do but wait. We sent Khalid out into the car park to keep a lookout and usher him in as soon as he arrived. A full hour after the ceremony was supposed to start, he turned up, driving a minibus full of his relatives including seven or eight children. Dad came out to meet him and, in an attempt to get the show moving and not cause a fuss, told him it was all fine – the tardiness and the additional guests.

Bas and I were waiting in a side room when Khal came through the door, 'You'll never guess what your imam's done, he's only shown up with his whole bloody family!'

'What? Why's he done that?' I asked.

'Free food!' Khal said, 'These idiots will do anything for a free meal!'

No one in that side room showed the appropriate reverence for a holy man, but he had tried our patience. He settled into a side room to prepare himself where he stayed for another twenty minutes. In the meantime, he made no attempt to wrangle the children he'd brought with him. They ran riot around the venue. One of them took a can of Coke from the bar at the back, shook it and then sprayed it everywhere, showering the string quartet and their instruments. By the time the imam was ready for the service and had taken his place centre stage, we still had to wait another five minutes for the musicians to mop down their instruments and be ready to play again.

With the band dry, the imam in place and Khal trying to corral the feral kids, Laura was ready to walk down the aisle. I sat on the stage watching her, trying to ignore the sea of faces looking up at me and just focus on her. My girlfriend, fiancée and now bride. I had loved her and fought for her for years, and now we were finally getting married. She looked breathtaking. The years of conflict and fighting for the relationship and even the frustration caused by the errant imam melted away when I saw her walking down the aisle towards me.

Laura took her seat on the other side of the stage, as is customary in Islamic weddings. When we sent out invitations to the event, we had included a little card that explained to our non-Muslim friends and guests what to expect from the service. The imam would spend the service addressing us separately until after we were officially married.

The imam welcomed the room in English and then completed the ceremony in a combination of English and Arabic – as this is the language of the Qur'an and all Muslim religious proceedings. When the formalities were complete, he faced the guests and said, 'Now they're married.' Which was met with a big cheer. The Islamic ceremony doesn't include a 'you may now kiss the bride' moment, so this was it. We were ready to conclude the service and start with the eating and dancing. Or at least we would have been if the imam hadn't chosen that moment to take matters into his own hands.

'Because there are a lot of people here today that don't know about Islamic weddings, I just want to explain what weddings mean in Islam,' he said. I felt myself getting tense; this wasn't a part of the script and we were already well behind on the schedule for the day. I hoped he would say a few nice words and send us on our way in two minutes.

He took a moment to explain why marriage was important to the Islamic faith, much like he had when we visited him at his house. 'It is a man's duty to look after the wife. And a wife's duty is to look after the house and the children.' That was not how we saw our marriage, and I was concerned her friends and family would start to worry about what she'd signed up for. Then he said, 'Sajid has married Laura today and Laura has married Sajid. In Islam, it is very equal to the man and woman. Islam understands that not all weddings work out the way you want them to. Allah has said that a man and a woman must be allowed to divorce if they're not getting on. It's very easy to get a divorce after an Islamic wedding.'

He made direct eye contact with me and then turned his head to look at Laura as he made this point. I felt tetchy. I wanted to show him respect but I also wanted him to shut up and sit down. I started jogging my left knee up and down. Tariq put his hand on my anxious leg and whispered, 'Do you want me to stop him?' Dad looked over at us both to shut any plan down with a short, sharp shake of his head.

Without noticing, the imam went on, 'In fact, the way you do it is very straightforward. All you have to do is, the man or the woman just needs to say: "I divorce you" three times. So, for example, if Laura wanted to divorce Sajid at any point in their relationship, all she has to do is say: "I divorce you, I divorce you, I divorce you."'

Our guests' faces looked frozen, although Bin and Marcus seemed to find the whole thing mildly amusing from their positions in the back. Tariq went to stand up and Dad put out his hand to signal for him to sit back down. My dad's face was stern and straight.

The imam, completely unfazed by the reaction he was receiving, went on, 'And when you get divorced the husband has to pay for his wife. He has to give her a special payment and the Qur'an suggests that payment is five hundred dirhams. Five hundred dirhams is not any amount. In today's money in pounds, it's like one hundred pounds! And the woman can spend it on anything, perhaps a holiday!'

This seemed to be the moment when Dad snapped. He no longer needed to send Tariq up for him as he leaped at the holy man from his seated position. Muttering a serious Punjabi expletive – an insult that implies an inappropriate relationship with one's mother – he bundled the imam off the stage and back into the side room. Bas took the cue and signalled for the music to start up again. I didn't see the imam for the rest of the event. I assume Dad hustled him and his family back into his minibus and sent them back on their way.

The rest of the night carried on as planned with people in high spirits. We did our first dance to an English and Urdu hybrid version of Whitney Houston's 'I Will Always Love You'. While Islamic weddings cannot serve alcohol, I was conscious that many of the guests would probably want to drink. I instructed my brothers that they could buy alcoholic drinks for whoever wanted one from the main bar in the venue and I would reimburse them afterwards.

As a gift, Laura's parents had booked us a fancy suite in the beautiful Swallow Hotel where we'd had our civil service. We were wearing full Pakistani dress as we turned up at 1 a.m. to the honeymoon suite. I wore a cream three-quarter-length embroidered jacket with a traditional Nehru collar and covered buttons down the front and on the cuffs. On my head, I had a matching turban with a fan of material emerging from the top. I looked regal and grand.

We checked in at the hotel and were given the key to the suite on the top floor. We let ourselves into our room. Laura went straight into the bathroom and I dumped our bags on the sofa in the living room, walked into the bedroom and turned on the light.

There, in the bed, was another couple. They woke up immediately and looked terrified to see me standing over them from the doorway in full Pakistani dress. The woman clutched the sheets around her and said, 'Who are you, and what do you want?' Laura came up behind me, peered over my shoulder and gasped.

'I'm so sorry,' I said. 'We've got the wrong room.'

The apologies came thick and fast from that point on as we backed out, grabbed our bags and stormed back down to reception. It turned out that we had been given the wrong key and our room was across the hall. We were furious and as the night manager walked us up to the correct suite he asked several times what he could do to make it up to us. In the end, so tired and unable to think, I told him to 'surprise us'. The following morning we were greeted with a series of breakfast trays stacked full of champagne, pastries and every type of breakfast imaginable, along with a handwritten note of apology. I understand the couple across the hall got the same gift. Apparently the woman thought she was being attacked by a Rajasthani assassin after watching one too many Bond films.

23

Goodbye Dad and Tariq

Throughout his life, my dad never felt financially comfortable. He worked every hour that God provided but, like a hamster on a wheel, never seemed to make any progress. Peacocks had opened on East Street and taken much of the low-cost women's clothing market away from our shops.

By 1995, my parents were down to just the one store in St Catherine's precinct and it was a shadow of the shops we once owned. Unable to break a profit on clothes alone, they started selling accessories and handbags, then luggage and homewares and eventually garden supplies. The pavement outside the shop was a metre deep with a shoddy display of Tupperware boxes and slug pellets, their bestselling item.

Inside, it was cold and damp and the stock was stacked haphazardly, making it near impossible for customers to find what they wanted — which may well have been in there somewhere. The shop had become an eyesore. Only Mum and Dad worked in the shop by this point as they couldn't afford a salaried member of staff.

That final shop represented a real sadness for me. It was a

tangible display of the decline of my dad's dream of becoming a successful businessman. It was never a job that was suited to him; he always should have been in the community, using his passion and love for people to affect real change. But he did what he could to survive.

These days, though, he didn't need the shop for his survival. He was of retirement age. They barely broke even on a good day. My parents were working to make no profit at all. I was working in the City, Tariq was a manager at Tesco, Khalid was doing well at Sun Life, Bas had left the Navy to join the Avon and Somerset Constabulary as a PC, and Atif was at City University, studying law. We all encouraged Dad to close the shop, to collect a pension and allow us to supplement any additional outgoings they had.

My mum was keen. She had spent every day working for her entire married life while raising five boys. She had made clothes well into the night in our childhood and worked up to fourteen-hour days in the warehouse and shops, trying to will the 'toe-taal' high enough to get Dad in a good mood that day. She was tired, and with good reason.

Dad was more reluctant to let go. His work had been his life. It was all he knew and all he could remember. He couldn't imagine not waking up and going to the shop in the morning. He was worried that he would be bored in retirement and feel useless.

As my parents spoke about it, Dad expressed regret that he never studied at university. He said he'd always wanted to learn more and maybe get a degree. Mum insisted that it wasn't too late and that, if they retired, he would have time to apply and go back to studying. Offering Dad something else to invest his energy in was the only way to get him on side. He agreed and applied to study Islamic history at the Open University.

There was no business to sell, no one to hand over the keys

to. They just made a final lease payment, sold the stock to market stalls and fellow business owners, and then closed the doors. My dad's big empire going out with a whimper and not a bang. No other business moved in. The shop remained empty for years, one of many in the precinct that the shopping centre was unable to fill.

The extra time allowed Dad to study. He would regularly go to the library and the brothers clubbed together to buy him a desktop computer to help with his work. Mum got to spend more time with her sons and her ever-growing brood of grandchildren. We had reached a nice point where the five of us boys were satisfied that they were comfortable and content, without working their fingers to the bone any more.

It was in September 1998 that I got a call from Dad out of the blue. Laura and I were living in Chelsea and hadn't had our first daughter Sophia yet, but she was on the horizon. We had settled into the rhythm of life nicely, having bought our first home, a flat on Tite Street. My phone rang on a Saturday morning, and it was Dad. I was used to hearing from Dad occasionally but I would speak to Mum far more often.

'Hi, Dad, are you all right?' I said.

'Yes, yes, puttar, I'm all right, but I need to see you.'

I had a familiar feeling, dreading what he wanted to say.

'Why Dad? What's wrong?'

'Nothing's wrong, I just need to see you. Can you come?'

'You want me to come now? To Bristol?'

'Yes, if you can.'

'I have so much on with work and I have to go away tomorrow, Dad. I can't come to Bristol. Can you tell me over the phone?'

'No, son, not over the phone. I have to see you.'

We settled on meeting halfway at Reading services on the M4 the next day. It wasn't a relaxing drive for me. Once again,

I had been summoned to a one-on-one meeting with my father with no idea what he had to say. Last time we did this, I ended up spending years fighting an arranged marriage.

I got to the bleak service station and got a cup of mediocre coffee from a machine in the WHSmith. I sat at a plastic table on a plastic chair that was bolted to the ground and waited for Dad. He was only ten minutes behind me and sat down without treating himself to the tepid coffee.

'Hi, Dad, are you OK? Is Mum all right?' I asked as he slid himself between the static chair and table.

'Yes, yes,' he said. 'I just need to talk to you.'

'What is it?'

'There's been something on my mind for a long time and I need to speak to you about it.'

'OK, Dad, what is it?'

'Do you remember when we lived in Bedminster and you and Tariq had a fight?'

'Yes.'

'And I came up into the flat and I hit you? I hit you a lot.'

'Yeah, I do, Dad. I remember.'

'I remember that too. And I remember that I tried to hit you with a hoover and I hurt you.' He sighed and sat back in his chair, making eye contact with me. 'I want to apologise. I'm really sorry. I never forgot that day. I know that you never brought it up with me again, but I didn't have the courage to bring it up with you. I thought you had forgiven me because our relationship is good. But I want to make sure you've forgiven me, because I never said sorry and I should have.' His eyes had swelled, and there were tears.

I was taken aback. I'd never heard an apology from Dad, let alone one so heartfelt. I was surprised that he had allowed himself to dwell on it for so long and that he had felt such urgency to have the conversation with me.

'Dad, it's all right.' I leaned forward and put my hand on his. 'Thanks for saying it.'

He carried on, 'You were right with what you said about Tariq. I should have known in my gut that you were being honest. I didn't listen to you and I lost my temper. By Allah's will you managed to escape and get away. And I'm pleased you did.'

I reassured him once again that I accepted his apology.

He said, 'When I was a kid, I used to get hit a lot. I thought it was OK but now I know it's not. I look at my grandchildren and think if someone hit one of them I would be furious. It's wrong in every way.'

He finished with, 'Will you forgive me? You don't have to.'

'Dad,' I said. 'Yes, of course I forgive you.'

We stood up from the table and embraced with a hug. He wiped his eyes. As he released me, he put a hand on each of my arms and said, 'I don't think I have the right to say this, but if you have children, don't ever be a dad like me with your kids. There's no justification.'

There were many ways I would love to be a dad like him to my kids. He's right, I would never lay a finger on my kids, and I never did. But his work ethic, his commitment to providing for us and supporting our education, the care he showed to my mum, even his faith and trust in people and their humanity... these weren't traits to ignore or disregard. In many ways, following his lead made me a better father and husband. That conversation meant more to me than I was able to say.

In 2008, Dad had a stroke. I was living and working in Singapore, and by this time Laura and I had three children: Sophia, Suleiman and Rania. We had our fourth and final baby, who would turn out to be a girl we named Maya, while we were living in Singapore. Getting a call like that, when you're so far away, is debilitating. Mum found Dad having a fit in the house and called an ambulance. Atif, who lived the closest, went with them to the hospital. When Dad had been brought back home, I tried to speak to him on the phone but his speech was slurred. It took him three or four months to be able to communicate fully again, but even then he never got back to full strength. He was weak and lacking energy.

One morning he was brushing his teeth when he started coughing up blood. The doctors ran several tests and he was diagnosed with colon cancer, which had already started to spread. The doctors made no promises about the outcome, but recommended a course of chemotherapy.

Dad agreed to the treatment, but it ravaged his formerly plump and full frame. He became weaker and thinner and had very little energy for anything. He had to stop his studies with the Open University and started to spend more and more time in bed between treatments.

Laura and I moved back to London in the summer of 2009, allowing us more time to spend with Mum and Dad. For the next few years, he grew increasingly weaker. Doctors tried a few different courses of treatment, but none eradicated the cancer, just slowed it, and him, down.

I was elected to parliament as the MP for Bromsgrove in 2010 and within a month of taking office, I arranged for my parents to come into Westminster for a tour of the Houses of Parliament and to see my place of work. I didn't want to wait any longer, in case I would miss the chance. Dad was so proud as we slowly guided him around, his walking stick tapping softly on the stone floors.

Knowing that Dad wouldn't continue for much longer, in 2011, Bas had the idea to arrange a family party marking the fifty-year anniversary of Dad moving to the UK. We hired Emersons Green village hall around the corner from where my parents were living and invited every family member under the sun. Majeed flew over from Pakistan, Rozina and her husband Aziz came from Rochdale, along with her brother Tes and Phopo Salima. Amna and Fatima drove down from Leeds and all five of us brothers were there with our wives and many children. Dad was in high spirits throughout the event. He proudly handed out little badges showing the UK and Pakistani flags intertwined – especially to his fourteen grandchildren – encouraging them to honour their roots while embracing their future.

It was after that event that he started to deteriorate quickly. In consultation with my dad, the doctors made the decision to stop chemotherapy, to allow him more comfort in his last days. He asked for them to add DNR (do not resuscitate) to his paperwork. We installed a stairlift in the house to help him remain independent for as long as possible, but it wasn't long before we had to put a bed for him in the living room on the ground floor. He would often cry out in pain in the night and need someone to turn him. Soon it became too much for Mum so the five of us brothers made a rota and arranged that one of us should be there every night of the week to help. With full-time jobs and families of our own, this was difficult but we jigsawed the timetable together. I would sleep in the spare room with the door ajar. When Dad called out, I told Mum to ignore it and to try to keep sleeping because I would go and care for him. Over those six months or so, I would hear him call out my name three or four times in the night, to bring him water or rearrange his bedding. For a while after he died, I kept hearing that same cry in my sleep. I would sit up thinking my dad needed me only to realise he was gone.

We never considered putting him into a hospice, for all of the wonderful work those facilities do, as it wasn't in our culture. We would care for the man who cared for us, no matter how taxing or inconvenient. There were a few nights when the doctors suggested Dad stay in a local Macmillan centre, for extra support for Mum when he was going through a particularly bad period. He thought the people in those centres were amazing but he always insisted that he wanted to die at home in his bed, with his family.

When it looked like Dad was in his very last days, we all went to Bristol. Laura and I brought all four of our children and stayed nearby. By the time we got there, he was in a hospital-type bed in the living room, and he could barely move or talk. I had to lean right in, with my ear next to his mouth, to hear his whispers. He was glad that I was there. We explained to the older of the children what was happening and asked them to say goodbye to him. He gave each a small kiss on the forehead and a squeeze on the hand.

Mum was sitting by his bedside with Auntie Salima at her side, both watching him, not breaking their gaze. Tariq, Khal and Atif were already at the house, and Bas was on his way from Cambridge, where he had just started a master's degree in criminology as part of his police training. There was a picture of him on the mantelpiece posing in his police superintendent's uniform, war and policing medals attached, by one of the old Cambridge colleges, a far cry from the boy who left school with no O levels and set fire to the train station.

The doctor came over to administer painkillers and run a few general checks. He confirmed that we were now looking at hours rather than days. I texted Bas to hurry his return. Before the doctor left I asked if there was anything we could do to help Dad in these last moments. He told me that Dad had virtually no energy, and it may be helpful for him to have some glucose lozenges, which were available from Boots. I was set that I would go and get them for my dad. I would get him whatever he needed.

I went over to his bedside and said to Dad to hold on for a little while longer, Bas was on his way. I said that he was rushing from Cambridge. 'He's coming now, Dad, it won't be long.' I took the photo off the mantelpiece and held it up to his face, 'Look, Dad,' I said. 'That's where he's been, in Cambridge.'

Dad's eyes took a moment to focus in on the picture. His lips pulled up into a smile and he raised his hand to touch Bas's face. 'That's my boy,' he said in his low, strained tone.

'Dad, there's something I need to get you from the chemist, OK? I just need to go and do that but I'll be back in ten minutes.'

I started to put my shoes on by the door when Laura came over. 'Do you think you should leave now?' she asked. Boots was only a six-minute walk away, less if I ran. I was set on getting Dad the lozenges.

'No, it's fine,' I said. 'I'll run there and back.'

Bas burst through the door to see us all crowded round Dad. He was just in time to say goodbye. Later, I told him what Dad had said when I showed him the picture and he was in floods of tears.

It took me exactly nine minutes to get to Boots, buy the lozenges and run back. But by the time I was home, Dad had died. I was furious with myself for leaving. I felt like I'd let him and Mum down by not being there, until later that night when Laura took me by the hand and told me, 'You *were* there.'

In Muslim tradition, when a person dies, they are buried within twenty-four hours of their death. As this moment was expected, much of the plans were in place. We called the doctor who came back an hour later to formally confirm the death. Then Khal, Bas and I went to the registry office to collect his death certificate the same day.

Dad's body was stored by undertakers overnight and then, the following morning, he was taken to the mosque in Easton.

The men in the family gathered in a special room where we washed and prepared his body. All five of us brothers, cousin Tes and Rozina's husband Aziz all gathered round him, laid out on a table ready for the soap and warm water. I had never done anything like it before. It was the first time I'd been involved in the process. It felt tender and intimate. I was pleased that the people to care for my dad's body after his death were the ones who cared for him most in life, and I was pleased to be doing this with my brothers. It felt like we were doing one final good thing for him.

As we applied the lathered soap and washed it away with warm water, I thought of us as children, jumping on his round, bouncy belly, trying to climb up into his vest in bed and tickle his feet to see if we could make him laugh. I hadn't seen his body since then, since we were children. He'd looked so big and sturdy when we were young. Cancer had taken the roundness out of him, he was frailer and weaker, but it was still him. It was still the dad I would collapse on top of in a heap in bed.

When he was washed, we applied talcum powder to his body and wrapped him in a white cloth. The shroud left only his face uncovered and this is how he was placed into his coffin. It was temporarily covered in glass and taken into another room in the mosque so that people could come and view his body and say their final goodbye. This was especially important for the women, who, according to tradition, don't attend the burial. There was a series of special prayers at the mosque and the room was packed with people from the community who came to pay their respects.

Finally, all the men proceeded to the Muslim burial ground where prayers were said and Dad's coffin was lowered into the ground. Each person added a handful of soil to his grave in a communal act, committing his body to Allah. Once the men had left, the women came to the graveside to say their prayers.

With the rush of the funeral over, I coped with my grief by redirecting my attention to Mum. This would be the first time that she had lived by herself. We had spoken to her about coming to live with one of her sons, but she was clear that she wanted to stay in their house and live on her own. In those first weeks I helped her sort through things and clean out all of the medical equipment Dad had needed. Dad was ill for such a long time that she had been able to do some mental preparations, if you ever really can prepare yourself for grief. She came to London a lot to stay with me and we went to visit her often too.

As a family we had a few years to adjust to life without Dad and, in time, we came to terms with our grief.

Khalid and Fouzia have three amazing children, Zaen, Yasmin and Azam.

Bas exceeded all expectations, becoming commander for frontline policing in London and later the Met's deputy assistant commissioner. As I write, he's director general of immigration enforcement at my old stamping ground, the Home Office.

Atif married Shehla's sister Humera. They are happily married today with three children – Zaib, Rehan and Zaynah.

When Tariq left home and married Katharine against my parents' wishes, it ruptured his relationship with the family but, as the years went on, all parties softened. I was proud to have him stand next to me at my wedding. As children, the age gap between us meant we didn't spend as much time together but I loved him all the same.

He struggled professionally, initially working at Tesco on the shopfloor and then moving over to Waitrose in Croydon. Sadly he and Katharine grew apart and they eventually separated. He saw his wonderful children, Samuel and Hannah, regularly, and eventually met a woman working in Waitrose called Sylvia who he was with for ten years.

Tariq and Sylvia rented a place in south London and he would make the trip back to see Mum in Bristol every couple of months. Of the five of us, he saw Mum the least. I think his lack of availability made his contact all the more desirable. She would often ask me why he hadn't called or what he might be doing.

In 2018, we had a big family get together as one of our cousins, Vaseem, was having a fortieth birthday bash in Birmingham. All five of us brothers were in attendance. We chatted and ate and smoked cigars together, generally enjoying the festivities. That night, despite usually checking himself into a Holiday Inn or some equivalent, Tariq asked Bas if he could stay with him for the night. At the time, Bas was based in Solihull so agreed to put him up in the spare room. Everything seemed normal. Tariq was a little nostalgic, reminiscing on times gone by, but we all assumed he'd just had one too many whiskies. He apologised to Bas that night, out of the blue, for borrowing some money that he'd never paid back years before, and Bas brushed him off, telling him it was a long time ago and not to worry about it.

It was a week later that I was in my ministerial car with Laura being driven back to London after visiting my mum in Bristol. I was Home Secretary at the time, which meant that as a 'protected person', I was escorted at all times by armed plainclothes police protection officers. My phone rang and it was Bas.

'Can you talk?' he said, forgoing the usual pleasantries.

'Yes,' I said.

'Who are you with?'

'Laura and I are being driven home.'

'OK, that's OK. I'm afraid I've got some really, really bad news. I'm really sorry but Tariq's dead.'

'What do you mean?' I asked, completely stunned.

'How far away from home are you?'

I looked out of the darkened windows to see the familiar

Goodbye Dad and Tariq

streets of west London flashing by. 'About ten minutes,' I guessed.

'OK, I should call you when you get home. I'm here at a hotel in Surrey. Sylvia is here and we've just found Tariq. He's dead in one of the hotel rooms.'

'I don't understand, what happened? Did he have a heart attack?'

'I don't know for sure, but I'm going to find out more and call you back when you're home,' he said. 'Also, Saj, I've just told you and I haven't called Khal or Atif, and Mum doesn't know. We need to decide how we're going to tell Mum.'

'OK, OK,' I said. 'Call me when you know more.'

I whispered the words to Laura in disbelief that I was saying them, 'Tariq's dead.'

She squeezed my hand and we raced home.

It transpired that Tariq had checked into the hotel on his own. Sylvia had been working that Saturday, and when she got back from her shift at Waitrose, it was to an empty home and a letter on the table. I've not seen the letter as the contents were addressed to her. I do know that he had said he'd left her the car and house keys and that she should 'carry on and enjoy life'. She knew he was saying goodbye but had no idea how to get to him and how to stop him. He didn't say where he'd gone.

In her panic she called Bas, someone who knew Tariq well and as a policeman may have a better idea of what to do. Bas headed straight to Croydon to help with the search but encouraged her to run through the different places he could have gone. They decided to check at the hotel, which was a special place for the two of them. She drove over and asked the receptionist if Tariq Javid had checked in. He had.

Frantic, she persuaded them that they had to open the door. She told them that he was going to do something stupid and that he needed protecting. It was too late. They went into the room to find him in the shower cubicle lying on the floor in a pool of blood.

He had checked himself in and drunk his way through a couple of bottles of whisky before taking his life. The staff took Sylvia into a different room to calm down and that's when Bas arrived.

He phoned me minutes later, still in shock, going through the motions that felt most appropriate, but unsure if he could actually stand or talk as he tried to make sense of the scene. By the time he'd called me back and relayed all the facts, he sounded more lucid and in control. I called Khal and Bas phoned Atif, who drove over to Mum's to break the news. We all agreed that, for now, we would just say that he had died. We would wait until we had formal confirmation that it was death by suicide before we said anything to Mum. For now, all she needed to know was that Tariq was dead and that we would try to find out more.

Phopo Salima and Rozina left Rochdale that day to go and be with my mum in her grief. She was inconsolable. No woman wants to bury their husband but understands that the day could come. But no mother ever expects to bury their own child.

Bas also called Katharine and broke the news to her, so that she could speak to their two children and tell them what had happened.

His body wasn't released soon enough for a burial twenty-four hours after death, and we waited for the doctors to perform an autopsy. The results showed that he had a chronic heart problem. It wasn't treatable. Sylvia didn't know about the heart condition; he didn't talk to anyone other than the doctor about it.

Then, because he was my brother, the media started to report the death in graphic detail, and while my mother didn't read the *Daily Mail*, we were worried she would speak to others who had. By the time we told her how Tariq had died, she had already realised.

In Muslim culture, to kill yourself is sometimes seen as an unforgiveable thing that brings shame to your family. We told Mum that she mustn't think of it in that way. We couldn't judge, we didn't know how he was feeling and what was going on in his mind when he made the decision. We told her not to blame him. She listened to us as we explained it to her. We encouraged her to take pride in his memory. She nodded as we spoke and then asked, 'Can we tell people it was a heart attack?' It felt like heavy words coming out of my mouth as I told her no. I said that we couldn't do that, because the coroner's report would be made public, and we didn't need to lie. We had nothing to be ashamed of. It took her a while to truly believe what we were saying but she did and does now. She doesn't try to hide what happened and speaks with pride of her oldest son and sorrow of the sadness he battled.

When the day of the funeral came, it was a different type of sadness to the one we experienced with my dad. We were back in the same mosque, in the same room, but this time, the brother who previously stood beside me to wash our dead father was laid out on the table. The six of us who remained gently cleaning his body. There was no lightness to this day. No reminiscing. No smiles tinged with sadness. The day was just heavy and completely impossible to understand.

I didn't see it coming. None of my brothers expected such a horrendous thing to happen. Even now, when I reflect on it, having spoken to Sylvia and learned more about his heart condition, I feel my own heart strain and tighten as I mentally will him to just speak to someone. I wonder what would have happened if he'd knocked on a friend's door or come to see one of his brothers instead of checking into the hotel.

My brother, who drove me mad and made little time for

me as a child, but stormed into the headteacher's office and demanded justice for me when I was beaten up. Who wouldn't stop pushing until the boy was expelled. Who hugged me on the bench in the playground while I cried. He was gone.

Epilogue

The process of recalling these stories, researching my history and speaking to family members has only reinforced for me just how extraordinary a decision my parents – and so many others – made in leaving everything they knew in Pakistan to build a new life in the UK. Accepting an invitation from a foreign nation to come, settle and work – only to be met with a sometimes hostile reception – required a level of resilience and resolve that our modern society rarely demands.

My parents sacrificed so that I could have a better life. While I'd always recognised their selflessness and work ethic, it's only through this intense reflection that the full weight of it has truly landed. The deep sense of gratitude I feel towards them is something I hope never fades with time.

As I look back on my dad's career, I feel a mix of great pride and great sadness. I'm disappointed that, despite his drive and determination to succeed as an entrepreneur, none of his business ventures ultimately flourished. But I also hope he knew, in his final years, that his efforts were not in vain. Through his commitment to work, his refusal to take handouts and his insistence that we apply ourselves with the same discipline, each of his sons went on to achieve things he could be proud of. Those achievements are his and my mother's, too.

Just as my father worked tirelessly, so did my mother. Without formal education or fluency in the language of her new country, she persevered, always putting her sons first. It is nothing short of remarkable how her work – both inside and outside the home – held our family together.

I'll never forget the look of joy on my mum's face at the 2019 graduation ceremony for the Strategic Command Course at the College of Policing. She was seated proudly in the middle of the front row, watching as the Home Secretary – me – congratulated each senior police officer graduating that day. When Bas's name was called, I shook his hand – and we hugged in front of everyone (before he mischievously tickled my hips!). I caught the tears of pride welling in Mum's eyes. Later, she turned to the two of us and said quietly, 'If only your father were here – he'd be so proud.' Proud of the same two boys who, decades earlier, had ended up in a police cell in Weston-super-Mare.

My parents inspired me never to shy away from life's tests. From a young age, I decided I wouldn't let others limit my opportunities. Sometimes those people had good intentions: to protect me from disappointment or to manage my expectations. Other times, they simply didn't believe in me. But I refused to be boxed in. I chose the school I attended, the subjects I studied, and the careers I pursued.

Many assumed my background would naturally align me with the political left. But I believed in opportunity – and in taking it. The belief that anything could be achieved with tenacity drove me forward. Each time I chose my own path and found success, I became more determined to keep pushing. That's what drew me to the Conservative Party – and its guiding principle that government should create a country rich in opportunity and individuals must take responsibility to seize it, while ensuring there is support for those who cannot. I believed that in the seventies and eighties, and I believe it still. I am convinced we live in a country where hard work can truly change your life – and the lives of those around you.

While the UK my parents arrived in was marked by widespread racism and exclusion, the country has changed immeasurably. It hasn't always been easy, and the journey has been far from perfect, but we've made real progress – in all communities. Today, I genuinely believe that Britain stands as the most successful multiracial democracy in the world. It's a place where people from all backgrounds can rise, contribute and belong. The fact that the son of immigrants – raised in a modest home above a shop – could rise to the highest levels of government is testament to that progress. And while we must never be complacent, we should be proud of how far we've come.

Growing up, I had two goals. First, to earn enough to give myself and my family a better life. One of my proudest moments was handing my parents the keys to a terraced house in Bristol – the first home they didn't have to share or rent, where they could decorate the walls and finally settle in. Second, to make a difference in society – which is why I went into public service.

My parents taught me a great deal – and sometimes, I grew just as much by learning from their mistakes. I didn't share their views on interracial marriage or same-sex relationships. I resolved that I would never object to my children's partners on the basis of race, religion or gender. I also knew, even as a child, that I would never hit my own children. The experience was so painful for me that I could never imagine doing the same.

If those are habits I've chosen not to carry forward, there is far more that I have: the sacrificial nature of parenthood, the need to pull together as a family, the instinct to protect your children at all costs, and the belief that a home should be a safe, stable foundation from which you can explore the world.

These are the principles on which this book – and my life – are built.

I am eternally grateful for them.

Acknowledgements

My grateful thanks go to the entire team who helped me get this book from just an idea to sitting on bookshelves; led by Clare Alexander, Richard Beswick and Lauren Windle, and the team of proofreaders, designers, production staff and others at Little, Brown who did the behind-the-scenes work on the project.

To Wilson, Charles, the person who left their *FT* on the bus, the Barclays bank manager who approved the loan in my dad's name, Cindy and anyone else who invested in me – I am so grateful for that gift. Together you changed the course of my life.

To Robin and Sue, for being such phenomenal parents-in-law and supporting Laura and me at every opportunity.

Bas, Khalid, Atif, Tes, Phopo Salima, Fouzia, Amna, Fatima and everyone else in our family who generously allowed me to tell my story from my perspective, even when it overlapped with theirs.

Rozina, who dug through our family history, corrected some of my errant memories and spent hours relating family stories that are told here.

Mum, for sharing her story and allowing me to share mine, even when that was difficult.

My children, Sophia, Suleiman, Rania and Maya, for the joy and challenges they have brought to my life.

Tariq and Dad. Writing about the times we shared together, both good and bad, only reminds me of the deep love I have for you both. Rest in peace.

And finally, Laura – for not giving up on me. I look at our story and am struck by just how much you believed in me, when you had every opportunity and reason to walk away; when my parents wouldn't support us, when they tried to convince your parents to break us up, when they arranged another marriage for me, when I ran out of money and borrowed it from you, and when I moved country. I will never take your belief in me for granted. It is remarkable, and I am unimaginably lucky to call you my wife.